Exploring the Land of Lincoln

Exploring the

LAND OF LINCOLN

The Essential Guide to Illinois Historic Sites

CHARLES TITUS

3 FIELDS BOOKS
An imprint of the University of Illinois Press

3 Fields Books is an imprint of the University of Illinois Press.

Library of Congress Cataloging-in-Publication Data
Names: Titus, Charles, 1942– author.
Title: Exploring the land of Lincoln : the essential guide to Illinois historic sites / Charles Titus.
Other titles: Essential guide to Illinois historic sites
Description: [Urbana] : 3 Fields Books, [2021] | Includes bibliographical references and index.
Identifiers: LCCN 2020045741 (print) | LCCN 2020045742 (ebook) | ISBN 9780252043697 (hardcover) | ISBN 9780252085673 (paperback) | ISBN 9780252052583 (ebook)
Subjects: LCSH: Historic sites—Illinois—Guidebooks. | Illinois—History, Local—Guidebooks. | Lincoln, Abraham, 1809–1865—Homes and haunts—Illinois—Guidebooks.
Classification: LCC F539.3 .T57 2021 (print) | LCC F539.3 (ebook) | DDC 977.3—dc23
LC record available at https://lccn.loc.gov/2020045741
LC ebook record available at https://lccn.loc.gov/2020045742

For Courtney, Whitney, and Elda

Apple River Fort

Old Chicago
Water Tower

The Eternal Indian
(Black Hawk) Statue

Haymarket
Martyrs' Monument

Jane Addams
Hull-House Museum

South Side Community
Art Center

Starved Rock

Bishop Hill

Nauvoo

New Salem

Vachel Lindsay Home

Lincoln Tomb
Old State Capitol

Moore
Home

Thomas Lincoln
(Shiloh) Cemetery

Lincoln
Log Cabin

Vandalia State House

Cahokia Mounds

Fort de Chartres

Old Shawneetown

Fort
Massac

Contents

Part 1. EARLY ILLINOIS

Part 2. FRONTIER TIMES

Part 3. THE PRAIRIE STATE GROWS

Part 4. AT THE TURN OF THE CENTURY

Part 5. ONLY YESTERDAY

Introduction

Illinois is a land of great variety and surprising contrasts. In one area the Grand Prairie (from which the nickname Prairie State comes), shaped millennia ago by enormous, grinding glaciers, stretches in unending, table-top flatness from horizon to horizon. In another, just beyond the reach of those same glaciers, a rugged region of craggy hills, gently flowing streams, and dense woods makes Illinois seem at once mysterious and enchanting. This landscape is the impressive stage upon which the story of the state has unfolded.

As I hope this book shows, that story is a captivating one, complete with important events, remarkable people, and interesting places, many of which are noted in its historic sites scattered across the state. From a nineteenth-century water tower incongruously standing amid the cosmopolitan glamor of Chicago's Magnificent Mile to the rugged stone walls of an old frontier fort near the Mississippi River to the silent, enigmatic mounds at Cahokia, these historic sites can help make the past tangible. As such they can also contribute to what is, perhaps, a key purpose of history: to gain a better understanding of the present.

The variety in the state extends to its people as well, for Illinois is a place of great human diversity. Millennia ago, American Indians occupied its prairies and woodlands. Europeans and others followed, and migratory streams from the Upland South, New England, and the Middle States made Illinois a potpourri of many folk. The Great Migration of African Americans to Chicago in the early twentieth century became another chapter in the story of the Black diaspora and added a new vitality. Thus, characterized by a remarkable cast of ancient peoples, old settlers, and new arrivals, contemporary Illinois is the heir of an exciting, variegated, and vibrant history.

Variety is here in other ways as well. Chicago is America's third-largest city and one of the most important metropolitan areas in the nation. And yet only a few miles to the south or west of the Dan Ryan's perpetual interstate traffic and Rush Street's sparkling nightlife are the innumerable small towns and seemingly limitless fields of corn, soybeans, and wheat that are so characteristic of rural Illinois.

For those readers interested in Illinois history, *Exploring the Land of Lincoln: The Essential Guide to Illinois Historic Sites* is an excursion into the state's past through stories and illustrations that lead to locations of events great and small and to places where persons who helped shape history are recognized. Of the dozens of myriad points of historical interest in Illinois, the twenty in this book were selected because they are especially informative concerning the variety of aspects of the past.

David E. Kyvig and Myron A. Marty, in their insightful book *Nearby History: Exploring the Past around You*, comment, "A good understanding of the past . . . needs to take into account nearby as well as national and international developments."[1] The sites described in this book can help us place specific events or personalities in Illinois history into the larger context of the American national story.

This book presents the sites in the span of time that ranges from earliest settlers in Cahokia to the Europeans' arrival to the early twentieth century. This chronological approach permits a broad view of the state's history and may encourage readers to learn more about those places or events or people about which they may be especially curious.

The historic sites in this book are found across Illinois. Each is a part of the colorful mosaic of the Prairie State's past, and collectively they constitute a valuable portion of its heritage.

How to Use This Book

The chapters are organized to show how the state's history has unfolded over time. I hope that this chronological arrangement will help you envision the broader trajectory of historical events in Illinois and assist in locating those individual places where Illinois history is braided into the larger fabric of the American story.

For those interested in visiting multiple sites while exploring the Prairie State's past, a geographical table of contents follows. This, along with the accompanying maps and mileage tables, can be useful in planning your journey of historical discovery. Illinois is a large state, and some sites even within the same geographical region can be distances apart. For example, the Apple River Fort and Starved Rock, while both in the Northern Illinois region, are 115 miles distant. The same holds true with two sites in the Southern Illinois region: Old Shawneetown and the Vandalia State House are separated by 130 miles.

Others, though, are close, and visits to two or more of these under normal traveling conditions can often be combined into one trip. Such is the case with the Vandalia State House and Cahokia Mounds. Both are in the Southern Illinois region and are separated by sixty-five miles. The Lincoln Log Cabin, Moore Home, and Thomas Lincoln (formerly Shiloh) Cemetery, in the Central Illinois region, are only minutes apart and could easily be viewed within a few hours.

The four sites in Chicago are relatively close, but visitors should keep in mind such factors as traffic and road construction, which frequently characterize travel in and near the city. An excellent source of information for the considerable number of places with historical significance in the Chicago area is Ann Durkin Keating, *Chicagoland: City and Suburbs in the Railroad Age* (Chicago: University of Chicago Press, 2005).

Geographical Table of Contents

Mileage Tables by Geographic Region

Northern Illinois

	Apple River Fort	Bishop Hill	The Eternal Indian Statue	Starved Rock State Park
Apple River Fort	-	96	61	115
Bishop Hill	96	-	90	75
The Eternal Indian Statue	61	90	-	70
Starved Rock State	115	75	70	-

Chicago Area

	Haymarket Martyrs' Monument	Hull-House	Old Chicago Water Tower	South Side Community Art Center
Haymarket Martyrs' Monument	-	9	10	15
Hull-House	9	-	4	5
Old Chicago Water Tower	10	4	-	7
South Side Community Art Center	15	5	7	-

Central Illinois

	Lincoln Log Cabin	Lincoln's New Salem	Lincoln Tomb	Moore Home / Th. Lincoln (Shiloh) Cemetery	Nauvoo	Old State Capitol	Vachel Lindsay Home
Lincoln Log Cabin	-	120	100	3	250	100	100
Lincoln's New Salem	120	-	21	120	115	21	22
Lincoln Tomb	100	21	-	100	130	3	3
Moore Home / Th. Lincoln (Shiloh) Cemetery	3	120	100	-	250	100	100
Nauvoo	250	115	130	250	-	130	130
Old State Capitol	100	21	3	100	130	-	1
Vachel Lindsay Home	100	22	3	100	130	1	-

Southern Illinois

	Cahokia Mounds	Fort de Chartres	Fort Massac	Old Shawneetown	Vandalia State House
Cahokia Mounds	–	55	161	150	65
Fort de Chartres	55	–	125	125	115
Fort Massac	161	125	–	75	145
Old Shawneetown	150	125	75	–	130
Vandalia State House	65	115	145	130	–

All distances are approximations.

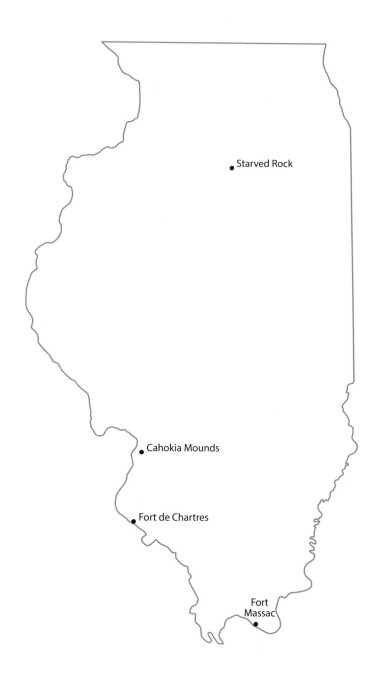

Starved Rock

Cahokia Mounds

Fort de Chartres

Fort
Massac

Part 1
EARLY ILLINOIS

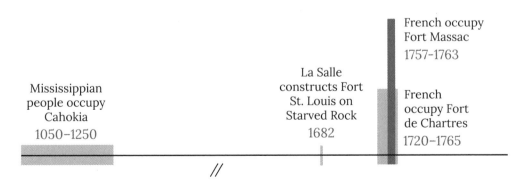

Mississippian
people occupy
Cahokia
1050–1250

La Salle
constructs Fort
St. Louis on
Starved Rock
1682

French occupy
Fort Massac
1757–1763

French
occupy Fort
de Chartres
1720–1765

Prologue

Illinois, situated near the heart of the North American continent, has for millennia been home to a variety of inhabitants. Its prairies, woodlands, and hills, blessed by fertile soil and plentiful in plants and animals, have offered a hospitable environment. Humans first appeared twelve thousand years ago, when people from what anthropologists call the Paleo-Indian cultural tradition inhabited the region. Over the next several centuries the Paleo-Indians were followed by the Archaic, Woodland, and Mississippian cultures. During the Mississippian period, a remarkable group of people appeared on the Mississippi River's expansive floodplain and built a large and elaborate settlement at what is now **Cahokia Mounds State Historic Site**, near Collinsville. There, from about AD 1000 to around AD 1250, the Cahokians constructed an extensive cluster of plazas and mounds that today provides evidence for what was likely an intricate, complex, and structured community.

Though much is yet to be learned about what happened here, archeological excavations at Cahokia Mounds suggest that the inhabitants knew about some aspects of astronomical phenomena, likely played games and participated in sports, and engaged in elaborate funerary practices, some involving human sacrifice. For unknown reasons these mysterious people abandoned their settlement around AD 1350 and drifted from the stage of history.

Later, other American Indians, especially those in the tribal confederation Illiniwek, also found the region congenial. Spread across much of what is now Illinois, they lived relatively undisturbed until Europeans appeared in the seventeenth century. With these newcomers, however, the destiny of the region's native people was forever tragically altered. When the French explorers Louis Jolliet and Father Jacques Marquette paddled their canoes along the tree-fringed banks of the Mississippi River in the spring of 1673, they were the first of countless travelers who, in a remarkably brief time, wrought enormous changes to what had been an extensive and undisturbed wilderness.

The French quickly grasped the many possibilities available in what they called "Le Pays des Illinois," or the land of the Illinois. Catholic missionaries, committed to converting the natives to Christianity, moved at great risk alongside others with worldlier goals. Among those with more secular ambitions for the Illinois Country was René-Robert Cavelier, Sieur de La Salle, a courageous and determined French explorer and entrepreneur. La Salle hoped to make the Illinois area the keystone of an enormous mercantile empire, an extensive realm centered in the Mississippi Valley, and on both resource exploitation and trade with the area's native inhabitants.

Following a series of difficulties, La Salle finally established Fort St. Louis on the summit of a striking, 125-foot-tall bluff on the Illinois River. Built at what is known today as **Starved Rock**, not far from the present-day community of Oglesby, it was to be the centerpiece of La Salle's great plan. Though no trace of Fort St. Louis remains atop Starved Rock, it was here briefly that La Salle envisaged his dreams. La Salle's enterprise ultimately failed, but his explorations of the Mississippi River were central in expanding France's claims to an enormous area extending from New France (Canada) to the Gulf of Mexico. Following La Salle's expeditions, the French presence in Illinois grew, and the area became increasingly important to France's colonial ambitions.

French authorities believed a military presence was necessary to protect their interests in the Illinois Country. Like other European nations, the French constructed fortifications at critical places in the territory they claimed. One of the most impressive of these was **Fort de Chartres**, near the present-day town of Prairie du Rocher. With massive stone walls standing near the Mississippi River, it was once a remote and lonely emblem of the French empire's global reach. The impressively reconstructed fort on the site today offers an excellent example of French military engineering.

A similar symbol of France's presence in Illinois was **Fort Massac**, built on a green bank that nudges the Ohio River at the state's southern tip, near today's Metropolis. The spot's defensive value was evident not only to the French but also later to the United States, which received the Illinois territory following the American Revolution. The fort standing at this strategic point today is a replication of an American installation built in 1802 on the site of the old French fort.

The mysterious mounds at Cahokia, the sharply ascending face of Starved Rock, and the impressive presence of Fort de Chartres and Fort Massac are all significant points of interest with much to say about the history of early Illinois.

Cahokia Mounds
State Historic Site
30 Ramey Street, Collinsville

On the western edge of the Prairie State, where the Mississippi River cuts its way between Illinois and Missouri, a floodplain extends inland until stopped by a range of rocky bluffs, covered with loess (windblown silt). This productive area stretches seventy-five miles from where the Missouri River dumps its muddy water into the Mississippi near Alton southward to the Mississippi's junction with the Kaskaskia River. Known as the Great American Bottom, it was shaped over time by the powerful force of the Mississippi.[1] It earlier served as home to peoples from what anthropologists call the Paleo, Archaic, and Woodland Indian cultures.[2]

But nine centuries after the Paleo culture and not far from present-day Collinsville, an extensive and vibrant prehistoric community flourished here. Those intriguing native people disappeared long ago, but the enduring signs of their presence are visible in dozens of mounds found throughout the twenty-two hundred acres of Cahokia Mounds State Historic Site, one of the most important pre-Columbian settlements north of Mexico.

The ancient peoples who eventually made their way into the Great American Bottom arrived on the North American continent from Asia thou-

Monks Mound on ancient plaza, Cahokia Mounds State Historic Site. *Illustration by Phil Glosser.*

sands of years earlier. Some traveled across the Bering Land Bridge, which appeared when the sea level dropped as water froze into glaciers while others possibly crossed the Bering Strait by boat. Examinations by archeologists and anthropologists of stone-tool artifacts found on both sides of the Bering Strait have long indicated that these items were produced by people of the same culture. More recently, analysis of DNA extracted from the twelve-thousand-year-old remains of a young boy unearthed in 1968 on a Montana farm has provided further evidence that Paleo Indians originated in northeast Asia.[3] Anthropologists believe the Paleo-Indians were nomads who moved southward while hunting the large game then found on the North American continent. The Paleo-Indian cultural period at the Cahokia area began twelve thousand years ago.[4]

With the arrival of a warmer climate and the resulting changes in the region's vegetation and animal population, an Archaic Indian culture developed, existing between about 8000 to 600 BC. Archaic Indians in the Cahokia region, perhaps, were less nomadic, practiced a primitive form of agriculture, and constructed some of the first mounds here.[5] Over time, the Woodland culture arose in the Great American Bottom. Emerging twenty-six centuries ago, the Woodland people continued to build mounds, make pottery, and engage in funerary practices.[6] Sometime around AD 700 to 800,

Indians during the Terminal Late Woodland period were living in various parts of the Midwest, including the Lower Illinois River Valley and the Great American Bottom.[7] Characterized by a structured, communal living pattern featuring courtyards, these were the immediate predecessors of those who built the Cahokia complex.[8]

The next group who lived on the northern end of this region and who constructed the mounds were there mostly during a time known as the Mississippian cultural period. The Mississippian people built other mounds nearby: some where the city of East St. Louis is now located, some farther south, and others across the Mississippi River at present-day St. Louis. The many mounds at the Cahokia site indicate that it was the core of an extensive native culture found throughout much of the American Bottom.[9]

Who Were the Cahokians?

Archeological study shows that the society at Cahokia was sophisticated and well structured, but it existed as a thriving community for only about three centuries. Then, for reasons yet unknown, it disappeared, and the people who lived here slipped into the haze of history. Although they left no written records, their former presence remains hauntingly visible in the impressive and fascinating complex of mounds, plazas, and other artifacts that give voice to a remarkable prehistoric society still not fully understood.

Archeologists and anthropologists have investigated Cahokia for decades, but many questions concerning its inhabitants and their social order remain unanswered. Those who have carefully dug into the site's mounds and examined the objects and other features revealed by their spades and trowels do not agree unanimously on several aspects of Cahokia. Still unclear are how many Cahokians lived here, the exact organization of their society, the nature of their religious beliefs, and the extent of their and Cahokia's influence.[10]

While it is known that a sizable number of native peoples established a broad-based and sophisticated community here between about AD 1000 and 1250, there is less certainty about how Cahokia was governed and structured. Some anthropologists theorize that Cahokia's society was a hierarchically organized chiefdom, where upper-class chiefs and their subordinates occupied leadership positions, and workers from among the other people built the mounds, cleared the plazas, cultivated the crops, created the pottery, and did the other everyday work that enabled their thriving society to exist.[11] Alternative opinions are that the central community was smaller or that Cahokia was not organized purely through a hierarchical kinship structure but was instead "heterarchical"; that is, both kinship and nonkinship groups in some way acted together to ensure that this complex community functioned.[12]

Although it is clear that Cahokia grew over the years, views concerning exact developments in its history differ.[13] Recent studies of the site conclude that a kind of cultural explosion took place here around AD 1050. Advocates of this "big bang" theory think the Cahokians in a key development had a swift and remarkable increase in population, construction, and influence over a short time and marked the start of the rapid ascendancy of the people who became dominant in the region and, perhaps, across the mid-continent for nearly three hundred years.[14]

A Place of Mounds and Plazas

The tangible signs of this well-developed and complex ancient settlement are the mounds the Cahokians constructed. Seventy-two mounds of varying sizes and conditions are preserved at Cahokia Mounds State Historic Site.[15] The mounds interrupt an area called the Grand Plaza, which itself was smoothed and leveled by the Cahokians to serve as the epicenter of their community. Although it is now a broad, rectangular greensward, archaeologists think the Grand Plaza was once mostly grassless, and perhaps covered with a thin layer of sand.[16] Here, it is believed, the Cahokians carried out community activities and played games, especially one called chunkey, a game in which a spear was thrown at a chunkey stone as it rolled along the ground.[17] Around this plaza and at least three others, Cahokia's residents carefully arranged their mounds, which vary in shapes and sizes. Some have flat tops; others are ridge-topped with sides that slant downward, rooflike.

Now grass covered, the mounds look almost lush, but this may very well not have been the case when the Mississippians were here. Some archeologists believe the mounds may then have been bare and that the residents worked as needed to keep them free of vegetation and to combat the erosion that must surely have resulted from such conditions.[18]

The most physically remarkable of the mounds and the one that impresses itself upon the senses with stunning immediacy is Monks Mound, which received its name from the Trappist monks who resided not far from it in the early nineteenth century.[19] A massive hill that in the summer stands green against the blue midwestern sky, Monks Mound emerges at the north end of the Grand Plaza. It is the largest prehistoric earthen mound found anywhere in North America.

Monks Mound is made up of four large tiers that climb finally to a flat top a hundred feet above the Grand Plaza. The mound's base spreads over fourteen acres, with a resulting footprint larger than Cheops' Great Pyramid at Giza in Egypt.[20] Archaeologists believe Monks Mound may have been the site of important religious ceremonies for the Cahokia community. Excavations on its top have exposed signs that a large building, perhaps built for that purpose or as the residence of an important leader, was once there.[21] When engaged in work to repair slumps in Monks Mound, drillers discovered a layer of stones that lies forty feet below the surface of at least a part of the mound. The stones, according to William Iseminger, assistant site superintendent at Cahokia, were in a layer "about ten meters" or about thirty feet thick and seemed to be "about a foot in size."[22] The exact purpose once served by these stones, which must have been moved a significant distance and with great effort, remains unclear.

Scientists have analyzed the soil the Mississippians used to build Monks Mound and found that the mound was constructed in stages over a period of years.[23] Archaeologists hypothesize that those who created it carried individual baskets of dirt, twenty-two million cubic feet of it, to the site of the mound until it reached its current height.[24]

The Strange Story of Mound 72

Another mound, tiny compared to Monks Mound but exceptionally important in helping decipher part of Cahokia's history, is Mound 72. This hill, only about seven feet in height, seems modest, almost insignificant. Yet, when it was excavated, Mound 72 told a strange and heretofore unknown story.

In the late 1960s, archaeologists began excavations at Mound 72 to determine if it contained evidence of a post the Cahokians possibly used as a marker in a planned, geometric design of their town. The remains of such a post were, in fact, present, but the excavations of Mound 72 also found much more.

First, they revealed that the mound concealed three other mounds. Then they disclosed the skeletons of two long-dead Cahokians, for several years thought to be two important males in their forties. A new examination of the skeletons, however, concludes that one set of remains is of a young male, the other of a young woman, both in their early twenties. The initial discoveries at Mound 72 were unexpected, and almost from the time of the mound's original excavation, archeologists and anthropologists have made various interpretations of their meaning. And as with nearly all such research, investigations continue.

Those who conducted the Mound 72 burials first put the woman on a bed of thousands of marine-shell beads under much of her lower body, a recent analysis of the Beaded Burial by University of Illinois anthropologist Thomas E. Emerson and his associates concludes. Next, the Cahokians put more beads over her legs and then placed the man's corpse on top of the woman's right side, and additional beads alongside his body, extending from his right shoulder. These beads seem to be in the shape of a bird's head, with its beak pointing away from the man's body. However, some scholars now question these earlier interpretations of the seemingly bird-like shape of the beads, which is associated with much-later American Indian iconography.[25]

Another part of Mound 72 contained a number of skeletons, including a group of fifty-three, mostly young women who were buried together, apparently with a few young males. Another thirty-nine individuals in the mound appear to have experienced inordinate violence, including in some cases decapitation, anthropologists conjecture, during a sacrificial procedure. Other artifacts, including chunkey stones and carefully crafted arrowheads, were also found in Mound 72.[26]

Ancient Astronomers

Although the sun has long been understood to have played a prominent part in the Cahokians' supernatural beliefs, findings at Mound 72 and at other sites in the greater Cahokia region now seem to reveal another aspect of their religious practices. Archeologist Timothy Pauketat speculates the moon was also important in the Cahokian cosmology.[27] The fifty-three bodies interred in Mound 72 lie at the same angle, almost exactly at the 130.07-degree azimuth of a lunar maximum standstill, which, Pauketat explains, occurs during "the year in which the rising and setting positions [of the moon] cover the longest stretch of the horizon north and south of the winter and summer solstice, respectively." Lunar azimuths are in the angles of other archeological sites in the greater Cahokia region, including the Emerald Site, a mound about fifteen miles east of Cahokia. Similar azimuths are also at the Lange Site, which archeologist think was likely used as some sort of ceremonial center.[28]

The significance of the sun and possibly the moon is seen, too, in Woodhenge, about a quarter mile west of Monks Mound. Warren Wittry, an archeologist excavating at Cahokia in the early 1960s, discovered the vestiges of five wooden-post circles whose purpose remains unclear.

The Cahokians arranged one circle so that the post near the center and some on the eastern side line up almost perfectly at dawn on the fall and spring equinoxes and the winter and summer solstices. On the equinoxes, the sun rises behind Monks Mound, and Woodhenge seems to be a solar marker. A more recent interpretation sees Woodhenge as possibly associated with lunar cycles.[29]

As with many aspects of Cahokia, determining what ended the community that flourished a thousand years ago remains yet another riddle. Anthropologists and historians have offered a variety of speculations for why the Cahokian society disappeared, including environmental factors, such as the overuse of nearby plants and animals; climate change; the presence of disease due to diet and the disposal of the refuse and human waste from thousands of people; and war.[30]

Although much remains unknown about the Cahokians, all who have studied them agree that Cahokia Mounds State Historic Site is a place of immense importance, one that holds an enormous amount of invaluable archeological and anthropological information concerning the inhabitants of this part of North America ten centuries ago.

The Twin Mounds seen from Monks Mound at Cahokia.
Photo courtesy of Illinois Department of Natural Resources.

Cahokia Today

The site's interpretive center judiciously reflects the significance of this place. It is an impressive venue. Prior to its construction, the space where it now stands was carefully excavated.

In 1981 the Cahokia Mounds State Historic Site was deemed so important that the United Nations placed it on its World Heritage List. And, as is noted on many of the placards near the mounds and at other locations across the site, it is significant, too, because it remains sacred to American Indians.

The top of Monks Mound, accessible now by a well-maintained stairway, offers a panoramic and stunning view of this mysterious place. Looking south from the edge of Monk's Mound and across the Grand Plaza, several other mounds are visible. Especially notable are the Twin Mounds, one circular, one rectangular. Just to the west is Mound 41. Past it, perhaps an eighth of a mile distant, Mounds 42, 43, and 44 contour the flatness. Then, just beyond them, the poles of Woodhenge stand again, casting their cryptic shadows, just as those emplaced by the Cahokians once did.

Eight miles from the windswept summit of Monks Mound, and slightly to the southwest, St. Louis's skyscrapers and iconic arch stand dimly etched against the blue-gray haze of the distant horizon. This juxtaposition of the emblems of two civilizations—one ancient, mysterious, and vanished, the other modern, bustling, and vibrant—offers a striking illustration of continuity and change in this place. The mounds, though silent and enigmatic, may ultimately tell much not only about how the Cahokians viewed their world but also of the challenges they faced here and how they responded to them. And, like the antiquities of Greece and Rome, of Egypt and Mexico and Peru, perhaps they can remind us of—and help us understand—the fragility of our own society.

Starved Rock State Park

2668 East 875th Road, Oglesby

A few miles east of where the westward-flowing Illinois River angles
its course to the southwest toward the Mississippi River, the towering,
sand-colored sides of Starved Rock stretch 125 feet into the air. This is one
of the Prairie State's most unusual geographic features, and it rises abruptly
from the river to dominate the nearby countryside like, as someone once
observed, a misplaced and smaller Rock of Gibraltar. Clumps of trees cling
precariously to a craggy, cliff-like face that plunges steeply to the river's
surface, and the water of the Illinois swirls and eddies at its base. This huge
outcropping of St. Peter sandstone is a dramatic reminder of a colorful
chapter in Illinois history.[1]

Starved Rock remained unknown for decades to the French, who began
to occupy the St. Lawrence River Valley in the early seventeenth century.
In those years, only American Indians passed by it, canoes gliding as quietly
on the Illinois as cottonwood fluff floating on an early summer breeze. Even
after the first Jesuit priests and French coureurs de bois began to push ever
farther westward along the St. Lawrence River and then into the forests
snugged against the Great Lakes, Starved Rock remained unknown to white
people. The first Europeans did not see Starved Rock until a century before

Starved Rock, the site of La Salle's Fort St. Louis, rising above the Illinois River.
Illustration by Phil Glosser.

American independence and a century and a half before Illinois became a state.

In the late summer of 1673, seven French explorers looked upon Starved Rock by happenstance. Within a few years from that eventful day, it transformed from an impressive but isolated landform into a point of strategic significance and geopolitical import. The change resulted from decisions made in the royal court of France, thousands of miles from the primeval stillness of the Illinois River Valley.[2]

King Louis XIV and his influential minister Jean-Baptiste Colbert hoped to increase French influence in Canada, the New France, which the French had claimed since Jacques Cartier's voyages of exploration in the late sixteenth century and the settlements by Pierre Dugua de Mons and Samuel de Champlain in the early seventeenth century. The French wanted not only to open a route to the Pacific Ocean but to also counter the growing Spanish influence coming from Mexico.

In their isolated missions near the Great Lakes, the Jesuit fathers had heard American Indians relate wondrous accounts of an enormous river someplace in the wilderness to the west and south. Though to the priests it was shrouded in the mists of the unknown, the river was familiar to the Indians.[3] These stories stirred the old visions of a passage to the Pacific Ocean. Was this the legendary shortcut to the East? To answer this intriguing question, Jean Talon, the intendant of New France, formed an expedition to locate and map this strange stream the American Indians called the Mesippi.

Officials in New France soon chose Louis Jolliet, a twenty-seven-year-old explorer, hunter, and merchant, to lead this dangerous foray into the wilderness. In the autumn of 1672, Jolliet journeyed by canoe to the Jesuit mission of St. Ignace, on the southern shore of Lake Huron. There thirty-five-year-old Jacques Marquette, a Jesuit priest with knowledge of American Indian languages, joined him.[4]

In the early spring of 1673, Jolliet, Marquette, and five voyageurs traveled by canoe and portage through the woods of what is now Wisconsin to the Mississippi River. There they turned southward, and the current carried their canoes downstream past a riverbank displaying a faint gauze of springtime green. The little party pushed ever deeper into geography unseen until then by European eyes. Moving steadily, following the great stream's course south, they passed the raging turbulence where the Missouri Rivers dumps its muddy, debris-choked waters into the Mississippi. Finally, they came to the mouth of the Arkansas River, not far north of modern Greenville, Mississippi.

There, the explorers concluded that the Mississippi River led to the Gulf of Mexico and not to the Pacific. Fearing the presence of hostile Spanish explorers, Jolliet and his party turned around. They ascended the Mississippi and entered the Illinois River, where, American Indians said, their trip could be shortened to what is now Lake Michigan.[5] In August 1673 these seven Frenchmen were surely the first white people to view Starved Rock, a feature they could not have missed as they passed between the banks of the Illinois.

Dreams of an Empire

Starved Rock's most important time was yet to come, however, and it stood in obscurity for another decade, when it became one of the most important outposts of the Mississippi River Valley. French explorer René-Robert Cavelier, Sieur de La Salle, established on its top Fort St. Louis of Illinois, a frontier post that he saw as the center of an enormous and bountiful entrepreneurial empire.[6]

La Salle had an ambitious plan. Aware of the potential of the unexplored western wilderness, he hoped to build an even-larger New France in the forbidding remoteness of the Mississippi Valley. In the scheme pictured in his mind, the area's American Indians would be drawn to the French government by the promise of protection from their deadly enemies, the Iroquois, who, though they mainly inhabited an area to the east, often threatened the Illiniwek and others in the Mississippi region. In return, La Salle would receive the hides and furs the Native Americans provided—furs now so highly demanded for their use in making apparel for the fashionable in Europe.[7]

La Salle's strategic vision was prescient of today's globalization, and the pieces of his plan interlocked with precision. He determined to find the mouth of the Mississippi first. Once he had achieved this, outposts were to be established, including a fort he envisioned at Starved Rock. These outposts were to attract the tribes of the Illinois Country. Trade for the furs and

One of many scenic spots at Starved Rock State Park. *Photo courtesy of Illinois Department of Natural Resources.*

other commodities could be conducted, the word of God could be spread, and the glory of French civilization could flourish in the forests and prairies of the west.

In January 1682 La Salle and a party of American Indians and Frenchmen began their journey toward the mouth of the Mississippi. Among the group was La Salle's confidante and assistant, an experienced and capable soldier of fortune named Henry de Tonty, known to the American Indians as "iron hand" because of the prosthetic device he wore to replace the hand he had lost in a European battle. In early April, as the Louisiana woods displayed the lacy green of spring, they reached the gulf. In one grandiose gesture, La Salle claimed the region for Louis XIV and France.[8] Like other European adventurers before and after him, he was likely little concerned with the consequence of his claim for the people whose home the region had been for millennia.

La Salle soon started his party upstream, though he became ill and was forced to send Tonty ahead with the news of his great achievement. He rejoined Tonty later at Michilimackinac, located at the straits between Lake Michigan and Lake Huron.[9] Abandoning plans to rebuild a fort destroyed earlier during a mutiny, the two then traveled to Starved Rock, arriving as winter descended on Illinois. There La Salle hoped to put the next phase of his plan into operation.

Le Rocher and Fort St. Louis

La Salle seemed to have found a superb headquarters for his efforts. The rock's crest stands 125 feet above the waters of the Illinois River. Steep and cliff-like on three sides, the rock's fourth side was accessible then only with much effort. The summit, almost an acre, provides a natural observation post along the Illinois. To La Salle these features must have made le rocher ("the rock") as the French called it an ideal location for the center of his operations. It was here, late in 1682, that La Salle and Tonty began to build Fort St. Louis of the Illinois.[10]

La Salle, however, found himself in difficulty with the new governor general of New France, Antoine Lefebvre, Sieur de La Barre, and felt compelled to return to France where he hoped a royal audience could solve his growing problems. La Salle turned command of Fort St. Louis at Starved Rock over to Tonty. La Barre sent a representative to claim Fort St. Louis from La Salle but allowed Tonty to remain. As the representative and Tonty held joint command over the fort, a band of Iroquois Indians attacked. Throughout the six-day siege, the fort sustained La Salle's earlier judgment that it would be nearly impossible to capture. The fort held, and the Iroquois eventually departed.

La Salle had received a favorable hearing at court. Promising to build a fort at the mouth of the Mississippi that could be used to stage attacks against the Spanish in Mexico, he set sail for the gulf. Unfortunately, his plan failed. For whatever reason, he passed the Mississippi's mouth and landed in what is now southeast Texas. Realizing his error, La Salle made repeated efforts to reach the Mississippi. During one of these, as he struggled desperately overland through the inhospitable reaches of this strange and hostile country, his own men rebelled and murdered him.[11]

Tonty remained at Starved Rock, learning finally in 1684 that La Salle had been murdered. In 1690, with La Salle gone and his dreams dashed, the king granted Tonty and François Dauphin de La Forest, another Frenchman who had worked closely with La Salle, each a half-interest in the fort in recognition of their services to the Bourbons, the royal family of France.[12] But the fort's days were numbered. Continued hostility by the Iroquois made trade with the Illinois Indians difficult, and the French settlers nearby relocated, establishing farming settlements farther south. The once-thriving centerpiece of La Salle's great dream, so prominent high atop the sandstone bluff of Starved Rock, fell into disuse. The fort was likely abandoned in 1691 or 1692, although it may have been in use somewhat longer.[13] A few years later, little was left of the place but some charred remains.[14]

The event that gave Starved Rock its name is supposed to have occurred in 1769, eighty years after the Rock played its busy, important part in La Salle's collapsed dream. According to a story that has now been shown to almost certainly be false, a group of Pottawatomi, Ottawa, and Fox, working together, drove a band of Illinois to the summit of Starved Rock. The assaulting tribes forced the Illinois to remain there until their food and water were gone. The Illinois, who were so starved and desiccated by lack of food and water that their resistance flagged, tried in desperation to escape but were destroyed by their enemies.[15]

Thus, Starved Rock's name was etched into the history of Illinois. Without question the place was for a short time one of the most significant spots in the Mississippi Valley during the French period there.

After the close of the seventeenth century, however, little was heard of Starved Rock except for the legendary event that gave the place its name. It remained unnoticed during much of the rest of the eighteenth century. After the frontier reached the area, and Illinois joined the Union in 1818, it was noted, if at all, for its stunning beauty. Yet, Starved Rock was largely overlooked throughout the remainder of the 1800s. In 1835 Daniel Hitt bought Starved Rock and several nearby acres. Fifty-five years later he sold the Rock and one hundred acres of land to Ferdinand Walther, who turned the area into a private resort. It was not until 1909, however, that any official action was taken to preserve the place's grandeur and historic significance. In that year, the Forty-Sixth General Assembly formed the Illinois Parks Commission, which was to investigate the possibility of establishing a state park at Starved Rock. In 1911 legislators in the Illinois House introduced and passed a bill to purchase the area for $225,000. The senate approved the measure for $150,000. On December 15, 1911, the state bought Starved Rock and 290 adjacent acres from Walther for $146,000, and the area became an Illinois state park.[16]

Starved Rock Today

Today Starved Rock is the focal point of a state park many times the size of the original one. The Rock looms up from the south bank of the Illinois, looking much as it must have when Marquette, Jolliet, La Salle, Tonty, La Forest, and the other early French adventurers first saw it more than three centuries ago.

The summit, so isolated then, is accessible now by a well-maintained stairway that leads to the top. There, on a bed of grass and moss, white and red cedars and oaks grow. A panoramic view of the extensive countryside stretches away in all directions to the horizon. Starved Rock itself is surrounded by a system of strikingly lovely natural canyons, unlike any found elsewhere in the state. The high precipice, the steep, wooded canyons with their effervescent streams, the foliage and the wildlife and the stillness—all combine to make this a place of enchanting beauty.

A visitor's center, staffed by park rangers, contains maps, exhibits, and displays about the park and Starved Rock itself. In 1935 the Civilian Conservation Corps constructed a large log lodge and several other buildings. A modern hotel, complete with swimming pool, along with a café, banquet and conference rooms, and numerous cabins, provides comfortable accommodations for today's visitors.

On the summit of Starved Rock, a bronzed plaque and a flagpole with an American flag fluttering in the breezes that blow softly across the crest are the only evidence to signal the historic significance of this strangely captivating place. No vestige at all of La Salle's Fort St. Louis meets the modern eye— only the towering rock, the eddying waters of the Illinois far below, the slanting shadows and golden lances of sunlight in the nearby canyons, the trees, and the sky. But, looking across the river, past Plum Island and into the northwestern haze of a late-summer day, a visitor can view in reality what La Salle and Tonty saw only in their dreams—a vast, rich, productive land, a place in many ways now wealthier by far than any even they could have imagined.

Fort de Chartres
State Historic Site

1350 State Route 155, Prairie du Rocher

The flat, alluvial landscape of rural Randolph County stretches away to the north and east from the tree-shaded banks of the Mississippi River until it is abruptly stopped by towering, tan-colored bluffs three miles distant. In summertime, fields of corn and patches of wheat, interspersed with small groves of trees, checker the expansive floodplain. Tucked into the southern tip of the Great American Bottom, this bountiful place is some of Illinois's most historic ground. Here, over three centuries ago in small villages not far from the sturdy walls of an impressive military post named Fort de Chartres, French colonists made their homes in what they called "Le Pays des Illinois," or land of the Illinois.[1]

Although by the 1680s French traders and missionaries were present in central Illinois at Starved Rock and near what is now Peoria, the increasing hostility of the Fox Indians had by the 1690s caused the French to relocate down the Mississippi to the American Bottom. One of the first villages, Cahokia, grew up near the Mission of the Holy Family, started in 1699 by Seminarian missionaries.[2] A few years later, in 1703, other settlers began the community of Kaskaskia, farther down the Mississippi.[3] Within the next two decades, the establishment of yet another community, Prairie du Rocher and the construction of Fort de Chartres provided evidence of the growing significance of the region.

Originally included in Canadian New France, royal officials in 1717 shifted governmental authority over the far-off but increasingly important Illinois Country to the French colony in Louisiana.[4] Much of the growing interest in the American Bottom was driven by the unusual ideas of John Law, a brilliant and charismatic Scottish economist, who in the financial chaos following King Louis XIV's death had gained influence at the French court. Law had more than a few notions about how to make money and convinced Louis XV's regent, Philippe II, duc d'Orléans, that through these he could extricate France from its economic crisis.[5]

To further Law's scheme, the crown also soon gave administrative control of this valuable region to the Company of the Indies, a powerful mercantile organization Law controlled. The company, with its royal monopoly, hoped to profit from the Illinois Country.[6] In France, Law sold shares of his company at greatly inflated prices and promoted the Illinois Country as a place of great possibilities, complete with precious metals and astounding wealth.[7] Ultimately, Law's scheme, often referred to as the Mississippi Bubble, collapsed. A lasting effect, however, was the introduction into Illinois of slaves brought from Haiti to labor in the nonexistent mines.[8]

A Faraway Fort

The Illinois Country was, in fact, a rich part of France's colonial enterprise, not in the way Law had envisioned it but as an important source of grain and several other commodities to send downriver to New Orleans.[9] Before Law's bubble burst, his Indies Company, to help secure this midway anchor, constructed the first Fort de Chartres, a military and administrative outpost that stood hard by the eastern bank of the Mississippi River. Named for Louis, le duc de Chartres, the son of the regent to Louis XV, it was completed in 1720. This fort was a square log stockade, with two extended bastions at opposite corners.[10] Though designed to serve as a symbol of the Company of the Indies' power in the region, this fort was short-lived because its wood deteriorated quickly.[11]

A sentry box in the wall at historic Fort de Chartres. *Illustration by Phil Glosser.*

The company replaced that rotting structure in 1725 or 1726 with another fort, also a square, wooden-log palisade, with projecting bastions at all four corners and four buildings inside.[12] But by 1731 the Company of the Indies was facing financial difficulty and, unable to make enough profit to continue operations in the Illinois Country, returned control of the region to the French crown.[13] The second Fort de Chartres, like its predecessor, also began to give way to the effects of time and weather. The place had declined into such disrepair by 1747 that the French commandant moved the garrison eighteen miles southwest to Kaskaskia, although some soldiers apparently continued to use the fort from time to time.[14]

By midcentury traders and a few settlers from France's longtime adversary Britain began to appear more frequently in the forests and prairies rimming the eastern side of the Mississippi River Valley. The presence of these British intruders prompted the French to increase security for this vital region that had been their province since the explorer La Salle claimed it for the Bourbons nearly a century before.

To meet this growing threat, the French in the early 1750s started work on a third Fort de Chartres (or, according to recent archeological findings, possibly a fourth), this one made of stone.[15] Construction began not far from the second (or third) fort, and by 1753 workmen had built the fort's foundations.[16] Workers were sent to the towering limestone bluffs that marked the edge of the Mississippi's ancient course, where they quarried the stone for the new fort. Teamsters using ox carts moved the blocks cut to the construction site, where they were used in the fort's walls and interior buildings.[17]

Construction of this Fort de Chartres took several years. A great improvement over its predecessors, the stone walls were nearly three feet thick and fifteen feet high, reflecting many of the fortification concepts of the great French military engineer Sébastien Le Prestre de Vauban.[18]

Like the preceding forts, this one was rectangular and enclosed a parade ground of four acres.[19] Large, acutely angled bastions, each with its five-sided sentry box, or guerite, extended from the fort's four corners. Inside the walls, around the perimeter of the parade ground or tucked within the bastions, were several substantial stone buildings, including barracks, a guardhouse and chapel, the fort storehouse, a powder magazine, a jail, and others.[20]

Flags Change over Fort de Chartres

Soon after the fort was finished, events far distant from the Illinois Country again intruded to shape the destiny of its residents and of Fort de Chartres. In 1756 France had once more gone to war with Great Britain. Fort de Chartres played no direct role in the Seven Years' War (or French and Indian War) although it furnished some troops, supplies, and weapons for the fighting far to the east.[21] The war did not end well for France. By the Treaty of Paris, signed in 1763, France lost to Britain most of its North American empire, including the small, remote settlements scattered along the Mississippi River in the Illinois Country.

On October 10, 1765, under the command of Captain Thomas Stirling, soldiers from Britain's famed Black Watch Regiment took possession of Fort de Chartres. In a highly formal ceremony held at about ten o'clock that autumn morning, the white-and-gold flag of the Bourbons was lowered, and the colors of Great Britain were raised to unfurl in the fall breezes wafting above the fort's ramparts.[22]

The British renamed the place Fort Cavendish, but they did not stay there long. In London, King George III's cabinet decided to reduce Britain's military presence in the Illinois Country. In addition, the current of the Mississippi River increasingly threatened Fort de Chartres and made the fort's continued use as a military post questionable. When Stirling arrived, the river had slipped by nearly a hundred yards from the fort's west wall. Five years later, despite efforts to stop the ongoing erosion, the Mississippi's brown water was persistently gnawing at a bank now only thirty feet away.[23] In 1771 those at the fort were ordered to evacuate. In 1772 the Mississippi flooded much of the area, and a part of the fort's west wall, including its bastion, disappeared into the river. At that point the British garrison abandoned Fort de Chartres and relocated near the village of Kaskaskia.[24]

After the British departure, the old fort rapidly declined. With an American victory in the Revolutionary War, the region fell under the control of the Confederation Congress, which prohibited settlement in a square-mile area around the fort. In the nineteenth century, the US government opened the area as public land, and farmers occupied the nearby acres.

Several accounts of Fort de Chartres in the century after the British left describe that it had fallen into extensive disrepair.[25] The unforgiving Mississippi currents had long ago caused the southwest rampart to vanish, and parts of the remaining walls and bastions had tumbled down. The parade ground, where French soldiers had once proudly stood in formation as the Bourbon flag floated above them, was now thickly overgrown with trees and brush. Nearby residents plundered the dilapidated old fort of stones from its walls and buildings for their own use. By the beginning of the twentieth century, only the powder magazine remained extant.[26]

Citizens from the surrounding area banded together to save what remained of Fort de Chartres, and through their efforts this significant artifact from an important period of the state's history was rescued from complete oblivion. Thanks to these citizens' exertions, the State of Illinois purchased Fort de Chartres in 1913. Work to rebuild the fort extended over a number of years. Careful excavations revealed the foundations of the walls and the interior buildings. Using the foundations of one of the buildings, the state in

1928 built a museum and office for the site. Parts of the fort's walls, built on the original foundations, were constructed in 1989.[27]

Fort de Chartres Today

Fort de Chartres emerges out of the rural landscape on the southwest side of Illinois Route 155, a two-lane road that winds its way in one direction to the village of Prairie de Rocher and in the other northeast to Bluff Road, which runs along the base of the bluffs that mark the ancient course of the Mississippi. The massive stone walls seem oddly out of place in this rural countryside. The fort sits back about two hundred yards from the road, beyond a rustic rail fence. A broad lawn, dotted with a few trees, sweeps away toward the fort, which is surrounded by a shallow, grass-covered ditch.

Two verdigris-coated replica cannon stand guard nearby. A gravel path from the large parking lot leads to a gateway in the center of the eastern wall. Because the front of the original fort faced the Mississippi, the main entry is now in what was once the rear wall. The gateway was originally reconstructed in 1936 by the National Society Daughters of the American Colonists and was modeled on typical, similar entryways found in French fortifications contemporary with Fort de Chartres.[28]

The sally port itself is arch-like. In those distant, more dangerous days three centuries ago, two sets of enormous oak doors, nearly eight feet tall and six inches thick, once blocked entry here. The dark-red doors, now open during visiting hours, have heavy bands of iron at the top and bottom, with narrow windows equipped with thick bars at either side. Above the entryway's arch is a crenelated wall on which is mounted a rectangular wooden plate featuring a shield outlined in gilt. On the shield is the fleur-de-lis, and on the shield's top edge is a crown—all reminders that this place was once a distant outpost of the Bourbons. Towering over all this is a roof of wooden shakes, supported by large, heavy timbers. This impressive entry opens to a lawn-like interior, where a few sweetgum and cypress trees grow.

The foundation stones of the fort's walls and buildings inside are original, as are the walls of the powder magazine. The interior buildings are reconstructions, as are the fort walls, including parts of the northwest and southeast walls and the northeast wall with its two acutely angled bastions, each bastion again with its five-sided sentry box. Like the original walls, these

Reenactors with cannon in one of Fort de Chartres's massive walls. *Photo courtesy of Illinois Department of Natural Resources.*

walls, too, are made of limestone, tan, with a dark stain of lichens ribboning the top, and feature musket embrasures spaced about every thirty-two inches. There are large, square portals with wooden doors for cannon.

Much of the old dome-roofed powder magazine, in the east bastion, remained intact over the years and has been restored to appear much as it must have in the 1750s. This is a building that was critical to the soldiers who garrisoned this frontier post. Inside the magazine are wooden racks, holding many wooden kegs similar to those that contained Fort de Chartres's vital supply of gunpowder.

Some of the other buildings in the fort have been "ghosted." This is a technique found at many historic sites that uses only a skeleton frame to represent the shape and structure of a building that formerly existed. The ghosted structures here are the east barracks and the government house.

The reconstructed king's storehouse is now the Fort de Chartres museum, which houses an important and carefully arranged collection of artifacts and replica objects associated with the fort and the Illinois Country as it existed three centuries ago. Among the many valuable exhibits are wall panels detailing the inhabitants, French village life, Americans, Virginians, British, and arms and accoutrements. An additional display focuses on the American Indians who lived near the fort and includes replicas of Amerindian artifacts and a diorama of an American Indian village.

An important stockpile of Illinois history in the area surrounds Fort de Chartres. Not far away a prehistoric, eight-thousand-year-old early American Indian site is visible at Modoc Rock Shelter. A few miles southeast is the lovely home of Pierre Menard, the first lieutenant-governor of the state. The lingering, attenuated residue of the French culture that once predominated in this region is yet found here. But it is the massive limestone walls of Fort de Chartres, standing silently in this pastoral place, that, perhaps, most powerfully evoke those long-past days when a part of the once-great French empire was found here in the Prairie State.

Fort Massac State Park

1308 East Fifth Street, Metropolis

Southern Illinois is a place of great diversity and captivating beauty, an area where sparkling streams at the foot of craggy limestone bluffs carve their way through a rugged and enchanting landscape. Here the Shawnee National Forest is filled with a seemingly endless variety of trees. Oaks, beeches, maples, hickories, sycamores, and cottonwoods stand green in summer and are painted with striking hues of saffron, crimson, and orange in the autumn. Winter brings woods that are bare and gray, but on early spring days the recurring promise of new life returns with bright splashes of fuchsia or white from the redbud and dogwood trees. Not far away flat, alluvial bottomlands, with their productive cornfields and wheat fields, border the region's rivers.

The southern part of the state is attractive not only because of its striking loveliness and geological variation but also because of its history. This is a place of venerable towns and ancient forts, of vivid personalities and memorable events, of fascinating stories and legends.[1] One part of that colorful past is old Fort Massac, nestled on a bank of the Ohio River near where the river cuts an enormous inverted "U" into the bottom of the state.

Two block houses, silent guard at Fort Massac. *Photo courtesy of Illinois Department of Natural Resources.*

Located in Fort Massac State Park, the fort is a short distance east of the town of Metropolis and sits on a slight bluff above the river. It replicates an American military installation constructed in 1802, but its buildings and blockhouses represent only the latest of several forts that once stood here.

More than two centuries ago, when the Illinois Country was a key part of the great empire of France, French army officers early understood the military value of this place and its importance in controlling the waterways that dominate the region. As early as 1745, a French military engineer, Bernard de Verges, suggested building a fort here, but nothing came of his proposal for more than a decade.[2] Twelve years later, though, when war with the age-old enemy Britain again resumed, France reconsidered. In the spring of 1757, as the countryside displayed the green of the new season, authorities at Fort de Chartres sent Captain Charles Aubry, accompanied by a military engineer, to construct a fort here.[3]

Because he and his soldiers began their work on May 19, Ascension Day, Aubry called the new post Fort Ascension. Working swiftly, Aubry's troops were able to complete their mission by the third week of June. The fort, though constructed quickly, followed the accepted design of fortifications of the time. It was quadrilateral, with each side about 168 feet long. Acutely angled bastions were at each corner. The wooden walls of Fort Ascension's vertical stockade were made of a double row of logs standing approximately thirteen feet tall. Six feet above the interior banquette, or earthen firing platform on which the soldiers stood, Aubry's engineer fashioned loopholes for muskets. Inside the fort the soldiers built two post-in-ground barracks.[4]

Most of the fighting in the French and Indian War occurred far to the north and east, and the soldiers at Fort Ascension never saw the scarlet coats of the British army. A band of Cherokee, however, did ferociously attack the fort but were driven off. By 1759 this first fort, probably due to its hurried construction and, perhaps, because of the inferior wood used, had apparently deteriorated enough to cause the French to rebuild it.[5] The second fort, named Fort Massiac (later mispronounced and misspelled as "Massac" by the English and Americans), was improved with the addition of a ditch and a row of defensive pickets positioned beyond the walls.[6]

When diplomats finally ended the French and Indian War in 1763, the defeated French lost most of their North American territory. The Illinois Country, first explored for France when Louis Jolliet and Jacques Marquette and René-Robert Cavelier, Sieur de La Salle, and Henry de Tonty paddled their canoes down the Mississippi River nearly a century before, now fell to the British crown. Soon after the war's end, the French began to remove their military presence from the area over which the fleur-de-lis had flown for decades. It is unclear, however, exactly when French troops finally abandoned Fort Massac. The evacuation may have occurred late in 1763 or perhaps in the spring of 1764.[7] The fort itself did not long survive their departure. Sometime after the last French soldier marched out of the gate, a band of Chickasaws set it ablaze. The British expedition on its way to Fort de Chartres found only Fort Massac's burned remains.[8]

Into the Shadows

Although the British understood its strategic position, they chose not to rebuild Fort Massac.[9] It likely mattered little, for the Union Jack did not fly long over the Illinois Country. In the spring of 1775, on a cool April morning in the faraway colony of Massachusetts, a brief battle on a village green opened the American Revolution. Fort Massac was on the fringes of the Revolution's fighting. It played no role in the war except that Lieutenant Colonel George Rogers Clark and his troops, on their way to capture Kaskaskia and Cahokia, landed there briefly on a late June day in 1778.

Finding the place unoccupied, Clark and his men spent only one uneventful evening near the fort before disappearing into the Illinois woods on their clandestine way to objectives on the Mississippi.[10] When the Revolution ended with an American victory, Britain ceded all its North American holdings south of Canada and east of the Mississippi, except for Florida, to the United States. Still unused, the old fort slipped into the shadows and remained abandoned for another decade.

New Life for an Old Fort

Fort Massac's importance as a military post on the Ohio was not yet over. In 1794 General Anthony Wayne, commanding officer of US Army operations against American Indians in the Northwest Territory, sent Major Thomas Doyle to rebuild the fort. Fort Massac once again became a military presence in a period still marred by ongoing conflict with American Indians and troubled by uneasy relations with France during the infamous Citizen Genet affair. The disturbing presence of the Spanish just beyond the Mississippi also in part gave new life to the fort.[11]

Arriving at Fort Massac in the early summer of 1794, Major Doyle beached his ten riverboats on June 12 and began building the new fort. He finished his work a little more than four months later.[12] Doyle's fort was similar to those the French constructed earlier. Built of wood, it was a square stockade with four blockhouses, one at each corner of the walls.[13]

Although it was a military installation, Fort Massac was destined for an important new role as a port of entry where officials collected federal taxes on

Lt. Col. George Rogers Clark at the Ohio River. *Photo courtesy of Illinois Department of Natural Resources.*

products shipped on vessels plying the Ohio and Mississippi Rivers.[14] Except for this river traffic, the next decade at the fort was for the most part uneventful, but it was still destined to play a minor part in two episodes of US history.

The first of these occurred on an autumn day in 1803 when the explorers Meriwether Lewis and William Clark, on their way to their great "voyage of discovery," landed at Fort Massac on November 11 and remained until November 13. While at the fort they employed French-Shawnee frontiersman George Drouillard, who became an important addition to their expedition.[15]

Fort Massac was also peripherally involved with the so called Burr Conspiracy, a bizarre plot involving former Vice President Aaron Burr, General James Wilkinson, and others. The exact dimensions of Burr's scheme remain murky. He, perhaps, hoped to become the head of a group of western states that he thought he could somehow pry from the Union or to establish a separate nation in land held by Spain. Wilkinson himself claimed he wanted to simply settle as a farmer someplace in Spanish territory. Whatever the plan, Burr and Wilkinson met at Fort Massac in June 1805.[16]

Later, as Burr and a group of associates traveled down the Ohio, Captain Daniel Bissell, commander at Fort Massac, permitted Burr's boats to pass by undisturbed. Questions were initially raised about Bissell's actions, but he was later cleared of any wrongdoing.[17]

When America and Great Britain again went to war in 1812, Fort Massac once more briefly seemed important. The fort had been damaged by the enormous New Madrid earthquake of 1811, but the War Department chose it as a marshalling area for the 24th Infantry Regiment in the late fall of 1812. As the 24th began to assemble, they found the fort in poor condition. The situation worsened as additional members of the unit continued to arrive, and the soldiers, short of housing, clothing, and food, huddled for several miserable months there.[18]

Fort Massac played no other part in the War of 1812, and in 1814 it was abandoned yet again. And, once deserted, Fort Massac, like another former French military post, Fort de Chartres, became a rich lode of resources for nearby residents as they looted it for construction materials. Some accounts state that even the caretaker appointed to safeguard the place sold timbers from the fort for use as firewood by steamboats navigating the Ohio.[19]

In the early days of the American Civil War, two Union army units, the 3rd Illinois Cavalry and the 131st Illinois Infantry, briefly trained here but withdrew after an outbreak of measles killed several troops.[20] The fort, again abandoned, was for decades almost forgotten.

Fort Massac Today

Fort Massac was finally saved from vanishing into the mists of history when in 1903 the Daughters of the American Revolution convinced the State of Illinois to purchase the fort and another twenty-four acres for use as Illinois's first state park, dedicated in the fall of 1908.[21] The park is just east of Metropolis. A walkway leads from a modern visitors center across a tree-shaded lawn toward the fort, which sits very near the Ohio, perhaps seventy-five yards north of the river. Just past a seawall at the park's edge, a gravelly, driftwood-strewn beach extends to the water.

Beyond the fort's buildings is a striking background formed by an expanse of river and sky. Here a splendid view of the flat Kentucky shoreline is visible perhaps three-quarters of a mile distant across the silver-brown

Ohio. It is an imposing vista altered only by an occasional passing of a tow of barges, nudged along by its towboat. Nearby, not far from where the park's grounds end, stands a heroic-sized statue of George Rogers Clark, glazed green by time. Clark, map in one hand, musket in the other, stares intently across the Ohio toward the far shore.

The buildings here replicate the 1802 American fort, one of the fortifications that once stood on this spot. The reconstruction of Fort Massac began in 2003 and is ongoing. To preserve the archeological integrity of the original forts, the 1802 replication was built just a few yards east of where the originals were located. The outline of those forts is visible in the contours of a shallow, grassy ditch and wooden posts that trace where the stockade's walls formerly stood. Remains of foundations reveal the locations of buildings once enclosed by the walls.

The reconstructed fort consists of several buildings, including two long, narrow, two-story soldiers' barracks that front on a square parade ground; three blockhouses, square two-story structures, one with a watchtower, and with walls laced by rectangular musket loopholes; and another building just west of one of the blockhouses.

Made of heavy, hewn timbers and roofed with dark wooden shingles, the buildings are gray and weather-beaten, and their windows are covered by heavy planked shutters. A grass-covered ditch, perhaps six feet deep with gently sloping sides, surrounds the fort. Fort Massac's quadrangle and sharply angled bastions at each of its four corners conform to the classical configuration of eighteenth- and nineteenth-century fortifications.

Just north of the reconstructed fort is the park's excellent visitors center, whose museum houses exhibits that chronicle the various periods in Fort Massac's history. These have included interesting wall-mounted displays and a large detailed, glass-enclosed tabletop model depicting the American Fort Massac. One of these displays provides information concerning the excavations directed by archeologist Paul Maynard between 1939 and 1942 that revealed much of the knowledge of the various forts built and rebuilt here. Other panels trace the history of these forts.

Another room holds a collection of Amerindian stone projectile points and tools, such as arrowheads, spearheads, and other items in glass cases on the walls. These objects date from the time of the Paleo Indians millennia ago through the more recent Mississippian period.

Other than attacks against it by American Indian warriors, no great battles were fought at Fort Massac. For most of its history it existed, as it does now, undisturbed on its verdant bluff above the Ohio. Those who garrisoned this far-distant post kept the long watch for an enemy who did not appear. But whether they served under the fleur-de-lis or the Stars and Stripes, the sentinels who stood at this fort's walls not only endured the loneliness and hardships of a soldier's duty but displayed the fidelity demanded by that duty. In so doing they played their individual but important parts in the unfolding story of Illinois.

Part 2
FRONTIER TIMES

Battle of Apple
River Fort

1832

Vandalia
State House
constructed

Federal
land office
established at
Shawneetown

Abraham Lincoln
arrives in
New Salem

1836

1812

1831

Prologue

As the American frontier moved steadily westward during the eighteenth and nineteenth centuries, Illinois, like the rest of the nation, underwent a remarkable change. Claimed by France for nearly a century, the area that became the Prairie State was briefly under the British flag until ceded to the United States following the American Revolution. Long before that war ended, however, a few adventurous settlers had pushed beyond the Appalachian Mountains and entered an expansive region to the west, an area that had for millennia been home to several American Indian tribes. Some of these pioneers made the arduous journey overland, at first following trails and then a few primitive roads that had been scratched through the woods and across the prairies. Others chose to travel by water, especially on the Ohio River, called by historians Stephen Leonard and Melinda F. Kwedar the "great river road into the western frontier."[1]

Some of these westward-bound pioneers settled in what is now Ohio, Indiana, Kentucky, and Tennessee. Others who traveled on the Ohio found their way into Illinois at a place known today as **Old Shawneetown**, close by the contemporary community of Shawneetown, established in 1937 when repeated flooding caused most residents to move to higher ground. Snugged against the western bank of the Ohio, not far from where it joins the Mississippi, Old Shawneetown was one of the most important gateways into the Illinois Country. For a fleeting time, the village prospered as a boisterous, thriving port of entry and an early banking center. Old Shawneetown's economy rested in part, too, on salt extracted from the nearby saline springs, though this portion of the village's prosperity was darkly shadowed by the slave labor used in the production process.

Among those who journeyed into Illinois was the family of Abraham Lincoln. Like many others, the Lincolns moved first from Kentucky to Indiana and then to Illinois. Lincoln's father, Thomas, and stepmother, Sarah, ultimately built a home in Coles County, where both lived until their deaths. Young Abraham however, after a flatboat trip to New Orleans, left his family and settled in **New Salem**, a rough-hewn village on a ridge above the Sangamon River and not far from today's Petersburg. It was in New Salem where Lincoln, as a friendly, likable young man, began to study law, where he entered politics and where, perhaps, he fell in love with Ann Rutledge.

While living in New Salem, Lincoln played a small role as a militiaman in an unfortunate chapter in Illinois history known as the Black Hawk War. The war was yet another example of the many confrontations that flared between white settlers and American Indians as the frontier pushed ever farther to the west. Some of the sporadic fighting in this regrettable and ill-starred conflict occurred in southern Wisconsin. Other battles were fought in northwestern Illinois, where the Sauk chief Black Hawk and his warriors attacked area residents and local militia huddled in the hastily built **Apple River Fort**, a reconstruction of which is near the present-day town of Elizabeth.

Illinois achieved enough population to enter the Union and became the nation's twenty-first state in December 1818. The new state government met first in Kaskaskia but in 1819 moved to Vandalia, on the Kaskaskia River's west bank, where the legislature, governor, and other officials conducted the state's business in a series of capitol buildings. The third of these, and the last to be used before the government once again relocated, this time to Springfield, is the **Vandalia State House**. Though it was used for only a few years, the striking building still found here played an important part in the state's history and is where Abraham Lincoln, Stephen A. Douglas, and other notable figures from the state's past appeared early in their political careers.

The story of the frontier, with its courageous characters and mythic events, has long captured the imagination of Americans and the world.

Illinois played its role in this exciting era with Old Shawneetown and its boisterous inhabitants, New Salem and its early entrepreneurs, Apple River Fort and the gripping encounter between Black Hawk's braves and pioneer settlers, and the Vandalia State House where soon-to-be-famous legislators helped set the state's course—all part of the stirring frontier period in the Prairie State's past.

Old Shawneetown

Gallatin County

One of America's great rivers, the Ohio, makes a long, southwestward run of nearly a thousand miles from Pittsburgh, Pennsylvania, to Cairo, Illinois. The river's water, often coffee brown or sometimes glossed with a quicksilver sheen, is channeled between widely spaced banks. The river laps against six states until it finally reaches the even more massive Mississippi River. Though it suffers to some extent from pollution today, the Ohio remains a magnificent river.

Not far downstream from the Ohio's junction with the Wabash River, which separates Indiana and Illinois, the village of Old Shawneetown hugs the Ohio's west bank. Named for the Shawnee Indians who once lived for a short time in the area, Shawneetown is hidden and protected now by the mounding of an enormous levee.[1] Platted originally by the US government in 1910, this small community was one of the earliest and most important settlements in the state.[2] Although nearly deserted today, Old Shawneetown was once a rollicking and prosperous place and a focal point of civilization in early Illinois.[3]

A Port of Entry

The Ohio River was a major transportation artery at the dawn of the nineteenth century, a kind of superhighway that was a part of the great river system Americans used to travel inland. Flatboats carried freight and passengers on the long journey from Pittsburgh to Illinois or the Mississippi. Much of this traffic stopped at Shawneetown, and the village became a gateway to the frontier.[4]

Like Cumberland Gap in the mountains of Virginia, Kentucky, and Tennessee, and Independence, Missouri, and Santa Fe, New Mexico, Old Shawneetown, as entryway for migration to the west, witnessed the seemingly endless pageant of the great American westward movement. A stream of trappers, traders, pioneer farmers, mechanics, miners, and just plain adventurers, many of whom were from the Upland South region of the United States, passed through Shawneetown on the way to fulfilling their dreams.[5] Some of these decided to stay.

In 1812 the US government authorized a land office in Shawneetown, though selling didn't begin until 1814. Sales soon boomed, however, and by the end of 1819 government agents managed to sell 562,296 acres of public land at the Shawneetown land office.[6]

Old Shawneetown was also important because of the nearby salt deposits that had drawn American Indians and later the French to the area years before. In 1803 the federal government purchased the salt springs near Shawneetown and all the territory four miles around them from American Indians.[7] The government leased the saltworks to entrepreneurs, who conveyed the brine through wooden pipes from the salt springs to the "furnaces" in which well-stoked fires boiled away the spring water in large kettles, leaving a rime of salt. A bushel of salt could be produced from approximately two hundred gallons of brine.[8] The salt was then bagged and sold as a product of what was one of the state's first industries.[9] In one eleven-year period, 158,394 bushels of salt were taken from the Gallatin County salines.[10]

The saltworks operation was a lucrative enterprise, and Shawneetown flourished. But unfortunate counterpoints to the town's prosperity were hidden in the smudges of smoke from the saltworks fires. The salt entrepreneurs stripped away ever-larger areas of nearby timber for use as fuel. But the human toll for much of the profit resulted from the bone-wearying labor of slaves, who endured the drudgery of most of the difficult work required there.[11] Slave labor seemed so necessary that when Illinois became a state in 1818, the state's founding fathers permitted slavery in the Shawneetown area until 1825, though the 1818 state constitution banned it elsewhere.[12]

A traveler passing through in 1823 reported that Shawneetown had "eleven stores and as many grocery or grog shops." Despite the thriving businesses, perhaps reflecting on the unkempt surroundings so typical of frontier communities, this traveler felt that the residents "have not the appearance of being very industrious."[13] James Hall, who resided in Shawneetown between 1820 and 1828, painted a similar picture, noting that the community had "about one hundred houses of which five or six are of brick, several of frame, and the remainder of log."[14]

The Star Sets

After the mid-1820s, however, a darker shadow fell across Shawneetown. The state's population, along with trade, shifted northward. When the Erie Canal opened in 1825 and the Black Hawk War ended in 1832, settlers increasingly found the central and northern parts of Illinois more attractive.[15] Technological developments, too, added to Shawneetown's decline. John Deere's revolutionary new plow and Cyrus McCormick's grain reaper drew pioneers to the middle region of the state—an area friendly to wheat and corn production.[16] Railroads, most of which were built north of a line running from Alton, Illinois, to Terre Haute, Indiana, also made central and northern Illinois more attractive.[17] Shawneetown's star was clearly descending, but despite these changes, enough business remained for residents to open the first state bank in Illinois.

Prosperity, however, continued to drift away to the north and west as a growing market economy, the result of a spreading road network as well as the new technologies mentioned above, emerged in central and northern Illinois, just as it did in most of the northern part of the nation at large. Shawneetown changed. Once a bustling, busy pioneer entrepot, life settled as the frontier passed. The old village was quiescent during the last

The Ohio River inundating Shawneetown streets during the flood of 1898. *Abraham Lincoln Presidential Library and Museum (ALPLM).*

three-quarters of the nineteenth century though the turbulence of the Civil War and periodic floods from the Ohio sometimes broke the calm.

The possibility of flooding had threatened the village since its founding. Hall noted, "The town is often insulated, when not actually overflowed," and the Ohio had inundated the community in "1813 and 1815 when the water covered all the streets and entered the lower apartments of the dwellings, reaching nearly to the second floors."[18] High water swamped Shawneetown several more times between 1867 and 1884.

In 1898 the Ohio left its banks yet again, causing the levee built following an earlier flood to rupture. Thirty-nine years later, the worst flood of modern times and the one that finally prompted the residents of the village to move, took place in 1937. Many citizens of the older village founded a new

Old Bank of Illinois building in Old Shawneetown. *Illustration by Phil Glosser.*

community on higher ground, and over time the original village became known as Old Shawneetown.[19]

Old Shawneetown Today

The streets of Old Shawneetown are almost deserted now, lined mostly with vacant lots and empty buildings. Many of the town's historic structures have vanished, most likely the casualties of long-term damage inflicted by repeated flooding as well as simple neglect. A visitor, though, can still view landmarks from that thriving, vibrant village of the early nineteenth century.

The most striking of these is the former Bank of Illinois. Construction began in 1839, but the bank failed, and it was shuttered just a few years afterward. Several other financial institutions used the building later, but it was permanently closed in 1942.[20] It is an imposing structure, four stories tall. Made of red brick, the front facade and lower story are covered with limestone. Five fluted Doric columns support an impressive pediment of Greek Revival style that shapes the front portico, which shades two sets of double doors and two large windows, protected by heavy steel shutters.

The bank is owned by the State of Illinois and administered through the Division of Historic Preservation, Illinois Department of Natural Resources, but is an inactive site and is closed to the public. The old building today has a melancholy air of faded stateliness. The sixteen stone stairs that ascend from a red-brick sidewalk to the portico are sometimes strewn with litter. The rooms in the once-grand interior are now almost in ruin, the plaster from their walls crumbling and their lath exposed. But even with its time-worn exterior and darkened windows that stare blankly at Main Street, the splendid building dominates the downtown area still. Across the street from the bank, a plaque marks Meriwether Lewis and William Clark's celebrated 1804 expedition.

The John Marshall House, a reconstructed two-story, federal-style building made of orange-colored brick with white wooden trim, marks another of the town's most historic spots. The house is located at what was formerly the corner of Illinois Route 13 and Front Street. It stands almost in the shadow of the large levee that was built atop Front Street to hold the Ohio's waters at bay. The original structure, built in 1808, became the "birthplace of banking" in Illinois when the first bank in Illinois territory was chartered there in 1816.[21]

Inside, in a room replicating one used by Marshall as the bank's office, is a small, rusted safe, the only original object in the house. Four second-story bedrooms are accessible by a narrow, twisting wooden staircase. The Gallatin County Historical Society administers the John Marshall house and opens it May through October on the first and third Sundays or by appointment.

A third historic structure is the Rowan House, built in 1832. It is a handsome, two-story, federal-style, red-brick home with white trim. Located just north of Monroe Street on Market, the Rowan House remains a private residence and not open to the public.[22]

A more recent but still interesting building is Old St. Mary's Church, constructed in 1931. Made of dark-red brick, it sits on the east side of Market Street, between Jefferson and Monroe Streets. A walk leads to front stairs that ascend to a gracefully arched doorway, under which are two dark-brown doors. Above the doorway's opening are three Gothic arched windows with white intersecting tracery. A tall bell tower dominates one corner. Time has also passed Old St. Mary's by, and it, too, now seems forgotten. The church is on an unkempt lot, shaded by large maple, hickory, and sycamore trees. Owned now by the state, it also is closed to the public.

Today the hustle and bustle that must have been so much a part of Old Shawneetown more than two centuries ago have vanished. Despite its quiet streets and the silence of its aged buildings, Old Shawneetown represents a dynamic, exciting time in the American past. One part of Old Shawneetown's history frames a shadowed period when those who were enslaved suffered a tragic loss of dignity and freedom while the liberty of others was almost unfettered. But another, better chapter in this village's story offers a picture of an America that in an era of daily, almost unremitting challenge, managed through effort and innovation and hope to somehow hold fast to the promise of the future. In this way this small, nearly-forgotten town on the banks of the Ohio River can tell us much about an earlier and important time in the nation's history.

Lincoln's New Salem State Historic Site

15588 History Lane, Petersburg

Almost anyone who reads American history is certain to encounter a long roster of personalities who in some way are associated with the Prairie State. Cyrus McCormick, Ulysses Grant, Jane Addams, Carl Sandburg, Ronald Reagan, Bonnie Blair, Ernest Hemingway, Adlai Stevenson, and Barack Obama are only a few of these. By almost any reckoning, however, the figure of Abraham Lincoln stands above all these as the preeminent personage to emerge from Illinois and onto the wider stage of national and international prominence.

Lincoln as president is often considered epic in proportion, perhaps, only to George Washington. Even in an era when respect for national figures seems to have lessened and historians have focused less on the "great man," Lincoln has endured, and his visage greets us from currency and coins and from the solemn confines of his white-marble memorial in America's capital.[1]

Thousands of books have been written about Lincoln, whose craggy countenance remains familiar to millions. The books have plumbed his background, seeking the wellspring of his personality, hoping to find in that background what it was that formed Abraham Lincoln. Was it an allegedly difficult relationship with a demanding father in a home deprived early of a loving mother? Was it his poverty-laced backwoods childhood and adolescence in the primitive rawness of rural Kentucky and Indiana? Or was it the years spent in a rough riverside village in Illinois where as a likable, enterprising young man in his twenties, he hoped and worked for a career in politics and law?

It was, perhaps, all these, but some examinations of Lincoln's life have considered his years in the frontier community of New Salem, Illinois, as an especially important period in shaping his rise to legal and political success. Fascination with Lincoln has persisted for more than a century and a half, and as a result, this reconstituted little town where he once lived has exerted a remarkable pull on those who want to know more about this part of Lincoln's story.[2]

A Village on the Sangamon

When Abraham Lincoln first arrived in the summer of 1831, New Salem, located on a high, wooded ridge above the Sangamon River, was a typical Illinois pioneer community. Two enterprising southerners, James Rutledge from South Carolina and John Camron of Georgia, founded New Salem in 1829. The two constructed a mill and used the Sangamon's current to grind grain and saw wood. Before the place went into decline around 1836, thirty shops or offices and twenty-five families may have been clustered on the hill above the river, and a population of perhaps a hundred residents lived there at its height.[3]

In 1830 Abraham Lincoln, age twenty-one, had moved with his family from southern Indiana to central Illinois, where he lived in a cabin with his father, Thomas, and stepmother in Macon County near the Sangamon River. In 1831 frontier entrepreneur Denton Offutt asked Lincoln's stepbrother John D. Johnston to help crew a flatboat of goods to New Orleans. Johnston agreed and recruited Lincoln and Lincoln's cousin John Hanks to help. Working near the now-vanished hamlet of Sangamo Town, the three built the flatboat and started down the Sangamon toward the Illinois River.[4]

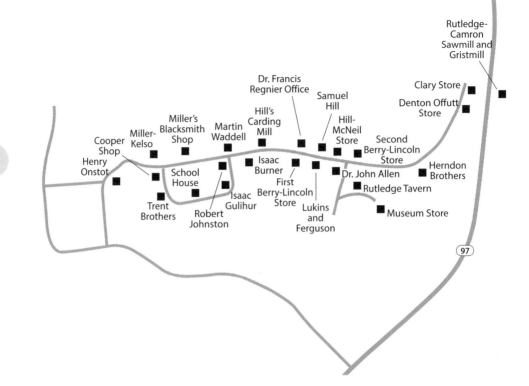

New Salem Village, ca. 1831

Life in New Salem

It was when Offutt's boat became wedged on Rutledge and Camron's mill-dam that Lincoln first visited New Salem. When water began to pour into the flatboat's stern, it started to sink. According to most accounts, Lincoln saved the craft when he shifted (or in some versions offloaded) its cargo and then drained the accumulated water by drilling a hole in the boat's bottom with a borrowed auger. When he somehow plugged the hole and reshifted (or reloaded) the cargo, the flatboat then cleared the dam.[5] Lincoln's quick thinking impressed Offutt, who was also intrigued by possible business opportunities in then-thriving New Salem. He decided to set up a store and offered Lincoln a job as his clerk.

Following the flatboat trip to New Orleans, Lincoln returned to New Salem. When he arrived, however, Offutt had not yet opened his store, and Lincoln engaged in miscellaneous employment to earn a living, including steering a raft carrying a family on the Sangamon to the village of Beardstown.[6] By September, however, the store was finally in business and, as promised, Offutt employed Lincoln as his clerk.[7]

Lincoln, however, soon faced an unwelcome challenge. Offutt, apparently a loquacious man, bragged frequently that Lincoln was the strongest and smartest person in New Salem. In the area's rough-and-tumble environment, Offutt's boasts brought Lincoln into conflict with the leader of a band of rowdies who lived around the nearby hamlet of Clary's Grove. The Clary's Grove Boys were led by a local roughneck named Jack Armstrong. Reacting to Offutt's boasting, New Salem resident and "grocery" (liquor-by-the-drink store) owner Bill Clary placed a bet with Offutt, wagering him Armstrong could best Lincoln in a wrestling match.[8]

The good-natured Lincoln was reluctant to participate but finally acceded to the wager. Accounts of the match, held near Offutt's store in front of a cheering crowd, differ. Some state Armstrong won, some say Lincoln was victorious, and some that the bout was a draw. Whatever the outcome, the match earned Lincoln the respect of Armstrong and the Clary's Grove Boys, who afterwards became his friends and advocates.[9]

Following only a few months of operation, Offutt's store, along with his other enterprises, failed, and Lincoln was left without work. Soon, however, when the militia needed men for the Black Hawk War in the spring of 1832, Lincoln volunteered. Initially elected captain of his militia company, he later reenlisted as a private and served a total of around three months before reappearing at New Salem.[10]

Before his enlistment Lincoln had expressed an interest in politics, and when he returned from his militia service, he made his first attempt at political office, declaring his candidacy for the state legislature in the election of 1832. Although he lost, he did finish eighth among thirteen contestants.[11] Remaining at loose ends, Lincoln tried his hand as a merchant and in 1832 went into partnership with fellow New Salem resident William F. Berry. The two ran their store for a brief period, but due to mismanagement by both Lincoln and Berry, it finally, as Lincoln later said, "winked out."[12] Berry died shortly afterwards, and Lincoln was left with the store's debt.[13]

Second Berry-Lincoln store in New Salem village. *Illustration by Phil Glosser.*

Lincoln was once more without employment. He had been named New Salem's postmaster in 1833, but the position did not pay enough to provide a living, and he again pursued a variety of odd jobs.[14] Fortunately, someone suggested to the county surveyor, John Calhoun, that he hire Lincoln as his assistant.[15] Though Lincoln knew almost nothing about surveying techniques, he apparently was a quick study, and after a brief but intense period devoted to examining some books on the subject, he began work for Calhoun.[16]

Lincoln's interest in politics had not diminished, and in 1834 he again became a candidate for the Illinois legislature. This time, drawing on the many contacts he had gained from his longer residence in the New Salem area and his experience in the Black Hawk War, he was successful, and he left to serve his first term as an elected representative.[17] When he returned to New Salem in the spring of 1835, Lincoln began to earnestly pursue the study of law, sometimes walking to Springfield (about twenty miles) to borrow law books from John Todd Stuart, a lawyer and future law partner, who had served as an officer with Lincoln in the Black Hawk War.[18]

Sometime during this period, Lincoln apparently fell in love with Ann Rutledge, a woman living nearby. Ann, four years younger than the twenty-six-year-old Lincoln, was the lovely and personable daughter of mill owner and village innkeeper Rutledge and his wife, Mary.

The relationship gained public attention years later through a Springfield lecture by Lincoln's longtime law partner, William H. Herndon, in November 1866. Shortly after Lincoln's assassination, with a biography ultimately in mind, Herndon had begun seeking information about the younger Lincoln from those who had known him in the years before his presidency. Included were several people who had resided in New Salem during Lincoln's time there. Their recollections indicated that there had been a closeness between the youthful Lincoln and Ann. They further revealed that Lincoln had appeared distraught by Ann's passing, to the point of being cast so deep into depression that a few even feared he might take his own life.

More than a half-century later, the Lincoln-Rutledge relationship was further ingrained into the public consciousness by Edgar Lee Masters's poem "Ann Rutledge," which was included in his enormously popular *Spoon River Anthology*, published in 1915.

The exact dimensions of this affair have never been precisely determined, and some prominent Lincoln scholars at one time relegated it to the status of near myth. More recent accounts agree, however, that the two did have some sort of association that was cut short when Ann died in August 1835, likely from typhoid fever.[19]

Lincoln was reelected to the legislature in 1836 and, to further his legal career, left New Salem, moving to Springfield in 1837. There he became Stuart's law partner. By the time Lincoln moved, New Salem's star was beginning to set. Menard County was created from Sangamon County in early 1839, and the county seat placed at Petersburg. As New Salem's importance lessened, several families moved away, many to Petersburg. By 1840 the little community was almost deserted.

New Salem as Consecrated Ground

After Lincoln's election to the presidency and his assassination, curiosity about places associated with him grew. New Salem was no exception, and within a decade of Lincoln's death, people started to arrive at the now-vanished village to see where the young Lincoln had once lived and worked.[20] As interest in New Salem grew, questions arose among several local groups concerning the best way it could fit into the Lincoln story. In 1906 members of the Old Salem Chautauqua Association attracted the interest of one of the Chautauqua's lecturers—newspaper publisher and US Representative William Randolph Hearst—in the site. After viewing the place, Hearst acquired the land where the village once stood and transferred it in trust to the association.[21] Nearby residents later created another local organization, the Old Salem Lincoln League, to further the site's preservation. In the summer of 1918, the league began construction of several log structures at New Salem.[22]

In 1919 the State of Illinois acquired New Salem. Later the earlier structures, now deteriorated, were dismantled; in 1932 the state, with a view of making the village as authentic as possible, began a new period of building there. English Brothers, a Champaign, Illinois, construction company, started erecting replica structures that year. Later the Civilian Conservation Corps also worked at New Salem, and through these efforts the present site was created.[23]

New Salem Today

As did the original, the reconstructed village, known as Lincoln's New Salem, stands on the high, forested ridge above the Sangamon. The river below is a muddy-looking stream that flows today through a broad, grassy bottomland, perhaps a hundred yards east of where it did when Lincoln lived here.

Entering New Salem at its west end, not far from the modern visitors center, one can easily gain a sense of a time nearly two centuries past when there was a hope for the future here. New Salem's main street, not much more than a wide path, runs generally east and west along a ridge that narrows as it nears the river bluff. Surfaced now, the street was likely dirt in Lincoln's time, and the areas on both sides are more park-like today. But the grass beneath the scattering of large trees here is uneven and coarse, perhaps akin to when the village flourished. Here and there, on a spring day, violets push their purple petals through the rough grass and fight for notice with the more aggressive and numerous bright yellow dandelions. In the distance the harsh cawing of a crow often breaks the rustic silence.

Split-rail fences border parts of the street. Scattered along both sides of the street are the sole original building and twenty-three reconstituted buildings, looking weather-beaten, that likely are similar to those of so many years ago. Most are constructed of hewn logs and are roofed with dark, heavy shingles. Many of the chimneys are made of pieces of stone, others of chinked logs. Blue-white threads of smoke rise from some of these, scenting the air with the pleasant smell of burning wood.

It is quiet on most days in New Salem now, with little of the comings and goings that must have once occurred when a busy village was here. From the far end of the street there occasionally comes the thin sound of a dulcimer. Costumed, well-informed interpreters are at work in some of the shops and houses.

Near the western end of the village is Henry Onstot's cooper shop, the only original building at New Salem. Once moved to Petersburg, it was returned here in 1922.[24] Onstot shaped by hand the white-oak staves that he then crafted into the barrels, churns, and buckets used in the village and surrounding area.

Hatter Martin Waddell's log house and shop are on the north side of the street, roughly in the village center. A heavy, black, iron kettle, once used by

Waddell to make felt, sits on the porch. A sign reveals coonskin hats sold for $2.00 ; those of rabbit-fur were 50 cents. Hat molds and other tools of the hatter's trade rest on a small table in one room.

Next to Waddell's is a two-story log structure representing Samuel Hill's carding mill. The contemporary visitor may find the extent of its technology surprising, especially in such a rural location as New Salem was in 1832. The mill was powered by two oxen walking on a circular platform, perhaps twenty feet across, which served as a treadmill. The treadmill turned a vertical shaft affixed to a large horizontal cogwheel. That cogwheel drove another shaft that connected to the carding machine. Made up of a series of large rollers mounted in a frame, the machine was designed to card (to untangle and comb) large quantities of wool.

Near the town's east end and on the north side of the street is the second Berry-Lincoln store, where they were merchants until their enterprise failed. The store is a one-story structure; attached to the back is an enclosed lean-to where Lincoln slept. Weathered and gray, the store is the only frame or clapboard structure in New Salem. The interior is whitewashed, with a floor made of wide wooden planks. A large stone fireplace on the rear wall likely would have kept such a building at least moderately warm on winter days. Shelves behind the counter hold items of merchandise typical of early nineteenth-century rural stores. The store was once also the New Salem post office, and a small set of cubbyholes, likely similar to what Lincoln used to sort the mail, sits on the counter.

Rutledge and Camron's reconstructed sawmill and gristmill is at the foot of the bluff that descends from the village's east end. Extending from the mill is a dam replicating the one on which Denton Offutt's flatboat lodged so long ago. The Sangamon River now slips by one hundred yards east of where it did in Lincoln's time, and thus the dam stops no water today.

At the top of the bluff, on the south side of the street, is the reconstructed Rutledge Tavern that was the village inn. A one-story building with a long front porch, the inn has two large rooms and a sleeping loft above. The original building was also the Rutledge home.

The site's visitor center, a large, low structure with a semicircular, columned portico, is on the west side of the village and is the entrance to Lincoln's New Salem. It is a welcoming place and close to a spacious parking lot. At the entry desk, friendly staff members answer questions and offer directions. The comfortable amphitheater features the film *Turning Point*, a chronicle of Lincoln's years here.

The center's exhibits offer much information about Lincoln's life at New Salem. Display boards show how the Berry-Lincoln Store was reconstructed and explain the Ann Rutledge story, the legendary wrestling contest between Lincoln and Armstrong, and about the Clary's Grove Boys. A series of exhibits trace Lincoln's life through brief biographical sketches titled "Young Cast About," "Wilderness Youth," "Springfield Lawyer," and "Wartime President."

Thousands of people visit here each year, and although New Salem is, as two historians who know much about it have written, an "imaginative approximation" of the village Lincoln once knew, it is, nonetheless, of undeniable importance.[25] Lincoln's persona has captivated our minds for nearly two centuries; and it is here, on this green bluff above the Sangamon where he once lived and worked and grew, that we can perhaps at least glimpse a place that surely in part shaped this remarkable man.

Apple River Fort
State Historic Site

311 East Myrtle Street, Elizabeth

One of the less-familiar parts of the Prairie State's past is the unfortunate conflict known as the Black Hawk War of 1832. Although a few historians have examined it and some of those who participated in it, such as Zachary Taylor, Abraham Lincoln, and Black Hawk, later became prominent nationally, the war is found today mostly at the margins of the state's history. As wars are now reckoned, the Black Hawk War was brief. Casualties were low. But for those families, both American Indian and white, whose lives were marred by it through the death or wounding of loved ones, this war was as heart-rending and sorrowful as any. And to the Sauk followers of Black Hawk, who were pushed by the war even further down a path away from their own way of life, the conflict was especially disastrous.

The violence of the war came suddenly late on a June afternoon in 1832 as a group of women left a small wooden fort near the Apple River in the northwestern part of Illinois. The women were off to gather gooseberries not far from the fort's newly constructed walls.[1] People in nearby settlements had quickly built the Apple River Fort a few weeks earlier when word

Stockade as it would have looked to Black Hawk's warriors at Apple River Fort in 1832. *Photo by the author.*

reached them that a band of American Indians had badly defeated a unit of Illinois militia on May 14. That encounter, the so-called Battle of Stillman's Run, had occurred at Old Man's Creek near the Rock River, thirty miles away. The fight was the beginning of the Black Hawk War, and it contributed markedly to the uncertainty and fear clouding northern Illinois and southern Wisconsin in the anxious spring and summer of 1832.[2]

The Black Hawk War was rooted in a variety of causes, many originating decades before the first shots were fired. At its base was the long-standing and tragic struggle between American Indians and white newcomers that had marred the westward movement of the frontier since colonial times. American Indians, pushed continually from ancestral homes, resisted the unrelenting demand for land by white settlers. As the frontier line extended, this resistance, often marked by violent and bloody conflicts, produced what one historian has called a "nativistic spirit," which from time to time coalesced around influential and charismatic leaders, such as Pontiac and Tecumseh.[3]

These chiefs attempted to unite Indians in their struggle against the white settlers, and though their efforts were ultimately unsuccessful, they contributed to a long-running "ideology of resistance" that surfaced among the Sauk prior to the Black Hawk War. Adding to this simmering discontent was the Treaty of 1804, negotiated between William Henry Harrison and a group of Sauk and Fox chiefs. The treaty, likely not fully explained to the chiefs, called for the Sauk to cede several million acres of land along both sides of the Mississippi River. In return the Sauk were to receive approximately $2,200 of gifts, followed by an annuity valued at $1,000 per year.[4] Though the Sauk were permitted to remain in the region, once white people began to settle there, the Sauk were expected to withdraw.

The Sauk chief Black Hawk had long considered the 1804 treaty invalid. However, in 1831, to avoid a confrontation with white troops, he took his followers from Saukenuk, their Rock River village, across the Mississippi River into Iowa. Shortly afterward, he signed an agreement that included a provision prohibiting him and his people from returning unless he was granted permission to the eastern side of the Mississippi.[5]

Black Hawk's Hope

The following April, however, at the invitation of Wabokieshiek, a Winnebago mystic better known as the Prophet, Black Hawk and his villagers, sometimes called the British Band, returned to Illinois.[6] Black Hawk's hope appears to have been to join a group of Winnebago followers of the Prophet at Prophet's Town, a village not far from where the Rock River meets the Mississippi River. He apparently believed that there he could resume a peaceful residence east of the Mississippi.[7]

Black Hawk seemingly acceded to the Prophet's contention that his return did not violate the agreement of the previous year. The Prophet interpreted the agreement to mean that Black Hawk had promised only not to return to his village at Saukenuk, rather than agreeing not to return to the eastern side of the Mississippi. He also probably aimed to peacefully unify the Sauk with members of the Winnebago and Potawatomi tribes and then reestablish their claims to the lands he believed were unrightfully ceded in 1804.[8]

Though Black Hawk hoped to avoid war, his presence alarmed white settlers living in the region. Units of US Army troops operating in the area soon became involved in monitoring Black Hawk's movements. The Illinois governor, John Reynolds, responding to the settlers' fears, called the Illinois militia into service, and more than a thousand mounted men were soon on the move toward the Rock River area.[9] When Black Hawk understood the building resistance, he knew his hopes for remaining east of the Mississippi had been dashed.[10]

On the afternoon of May 14, before withdrawing, Black Hawk sent a delegation of three braves to confer with members of an Illinois militia ranger unit commanded by Maj. Isaiah Stillman, camped near Old Man's Creek. Another small group of Sauk sent by Black Hawk to observe the proceedings remained at a distance. Like much of the militia, Stillman's troops were rowdy and ill trained. As the three emissaries approached, the undisciplined militia, suspicious of the Indians' intent, captured them. A detachment of rangers also spotted the Sauk observers and attacked them, killing two. The remaining Sauk escaped and returned to Black Hawk's location. The Sauk chief then led a party of his warriors forward, where they encountered the bulk of Stillman's command. In the ensuing battle, the rangers were routed, retreating in confusion and near panic to Dixon's Ferry.[11]

This episode, soon known as the Battle of Stillman's Run, quickly escalated into the full-blown conflict known as the Black Hawk War. Following the fight at Old Man's Creek, the Sauk and Fox, led by Black Hawk, as well as the Potawatomi and Winnebago allied with them, engaged in several other attacks. Much of the fighting consisted of small engagements, and though the Indians scored some victories, they were from the beginning disadvantaged by the large number of militia and regular forces they faced.

As a result of the battle at Old Man's Creek and the fighting that followed, the fear in the Apple River region was not without grounds. Warriors from Black Hawk's band had appeared at the fort earlier in the month, when on June 8 they fired at two people who had ventured outside. Although the two escaped harm, the attackers captured a number of horses.[12] But in the days since that skirmish, there was little further evidence of Sauk activity, and conditions near the fort appeared quiet and unthreatening.

War Comes to the Apple River Fort

By the afternoon of Sunday, June 24, danger, at least for the moment, appeared to have receded. Circumstances were tranquil enough that a few women left the fort on a berry-picking expedition. Suddenly, their seemingly carefree outing was interrupted by the frightening sounds of gunshots and shouting. The firing came from an unexpected encounter between some mounted messengers who had just departed the fort for Dixon, Illinois, and a group of Sauk warriors, headed by their leader, Black Hawk.[13]

The couriers, who had ridden only a few hundred yards from the fort when they received fire, shouted a warning. In the resulting uproar the gooseberries were quickly forgotten, and the pickers dashed to the security of the fort. One of the riders was wounded and fell from his saddle. Rapidly pulled from the ground by one of his companions, they rushed to safety behind the fort's walls.

Gathered inside the hastily built palisade were forty people. Women and children and the members of a local militia company under the command of Capt. Clack Stone waited uneasily for the battle they were certain loomed just ahead.[14] Black Hawk, leading 150 to 200 braves, did, indeed, quickly attack.[15] From behind the fort's wooden stockade, the militia returned fire. Women joined the heated fight by casting lead musket balls, reloading weapons, and handing them to the militiamen, who kept up a steady fire. Especially notable was Elizabeth Armstrong, who organized and led the critical support effort of the women.[16]

The battle continued for forty-five minutes with constant firing on both sides.[17] One of the couriers who had triggered the attack outside the fort fell as he was struck by fire from one of Black Hawk's warriors. Hit while attempting to aim over the top of the wall, George Harkleroad became the only fatality in the fort during the battle.[18] Black Hawk's band maintained an unremitting fire, wounding another militiaman. Although the number of casualties among Black Hawk's braves is unknown, apparently some were wounded or killed.

Finally, Black Hawk ended the attack and turned his attention to acquiring needed supplies from the abandoned cabins of the settlers, who were huddled inside the fort. After taking some horses, cattle, and other

Blockhouse at Apple River Fort. *Illustration by Phil Glosser.*

necessities, the warriors withdrew, and the Battle of Apple River Fort was over.[19] Black Hawk and the British Band were, however, at bay, and despite continuing to resist for a few weeks more, the Sauk chief at last decided his only choice was to lead his band back to the west side of the Mississippi. As he attempted to do so, regular and militia forces confronted the Indians at what became known as the Battle of Bad Axe, fought on August 1 and 2 in southwestern Wisconsin. This tragic encounter, during which many Sauk and Fox, including women and children were killed, brought the Black Hawk War to a close.

An Almost Forgotten Fort

With the arrival of peace, Apple River Fort was no longer needed, and its occupants returned home. Until 1847 the little stockade stood abandoned on the gentle slope where fifteen years before a desperate group of settlers had built it so quickly. The fort was on public property, and in 1847 the federal government sold the land to a local farmer named George Bainbridge.

Reflecting the frontier devotion to practicality, Bainbridge pulled the fort down and used the wood to construct a barn.[20]

The Battle of the Apple River Fort and the bravery displayed by all those present, settlers and Sauk, on a summer day in 1832 became almost legendary strands woven into the fabric of the surrounding area's history. The name of the town of Elizabeth, Illinois, where the fort is located, for example, recognizes the three women named Elizabeth who were active during the heat of the fighting. The battle has also been mentioned in several books that chronicle the history of the unfortunate war during which it was fought. With the passing of time, however, the Battle of the Apple River Fort and the little stockade where so much courage was displayed, both inside and outside its walls, mostly receded into the distant memories of many folk living nearby.

But among those attracted to the history of the Apple River region, the fort and the battle were not forgotten. In the mid-1990s a group of interested citizens formed the Apple River Fort Historic Foundation to retrieve the story of what had occurred on a June afternoon nearly two centuries before. The foundation consulted a professional archeologist, who, working in 1996 at the location where local tradition said the palisade had stood, soon found evidence of the fort.[21] Additional archeological excavations exposed the outline of the stockade and the presence of the buildings that had once been part of the fort's walls.

In 1996 and 1997, volunteers, using this archeological evidence, reconstructed a replica of Apple River Fort.[22] An interpretive center, built through fund-raising efforts by the foundation, was also completed. In 2001 the foundation made the site available to the State of Illinois, and the Historic Preservation Division of the Illinois Department of Natural Resources now administers it.[23] In recognition of Apple River Fort's historical value, the US National Park Service placed it on the National Register of Historic Places.

Apple River Fort Today

Today the reconstructed Apple River Fort stands on a gentle hill, about a quarter mile east of the site's interpretive center in the town of Elizabeth. It is easily reached by following Old Fort Road from the center to where the road forms a loop directly in front of the fort. A well-tended lawn surrounds the fort's stockade. Just beyond the street to the west, the hill drops away, and on the long gradual slope, prairie grasses grow, unkempt and wild, just as was likely the case in 1832. Yellow flowers speckle the hillside, and goldfinches, showing their black and yellow finery, perch precariously on tall, brown weed stems.

Perhaps thirty feet north of the present stockade, the approximate location of the original fort is indicated by a split-rail fence. Following the initial excavations, this area was left undisturbed for possible future archeological work.

The first excavations revealed that the original fort was rectangular, and the reconstructed fort was built using this information. The outer wall, a wooden palisade, is nearly seventy feet long and almost fifty feet deep, as was the case with the first stockade. The rough pickets, like those of the original fort, reach about ten feet above the ground. Today these are made of black locust logs five to seven inches in diameter. Because the logs used for the walls raised on those hurried days in 1832 were needed very quickly, they were likely made not from locust trunks but, rather, from any readily available nearby trees. Firing platforms extend from the northwest and southeast corners of the palisade and are accessible by crude ladders, built of small logs.

Three buildings are part of Apple River Fort. One is a small, rustic shed of round logs. It has a dirt floor and is roofed with rough planks with weight logs. The other two buildings help form part of the outer wall. One, a more substantial hewn-log cabin with a loft, is adjacent to the shed, at the northeast corner of the fort's wall. The third structure, on the southwest corner and incorporated into the stockade, is a two-story blockhouse, with heavy wooden shutters and loopholes in the walls.

As was the case with the original fort, the upper story of the blockhouse extends perhaps three feet beyond the lower part of the building. When area residents built the fort, the lower portion of the blockhouse probably already existed as a one-story structure of some kind. Because the second story was hurriedly added, the fort's builders likely did not take time to fashion hewn timbers but, instead, used quickly cut, round logs. The reconstructed blockhouse follows these architectural details.

Inside the palisade walls, the ground is bare. A large, black kettle hangs above a fire pit, and rough planks placed across wooden barrels form a crude but usable table. It must have been in a space much like this where, in the chaos and confusion of battle, Elizabeth Armstrong and the other women desperately cast ammunition and loaded weapons for the militiamen.

Much information about the fort and the battle is available at the Apple River Fort Interpretive Center, about a quarter mile from the fort itself. The interpretive center, 311 East Myrtle Street, is easily accessible from Illinois Route 20. It is a welcoming, friendly place with a suitable parking lot.

Inside, the museum store is stocked with books and other items related to the fort and to those who lived in the area nearby. The visitor will find much here concerning the Black Hawk War, those who were involved in it, and, of course, the Apple River Fort itself.

The interpretive center has several standing displays, which are highly informative and nicely illustrated with well-executed line-art drawings. The displays provide information about the Sauk and Fox, the settlers who lived in the area, and the background to the Black Hawk War and the attack at the Apple River Fort.

On the center's lower level, visitors can view an informative video, *Panic at the Apple River Fort*. A glass-topped case contains several artifacts discovered during archeological excavations of the fort site. The pieces are from the main collection of 632 others now housed at the Illinois State Museum in Springfield.

Above the artifact case, a wall board, "Pieces of the Past," outlines the archeological study of Apple River Fort, explaining how the archeological research carried out at the site supports and adds to the limited written sources available. Another display presentation, "Finding the Apple River Fort," describes how the fort was located through the efforts of the Apple River Fort Historic Foundation.

The reconstructed Apple River Fort exists today because of the dedicated efforts of many men and women who understood the importance of—and wanted to know more about—what happened there nearly two centuries ago. This small wooden stockade, now standing peacefully on its gently sloping hill, is emblematic of much from Illinois's past. It is illustrative of the kind of determination and perseverance that characterized life in a near-frontier area, such as this place was in 1832. But it recalls, too, the unquestionable valor shown by all those, American Indian and white, who were involved in that long-ago battle, a battle where opponents on both sides were convinced of the rightness of their cause. It is also a reminder that history is not always celebratory and that the Black Hawk War, like almost all wars, was deeply shadowed by tragedy and sorrow. Those shadows fell, of course, not only on Chief Black Hawk and his people but on all whose lives were marred by the war's violence.

Vandalia State House
State Historic Site

315 West Gallatin Street, Vandalia

Interstate 70's four pewter-gray lanes of asphalt and concrete slice diago-
nally through the prairie and scattered woodlands of south-central Illinois.
Thousands of cars and trucks move along the highway daily, passing just
north of the old town of Vandalia. About an hour's drive east of St. Louis,
Missouri, Vandalia is near the west bank of the Kaskaskia River, a stream
that ends farther south at the Mississippi River.

Vandalia is today a typical midwestern community, but in years past
it made a unique and important contribution to the history of the state.
Between 1820 and 1839, it was the second capital of Illinois and the location
of three early capitols, including the remarkable structure still present in
the city's downtown.

State officials founded the roughhewn village in 1819 at a place called
Reeve's Bluff on the western bank of the Kaskaskia. Delegates to Illinois's
first constitutional convention in 1818 decided to establish a new seat of
government to replace the old territorial capital at Kaskaskia.[1] Surveyors laid
out the town that summer, and auctioneers began land sales in September.

Vandalia State House. *Illustration by Phil Glosser.*

Later in the fall, as historian Paul Stroble Jr. tells us, "The chimneys of new houses and a few businesses sent wood smoke into the chilly air."[2] As axes thudded against trees ablaze with autumn foliage, woodchoppers pushed the forest back, and the primitive capital began to emerge.

This pioneer village, tucked among the woodlands of Southern Illinois, was the seat of the state's government for the next two decades. Those years were important in the new state's history, and they saw some of the most prominent of Illinois's political figures appear, among them the future president Abraham Lincoln and Stephen A. Douglas, later an influential US Senator.

By 1840, however, Vandalia was no longer the state's capital. The rapidly unfolding forces of a new era in American history had passed it by. Although it did not fall into the obscurity Kaskaskia, the state's first capital city, experienced, Vandalia's prominence after 1839 declined.

A New State House for Vandalia

The town's once-significant role in Illinois history can still be seen, however, in the Vandalia State House, an imposing building that was the state's capitol from 1836 to 1839. The state house is about a mile directly south of Interstate 70, surrounded by the stores and restaurants and shops of contemporary Vandalia. This impressive structure is not the first capitol constructed here, however. The state used the first of these from 1820 until 1823, when fire destroyed it. Legislators and other functionaries then occupied a shoddily built second state house in 1824 that, because of its dilapidated condition, was replaced in 1836.

The state's third capitol was the striking building that now dominates modern Vandalia's downtown. Constructed in 1836 for about $16,000, it replaced the decrepit second capitol, so dilapidated it was in danger of collapsing. Between August and December of that year, the new building emerged in an astonishing flurry of energy and effort. Early in December, it was ready for limited use by the members of the tenth session of the legislature—though lawmakers encountered damp plaster in the walls of the legislative chambers.[3]

The Vandalia State House is a large two-story brick structure, administered as a state historic site by the Historic Preservation Division of the Illinois Department of Natural Resources. When the state house opened on a December day in 1836, the building had no columns, and its exterior was unpainted and plain. Now painted a dazzling white, it is topped by an abbreviated rectangular tower crowned by an octagonal, windowed cupola that extends upward from the center of the roof. The cupola's cap is coated now with a celadon patina, and the slender mast of a weathervane points skyward from it.

Four Doric columns support classic pediments added after the county purchased the building in 1856. These form Greek Revival porticoes, each of which is centered in the north and south walls. Along those walls, the building's second-story windows form dark rectangles that march in precisely ordered intervals across the brilliant white of the building's exterior. A similar arrangement, of six windows and a centered doorway, is directly below on the first-floor walls. On the east and west ends of the second story are three identical windows, and under these, on the first floor, are two windows and a doorway, all beneath a gabled roof. The structure's design is an example of the orchestrated symmetry that often characterizes the more impressive of America's governmental buildings.

Seen from Gallatin Street, which fronts it on the south, the building immediately impresses itself upon the senses. The capitol is nearly in the center of a square city block. A well-tended greensward, shaded by large trees, surrounds it. The lawn is divided by a red-brick walkway that leads to the building's south entry.

Inside, the state house is redolent of history. From the reproductions of Lincoln documents in a wall display just beyond the south door to the reach of its lofty ceilings, the sense that this building played an important part in the state's past is almost palpable. On the first floor a spacious central corridor cuts south to north, passes by a wide, balustraded wooden staircase to the second story, and ends at doors submerged in the shadows of the north portico.

Another, narrower hallway runs the east–west length of the building and sections it into four large offices. The floor's wooden boards are dark and wide and, though not original, are reminiscent of those from an earlier era. The corridor walls are faced with white plaster and mounted at intervals along the halls are dark-metal sconces, each holding a single white candle.

The first-story offices are arranged to reflect their use between 1836 and 1839. The room in the southwestern quadrant once housed the state treasurer and his clerks. The office directly across the hall to the north was that of the auditor of public accounts. The space in the northeastern portion of the building was for the secretary of state. Directly opposite this, in the southeastern section of the capitol, is the chamber formerly used by the state supreme court. This is the only space in the building with a floor covering. A red, patterned, wall-to-wall carpet lends a magisterial dignity to the room. The dais, with its impressive desk and four comb-back Windsor chairs, enhances this effect.

These rooms are equipped mostly with reproductions of furniture, including several cabinets, tables, and sand-filled wooden spittoons and, in the treasurer's office, tall, narrow desks evocative of a Dickensian counting house. The wood-burning stoves that long ago must have struggled mightily but, perhaps, with only limited success to hold back the chill of Illinois winters are, however, original.

The wide central staircase, with its highly polished black-walnut banisters, climbs to the second floor, curving somewhat abruptly to open onto a large landing. From here was gained access to the legislative chambers through stairs at the south end the landing.

The senate chamber is on the west side, the house on the east. Each hall is crowded with wooden desks, tables, and chairs. On cloudless days, sunshine floods these rooms, and the furniture's polished surfaces glow softly as sunrays slant through the panes of nine large windows. Again, the furnishings here, except for one table in the house chamber, are not original but reproductions of those at which legislators once sat as they worked to shape the future of the state.

Fledgling Legislator

Though scores of lawmakers labored in these halls, the one who has evoked the most interest is, of course, Abraham Lincoln, who became the nation's sixteenth president. It was in Vandalia (although not in the existing state house) that a twenty-five-year-old Lincoln, tall, rail thin, rawboned, and, perhaps, a bit rustic, first held public office. The young representative's first term as a state legislator, in the ninth session, was spent in the second capitol. When Lincoln returned for the tenth session, however, he worked in the existing structure.

By most accounts Lincoln's record here was mixed. He supported increased expenditures on internal improvements though the state was near bankruptcy. Lincoln favored a bill to tax property at a rate of twenty cents per hundred-dollar valuation and opposed the elimination in the state of paper currency worth less than five dollars. He also was in the majority in the effort to stop an attempt to set up a legislative committee that would investigate banks.[4]

However, Lincoln, who was to become known as the Great Emancipator during a presidency dominated by the Civil War, also addressed the slavery issue, even if only peripherally, while serving in the Vandalia State House. Lincoln and Rep. Dan Stone, a fellow legislator from Sangamon County, filed a protest to a resolution concerning slavery that the legislature had passed earlier. Lincoln and Stone argued, "The institution of slavery is founded on both injustice and bad policy; but the promulgation of abolition doctrines tends rather to increase than to abate its evils. . . . The Congress of the United States has the power under the constitution, to abolish slavery in the District of Columbia; but that power ought not to be exercised unless at the request of the people of said district."[5]

While here Lincoln also closely associated himself with the so-called Long Nine, a group of Sangamon County Whig legislators who worked together on projects of common interest. In the 1836 session, one of those projects was to move the capital from Vandalia to Springfield, farther north and nearer to the center of the state. Following much political logrolling, the group was successful, and the legislature, after four ballots, voted in 1837 to relocate the capital to Springfield.[6]

A common story about Lincoln found in nearly every account of his time in Vandalia is that he jumped from a state-house window to avoid a quorum. Despite its persistence, several historians have concluded that the episode actually occurred later, after the capital had been moved to Springfield.[7]

A Capitol Lost

The last legislature to sit in the Vandalia State House was the Eleventh General Assembly, which met between December 1838 and March 1839. With its departure, Vandalia's growing prominence halted almost at once and then began to decline. The National Road finally reached Vandalia that year, but the US Congress failed to deliver additional funds, and construction stopped. Though hope remained that the road would provide a strategic link to the east, it came too late to have an immediate impact on the town.

During Vandalia's nearly twenty years as the state's second capital, the once crude, log-hewn frontier village matured by 1839 into a prosperous and settled town. But forces far from this small community on the hills above the Kaskaskia River worked to alter its destiny. Some of these were subtle and little noticed; others were quite visible and appeared with stunning speed. Population patterns that for years had steadily helped to fill the southern part of Illinois began to shift northward. A newly developing market economy, linked by canals and driven by innovative manufacturing processes as

Madonna of the Trail, sculpted by August Leimbach, southwest corner of the Vandalia State House grounds. *Photo by the author.*

well as by the promise of the exciting new technology of the railroad, ultimately favored the central and northern parts of the state.

When it departed for Springfield in March 1839, the state government gave the state house jointly to Fayette County and the town of Vandalia. The county used part of the building for the Fayette County Courthouse while the remaining portion was occupied by the Fayette Seminary. In 1856 the county purchased the remainder of the building from the seminary and renovated it for use as the county courthouse; the county occupied the entire structure until 1933, although it was leased from the state after 1919.[8] When Illinois bought the building and its grounds in 1918, a circle was completed—the state house once again became state property.[9]

Vandalia State House Today

The speeches and debates and deals that once were so much a part of this place have, of course, faded long ago into the past. But visitors arrive here daily to see this spot that was so significant in the early years of the state. The old structure projects a stately elegance, and the imposing columns, the impressive cupola, and the well-kept, tree-shaded grounds all evoke the sense that something significant happened here, that it was here that history was made, as it, indeed, was.

On the southwest corner of the state house's spacious lawn is the *Madonna of the Trail* statue of a pioneer woman and her two children. Sculpted by August Leimbach and placed in 1928, it is one of twelve monuments the Daughters of the American Revolution sponsored to commemorate those frontier women who traveled west on the National Road and played an often-unremembered but central role in the unfolding cavalcade of the American westward movement.[10] The statue and the state house are emblematic reminders of an important period in the state's past, material pieces of a history of how those who lived and worked in an earlier Illinois met with success the challenges of their time.

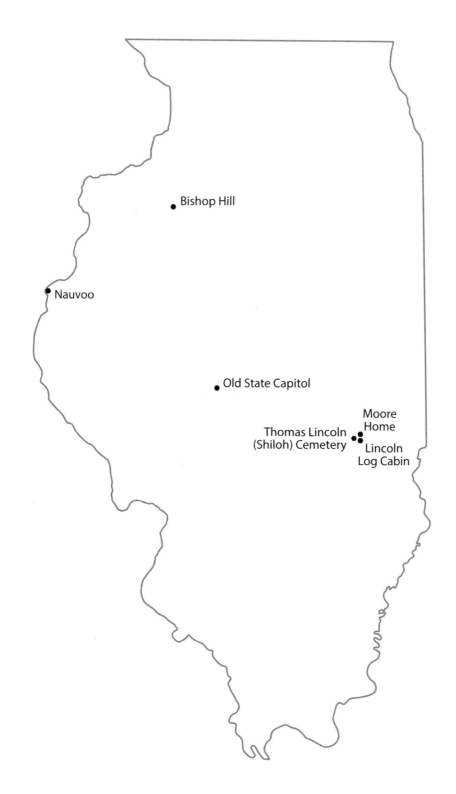

Bishop Hill

Nauvoo

Old State Capitol

Moore
Home

Thomas Lincoln
(Shiloh) Cemetery

Lincoln
Log Cabin

Part 3

THE PRAIRIE STATE GROWS

Old State Capitol
opens for use

Lincoln log cabin
constructed

1840

Lincoln visits
Moore Home, Th.
Lincoln/Shiloh
Cemetery

1861

Mormons
arrive at
Nauvoo

1839

Janssonites
arrive at
Bishop Hill

1846

Prologue

By the mid-1830s the frontier line had mostly moved farther west, beyond Illinois. In the first half of the nineteenth century, Illinois was a growing and promising place: increasing population, more farms and roads and towns, fertile glacially enriched land, and usable if not always easy routes of river transportation. Still, the state retained many of its frontier characteristics, which sometimes unfortunately involved instances of narrow-mindedness and violence.

Such was the case on a June day in 1844 when the leader and prophet of the Mormon Church, Joseph Smith, and his brother Hyrum were murdered while in jail in Carthage, Illinois. Hundreds of Mormons had begun to arrive in Illinois in 1839. Many settled around Commerce, a ramshackle village on the Mississippi River, near Quincy. Smith renamed the village **Nauvoo**, and it soon became a vibrant city.

Soon, however, conflict emerged with nearby residents who were suspicious and distrustful of the Mormons and their religious beliefs. Following Joseph's attempt in 1844 to close a Nauvoo newspaper with which he was displeased, he was arrested and jailed in nearby Carthage. A mob attacked the jail, killing Joseph and Hyrum. Within a few years of the death of their leader, the Mormons departed Nauvoo for Utah.

But the promising possibilities of the Prairie State still beckoned, and they appealed to the leader of yet another religious movement. In 1846 the

Swedish visionary Eric Jansson and his followers built a utopian community at **Bishop Hill** in Henry County. The village soon became a flourishing enterprise, known for producing flax and brooms, among other products. Though the colony ultimately failed, the Janssonites left behind a fascinating collection of buildings and other objects that provide a glimpse into this unusual community and its place in the state's history.

Representative, too, of Illinois's ongoing transformation was the decision by the legislature to relocate the capital city. The state's population continued to shift northward and, hoping to place the capital closer to what seemed an area of future growth and development, lawmakers abandoned Vandalia in favor of Springfield in 1839. Even before the legislature convened for the final time in Vandalia, the cornerstone for the new capitol had been laid. Now known as the **Old State Capitol**, it was evidence of a growing confidence that Illinois was on a trajectory of unparalleled growth. Though it was used for only thirty-six years, the imposing building in downtown Springfield was an emblem of an optimistic view of the future.

Parts of Illinois remained almost untouched by the changes appearing elsewhere in the state. One example of the persistence of an older tradition of life can be seen at **Lincoln Log Cabin State Historic Site** in southern Coles County, south of Charleston. In an area known as Goosenest Prairie, Abraham Lincoln's father and stepmother, Thomas and Sarah Bush Lincoln, pursued a rustic existence at odds with the more modern developments appearing in other parts of the state. Living in a rough, two-room log cabin, Thomas Lincoln was largely a subsistence farmer, producing only what he and his family needed for their own use. Lincoln's lifestyle was becoming less common, however, and it eventually would almost vanish among the state's farmers.

The Goosenest Prairie area is well connected to the larger story of Abraham Lincoln. Not far from Thomas and Sarah Lincoln's cabin, a modest building known as the **Moore Home**, sits alongside a rural highway in the hamlet of Campbell. Here, Lincoln, during the busy weeks following his election to the presidency and shortly before his departure to Washington, paid a sentimental and moving visit to his stepmother. A short distance from the Moore Home, the **Thomas Lincoln Cemetery**, sometimes called Shiloh Cemetery, holds the remains of both Thomas and Sarah Lincoln. This small burial ground, situated in a pastoral setting, is yet another cord tying Abraham Lincoln to the Prairie State.

As the third decade of the nineteenth century opened, Illinois was a land of both optimism and uncertainty, and the dual nature of the place is reflected in the historical sites from that era. The villages of Nauvoo and Bishop Hill are collective expressions of the confidence that when communities are bonded by religious unity, they offer a better way of life. The Old State Capitol, too, reveals a widespread optimism by state officials that Illinois was on a prosperous path.

But at the same time, the difficult nature of Thomas and Sarah Lincoln's lifestyle, evidenced by Lincoln Log Cabin at Goosenest Prairie, must have brought some uncertainty if not to the Lincolns, then to their neighbors. With the looming crisis of a divided nation before him, that same sense of an uncertain future surely accompanied Abraham Lincoln on his visit to his stepmother and as he viewed the place where his father lay in the cemetery.

Nauvoo
Hancock County

Emerging from Lake Itasca in central Minnesota, the Mississippi River begins its course to the Gulf of Mexico. At the Illinois-Wisconsin line, it sweeps into a series of large, graceful curves where, with nearly a mile of slate-gray water between its banks, it carves the border between Illinois and Iowa. On the Illinois side of the river, in the middle of one of the curves and not far from Quincy, the small town of Nauvoo nudges the Mississippi's east bank.

The shops and restaurants lining Mulholland Street, contemporary Nauvoo's principal thoroughfare, make this town at first glance seem like dozens of other communities across the state. The appearance is deceptive, however, for just a short distance to the west and closer to the Mississippi, it becomes apparent that this town is not what it first appears. The symmetrical grid work of the streets, the venerable buildings, the sense of history that seems to cling to everything here—all this is evidence that Nauvoo is different, and a place with a colorful, fascinating past. Not only was it once one of the largest cities in Illinois but it was also the "Zion" of a unique and energetic religious group, the Church of Jesus Christ of Latter-day Saints, or Mormons.[1] Later, after most of the Mormons had gone, the unusual story of

Nauvoo from across the Mississippi River in 1853. *Abraham Lincoln Presidential Library and Museum (ALPLM).*

the town continued as the home for the Icarians, who created a remarkable but short-lived utopian community here.

The Latter-day Saints came to Nauvoo in early 1839, after having settled first at Kirtland, Ohio, and later in northwest Missouri. When the Mormon leader Joseph Smith arrived in Illinois on April 22 of that year, he and the church officials made a momentous decision: they would build a new Zion, a place of gathering for the faithful in this quiet place on the banks of the Mississippi.

Church members purchased over $100,000 worth of property, trading Missouri land for tracts along the river in both Iowa and Illinois. Included in these purchases was Commerce, a rundown Illinois village of about a half-dozen dilapidated buildings. This area was to be the site of Nauvoo.[2]

Joseph Smith renamed Commerce "Nauvoo." Smith told his followers the word meant a place of "beauty and repose" or a "beautiful plantation" in

Reconstructed Mormon Temple, a replica of the original destroyed shortly after the Mormons' departure from Nauvoo. *Photo by Ryan Ballantyne. Wikimedia Commons, CC-BY-SA-2.5.*

Hebrew.[3] The town is on a stubby promontory that juts into the Mississippi from the Illinois side, the river forming the boundary of the village on the south, west, and north. Extending away from the uplands on the town's east side is the gently rolling prairie characteristic of so much of central and northern Illinois. The area next to the river, along with a portion of the prairie above, eventually became Nauvoo.[4]

By all accounts, Commerce gave little indication of its potential. Smith describes the village as it appeared when the Mormons arrived: "The place was literally a wilderness. The land was mostly covered with trees and bushes, and much of it so wet that it was with the utmost difficulty that a footman could get through, and totally impossible for teams. Commerce was so unhealthful very few could live there, but believing it might become a healthful place by the blessing of heaven to the Saints, and no more eligible place presenting itself, I considered it wisdom to make an attempt to build up a city."[5]

Despite daunting challenges, including an ongoing battle with malaria, the town grew. The Mormons worked quickly and effectively, and houses and other buildings appeared almost overnight. Frame structures and even some of brick soon replaced the crude log cabins and ramshackle buildings of the Saints' first difficult days in Nauvoo.

An emblem of the Saints' energy that soon became visible to both residents and visitors was the Nauvoo temple. Built of limestone, it was located at the highest point in Nauvoo, a hill in the center of the city. Of immense size for its day, it was 128 feet long by 88 feet wide and in its full height rose 165 feet. Around the building's periphery, spaced at carefully calculated intervals, were thirty large pilasters. The capstones and bases of these were sculpted with intricate designs of sunstones, moonstones, and starstones.[6]

A Time of Troubles

Despite their amazing progress, the Mormons were destined to remain in Nauvoo for only five years. The orderly growth and apparent prosperity of the town itself, when contrasted against the less-prosperous, less-orderly area surrounding it, triggered a jealousy among some living nearby. Concern about Mormon political power; fear of the Nauvoo Legion, the city's militia; and misunderstanding of and hostility toward some of the church's religious practices soon fractured the relationship between the Saints and their non-Mormon neighbors.[7] All these created an atmosphere thick with the poisonous fog of trouble, and a strong anti-Mormon sentiment was present in the area outside Nauvoo. The difficulties culminated finally in the jailing and murders in 1844 of Joseph and his brother Hyrum.

Joseph's death followed an incident in which he and the Nauvoo city council ordered the press of a dissenting newspaper, the *Nauvoo Expositor*, to be destroyed. Members of a group within the church who were opposed to some of the theological doctrines recently revealed by Joseph had started the *Expositor* to voice their objections. Prominent in the group was William Law, an important church member.

Following the destruction of the *Expositor*, Law quickly took legal action against Joseph in Carthage, a village about twenty miles from Nauvoo. Acting on Law's charges, local authorities confined the Smiths and two friends in the jail there.[8] On the evening of June 27, 1844, the long-simmering animos-

Carthage Jail, site of Joseph Smith and Hyrum Smith murders, June 1844. *Photo by Nyttend (Wikipedia)*.

ity toward the Mormons erupted in a bloody encounter. A mob attacked the jail, a sturdy two-story building made of rough, cinnamon-colored stone blocks. The mob, heavily armed and with faces blackened, stormed up the stairs and into the room where the prisoners were confined. Joseph and Hyrum died in a hail of gunfire.[9]

Joseph's death did not end the conflict with Nauvoo's neighbors. Law and his wife, Jane, fled Nauvoo to Iowa Territory, then to several other places, and finally to Wisconsin where William died in 1892. His brother Wilson was involved in the trouble and ended up in Wisconsin as well. Clashes, sometimes violent, between the Saints and the area's non-Mormons continued. Almost from the moment of the prophet's martyrdom, the church leadership considered moving, to relocate west, and ultimately the Saints decided to leave. In 1846 after a year and a half of almost nonstop preparation under the leadership of Brigham Young, who had replaced Smith as head of the church, the Mormons began an epic journey that took them to the unsettled wilderness of the Great Salt Lake Valley in present-day Utah.

The unusual days of Nauvoo, though, were not yet over. In 1849 the Icarians, a group of French utopians, moved into the town after attempts at a colony in Texas had failed. Étienne Cabet, a French attorney and author of *Voyage to Icaria*, founded the Icarians. The Icarians were totally communal. Their collectivist society produced and exported flour, shoes, clothing, and other products, and the profits were used for the good of the community. But a host of challenges leading to internal conflict soon appeared, and economic reverses quickly followed. The idealistic community disintegrated after some of the colonists became disenchanted with Cabet's leadership. By 1860 most of the Icarians, too, were gone, and Nauvoo began to slip into relative quiescence.[10]

Nauvoo Today

Although it has been nearly two centuries since its years as the center of the Mormon Church, Nauvoo has recaptured much of its past. Many of the impressive structures from those exciting, busy days when it was the Mormon Zion have been meticulously restored in a massive program of historic preservation. The streets of old Nauvoo, plotted so carefully by the early Mormons into a precise, geometric grid, are tree-lined and spacious. The soaring height of the Nauvoo temple draws one's eyes skyward, and the solid, red-brick buildings scattered across the town are reminiscent of New England. All these are hallmarks of the Mormon period and present a rich heritage of material culture, an immediate, physical narrative of this remarkable town's history.

Chief among these is the temple, on a hill in the town center. A tornado and a fire destroyed the original building shortly after the Saints' exodus. Between 1999 and 2002, the Church of Jesus Christ of Latter-day Saints, in recognition of the historical importance of this place, carefully rebuilt it in the original design. Located at 50 North Wells Street, it again dominates the town. Built on the site of the first temple, it is a stunning structure. An expansive greensward, dotted with trees, sweeps eastward up a gently rising slope toward the temple. The building's white limestone walls gleam in the sunlight, and a gracefully rising octagonal tower, surmounted by a gilded, angel-shaped weathervane, reaches toward the blue Illinois sky.[11]

The many other buildings include the striking red-brick, two-story federal-style homes of Heber Kimball and Wilford Woodruff, the impressive frame house once occupied by Brigham Young, and Joseph Smith's reconstructed, two-story red-brick store, where the Mormon leadership gathered upstairs for church meetings. Almost all this work was carried out by the Church of Jesus Christ of Latter-day Saints or the Community of Christ Church, formerly known as the Reorganized Church of Jesus Christ of Latter-day Saints.

Twenty miles southeast of Nauvoo, in Carthage, the jail where Joseph Smith and his brother were murdered on a June afternoon has also been preserved. The jail is flanked now by a visitor's center. A walkway of carrot-colored bricks, lined on either side by locust trees, leads to a courtyard with a statue of Joseph and Hyrum. Across the tree-shaded grounds is the jail with its second story window from which Joseph fell the day he died. Even when tourists are present, this place seems to have a stillness about it. Viewing this aged building, one sees no trace of these violent and bloody events.

In the north-central part of old Nauvoo, the Mormons have built a modern glass-and-brick visitor center. Inside, young Mormon men and women serving their church greet visitors, who view exhibits, artifacts, and paintings. For many Mormons and members of the Community of Christ Church, Nauvoo is a place of pilgrimage conserved as a prominent part of their churches' past. Automobiles with Utah, Idaho, Iowa, and Missouri license plates commonly sit in the large parking lot, evidence that many of the faithful visit this place.

To many who visit here, however, Nauvoo today offers a view of a unique time in the state's past, a glimpse into a remarkable, unusual, and important part of the history of Illinois.

Old State Capitol State Historic Site

Sixth Street and Adams Street, Springfield

The Old State Capitol is in downtown Springfield near the Abraham Lincoln Presidential Library and just a few blocks from the two-story, tan-and-brown home Lincoln and his family occupied before his election to the presidency. Construction of what was to be the Prairie State's capitol for three busy decades began with a cornerstone laying ceremony in 1837. Just three years later, in 1840, the capitol was first occupied.[1]

Two stories tall and built of large blocks of cinnamon-colored stone, it sits in the center of a city-block, bounded by Washington Street on the north, Adams Street on the south, Fifth Street on the west, and Sixth Street on the east. A well-kept lawn, enclosed by a dark, wrought-iron fence, surrounds the building. A flagstone walkway encircles the capitol and leads to porticoes on the north and south sides. The porticos feature four Doric columns and Greek Revival–style pediments. Rising from the capitol's center is a white, octagonal dome, topped with a brick-red roof supported by sixteen slender, white columns. Tall, narrow windows grace the dome's walls.

Built shortly after the legislature voted to relocate the Illinois government to Springfield from Vandalia, the capitol was designed by architect John Rague and held legislative halls, a chamber for the Supreme Court, and offices for other state officials, including the governor. As might be expected, this place is evocative of history. One of the events that helped make it so took place at eight o'clock on the evening of June 16, 1858, as the glow of gaslight reflected from the dark-walnut desks and speaker's dais in the Hall of Representatives. Standing at the podium, with a large portrait of George Washington behind him, Abraham Lincoln began one of the most memorable—and controversial—speeches of his career.

Earlier in the day Republican delegates had nominated Lincoln as their party's candidate for US Senator. Now, in accepting that nomination in the house chamber, he delivered his House Divided speech, in which he argued that the United States could no longer remain divided on the issue of slavery but, rather, would have to "become all one thing or all the other." Though Lincoln also said he did "not expect the house to fall," his speech foreshadowed the coming of the Civil War and the horrific violence that three years later tore the nation apart.[2]

From Capitol to Courthouse

Though this building was a magnificent structure in comparison to the earlier state houses in Kaskaskia and Vandalia, its place as the civic center of Illinois was to last only thirty-six years. As the state grew in the decades after the building's construction, the scope of Illinois's government increased beyond the Old State Capitol's limited capacity. In 1867, recognizing the need for additional space, the legislature approved a new capitol.[3] The state sold the old building to Sangamon County in 1869 for use as the county courthouse, with the caveat that it was to be occupied by the state until the new capitol was essentially completed.[4] It remained in use by the state until 1876 when officials finally moved into the present state capitol.[5]

To create more office space, the building was lifted for the addition of a story beneath the existing structure. Much of the original interior was renovated, and several features were lost that had characterized the building since Lincoln had sat there as a member of the legislature in 1840.[6]

Old State Capitol in Springfield. *Photo by Shadow2700 (Wikipedia).*

The Sangamon County government, like that of Illinois earlier, also grew and found the old capitol no longer able to accommodate its needs.[7] When the county constructed a new courthouse, the Illinois legislature authorized the purchase of the old capital from Sangamon County in 1961, and the county rented the building for the next few years.[8]

The American Civil War, which cost the lives of almost thirty-five thousand Illinois citizens, began a decade and a half before the government moved to a new capitol, eight blocks to the southwest. Abraham Lincoln, who spent his last term in the Old Capitol's Hall of Representatives in 1840, twenty years before the war, later used an office here as he prepared to go to Washington in the crowded weeks following his election as president.[9] Ulysses S. Grant, later to gain fame as one of Lincoln's favorite Union generals, also used an office here for a brief time in the early months of the Civil War. Then, in the somber days of early May 1865, with the building draped in mourning black, Lincoln lay in state in the same chamber where he had served twenty-five years before.

Rebuilding and Restoration

In the winter of 1966, over a century-and-a-quarter after the legislature had met there for the first time in 1840, the state began a massive reconstruction of the Old State Capitol. The walls were disassembled, the pieces numbered and stored, and the land formerly occupied by the building was excavated for three new floors for parking and office space. A steel framework was put into place, and the stone blocks from the original walls were affixed to it. When the renovation was completed, the building appeared much as it had during Lincoln's time in Springfield.[10]

The Old State Capitol Today

The Old State Capitol is a reminder of a pivotal period in the Prairie State's past. In the three decades when the building housed the state government, the population increased from 476,000 to nearly three million. During this same time the state's cities grew, and Illinois, especially after the 1860s, became less agricultural, more industrial, and ever more urbanized.

Today, the entrances to the reconstituted Old State Capitol open to an expansive lobby that makes up the middle portion of the building's ground level. The floor is made of wide, wooden boards, and the walls and ceiling are a pleasing white. In the center of this spacious room are two large staircases, one flight ascending from the lobby's north side, the other from the south. These steps lead to a middle landing from which two additional staircases, rising to the east and west, give access to the building's second (now fifth) floor.

In the large wings on either side of the lobby are spaces for the secretary of state, the state library, the state auditor, the supreme court chamber, the law library, and the treasurer. Although only a few original items are in these rooms, most of the furnishings here are period authentic.

The secretary of state's office, in the building's northwest corner, holds cabinets, desks, and tables. This is where another prominent Illinois politician, Stephen A. Douglas, worked when he held that position in 1840 and

1841. An oil portrait of Douglas, painted with a dark palette, hangs above a doorway leading to the state library next door.

The state library resembles a reading room more than a library, although some books rest in glass-fronted cases along the walls. On the several tables are copies of old newspapers. Lincoln spent much time in this room, and it was here that he composed a part of the House Divided speech. A replica of his familiar tall, black hat marks the place where it is believed he frequently sat as he worked.

The state auditor's office is in the capitol's southwest corner. Inside are desks and green-clothed tables. One of the desks, that of Orlin H. Miner, auditor from 1864 to 1869, is original. Miner's likeness is in a painting in the room.

The Illinois Supreme Court chamber, in the building's northeast corner, is directly across the lobby from the secretary of state's office. A chandelier with white candles hangs from the ceiling in the room's center. Four desks for the judges are on a dais, covered with a patterned, brick-red carpet and separated from the rest of the room by a balustrade of polished wood. A dark-red curtain, trimmed in gold, hangs ceiling to floor behind the judges' desks. At one side of the dais is a large wooden stanchion, topped with a gilded, wooden eagle. All these impart an air of dignity to the chamber. Several uncomfortable-looking wooden benches are here, presumably like those where visitors sat to observe the court's procedures.

A doorway from the supreme-court chamber leads to the adjacent law library, where wooden cabinets with glass doors hold impressive-looking books. Several desks and tables are also here, some draped with green cloth.

The capitol's second floor, the location of the legislative chambers, is accessed from the lobby by two broad flights of stairs that rise from a wooden landing midway between the first and second floors. The stairs emerge from a circular opening surrounded by an elegantly curved bannister, also of polished walnut as the two staircases' bannisters are. Four white, fluted Corinthian columns support an ornate, white interior dome, which rises to an oculus, which, on bright days, admits sunrays through the exterior dome's windows. The second floor's east and west walls are adorned with ornately framed paintings of Springfield views from each of the four compass points. Chandeliers with nine lamps and white glass shades hang from

A stovepipe hat on Abraham Lincoln's desk, House chamber of the Old State Capitol.
Photo courtesy of Illinois Department of Natural Resources.

the north and south ends of the ceiling. Sconces on the east and west walls hold similar lamps.

The representative hall is on the west side of this floor, and the senate chamber is on the east. On the north side two curved stairways lead upward, one to the house spectators' gallery, the other to that of the senate. Tucked between these stairways is a small committee room.

In the representative hall, twelve large windows admit a flood of light to the room, which, like the center portion of the building, has walls of white and a floor of wide, wooden boards. A striking dais and wooden lectern for the speaker face east. Immediately behind the speaker's podium is a large portrait of George Washington.

The furnishings of this room are made of polished wood. Three rows of desks for house members curve in front of the speaker's dais. Only one desk is original; the others are reproductions. A black stovepipe hat is on a desk placed where Lincoln sat as a legislator. The desks are just beyond a wooden balustrade. Eleven fluted Corinthian columns follow the curve of the balustrade's rail. Several green wooden benches are between the balustrade and the back wall, and above this space is the visitors' gallery.

The senate chamber is similar to that of the house, except that there are only two rows of desks here. Behind the speaker's dais, gold-trimmed burgundy draperies of heavy velvet adorn a large portrait of the Marquis de Lafayette. The painting is a copy of the original in Washington, DC, made when the old Revolutionary War hero visited the United States in 1824 and 1825. Two large, gilded eagles sit atop carved wooden columns flanking the dais. A brass chandelier with white candles hangs from a gently arching, sculpted ceiling.

The south side of the second floor has another committee room as well as the adjutant general's office. A portrait of Ulysses Grant, whose office was here, is close by. A hallway at the southeast corner leads eastward, past the office of the superintendent of public instruction and the governor's office and into the governor's reception room. Lincoln used this room, as well as the adjacent governor's office, for a time following his presidential nomination and as he prepared to go to Washington after his election to the presidency.

The reception room contains several chairs (all reproductions except for one original hoop-backed chair) and a large round table. A copper watercooler, believed to be original to the period when Lincoln was here, sits on a stand near one wall. A carpet of dark blue with a lighter-blue pattern extends from the reception room into the governor's office. It is a reproduction of the one here when Lincoln used the room.

The legislative halls of the Old State Capitol no longer ring with the sound of lawmakers' debates. Nor do the solemn arguments of attorneys echo today in the supreme-court chamber. Absent, too, is the busy hum of conversation that surely must have been heard daily in the lobby and offices of the first floor as state officials and visitors went about their business.

But the Old State Capitol has not receded into the mists of a vague public memory. It has, instead, remained an enduring emblem of the democratic processes of a free people and is used often for public functions yet today. A staff of friendly, helpful volunteers and professionals assists visitors in understanding the significance of this impressive old building.

The continuing symbolic character of this place was again evident on a chilly day in February 2007, when Barack Obama, then a US Senator from Illinois, used the Old State Capitol—bedecked in red, white, and blue bunting—as a backdrop for the announcement of his candidacy for the presidency of the United States. The building was again in the public eye when Obama introduced his running mate, US Senator Joe Biden, in August 2008 here.

The historic events that have occurred here ensure that the Old State Capitol has found a special place not just in the state's past but in the nation's history.

Lincoln Log Cabin State Historic Site

402 South Lincoln Highway Road, Lerna

In southern Coles County, near where the prairie's flatness edges into the low hills and woods of a glacial moraine, a rural road leads to Lincoln Log Cabin State Historic Site. Two buildings representing those once found on two very different kinds of mid-nineteenth-century Illinois farms are within just a few hundred yards of each other.

One, a diminutive saddlebag cabin, is in a small clearing shaded by locust and maple trees. Its roof sags slightly, and the walls of hewn logs are weather-beaten and gray. Four planked doors, two on either side and painted what seems an incongruous yet pleasing blue, open to a dimly lit interior. Occasional patches of dirt show in the cabin's lawn, and a rustic split-rail fence encloses a nearby sheep pen.

The second structure is a neat timber-framed farmhouse sided with white clapboards. A story and a half tall, it has an exterior chimney of red brick. The house has front and rear roofed porches, their planked floors painted a dark maroon, and a summer kitchen stands nearby. Though it was built in 1843, the house appears almost modern when compared to the plain log building a short distance away.

Wintery day at Thomas and Sarah Lincoln's cabin. *Photo courtesy of Illinois Department of Natural Resources.*

Stephen and Nancy Sargent's house, a sharp contrast to Thomas and Sarah Lincoln's cabin. *Illustration by Phil Glosser.*

The cabin replicates the Goosenest Prairie residence of Thomas and Sarah Bush Lincoln, father and stepmother of President Abraham Lincoln. The clapboard-sided house, previously located a few miles from the site and moved here in 1985, was once the home of Coles County farmer Stephen Sargent and his wife, Nancy. These buildings and their associated farms are quite different, but both tell the story of rural life in east-central Illinois nearly two centuries ago, for despite their dissimilarities they were, like their owners, contemporaries.[1]

An Itinerant Family

Thomas and Sarah Bush Lincoln, accompanied by Abraham Lincoln and several other family members, moved from Indiana to Illinois in 1830.[2] In March of that year they reached Macon County, where they lived in a log cabin near Decatur.

However, as had happened before in Thomas's life, things did not work out as planned. After an illness-plagued autumn and an exceptionally harsh winter, Thomas and most of those with him decided the following spring to forgo Illinois and return to Indiana.[3] It was then, in the spring of 1831, that Abraham Lincoln left his family, never to live permanently with them again. Abraham departed to help take a flatboat of goods to New Orleans, traveling first down the Sangamon River to the Illinois River and then down the Illinois to the Mississippi River. Upon his return, he settled in the New Salem area.[4]

On their journey back to Indiana, the Lincolns stopped in southern Coles County, where they stayed briefly with relatives who convinced them to remain in the state. Thomas and Sarah lived in several places in the region, locating finally in the Goosenest Prairie area in 1837.[5] There they likely moved into a cabin with Sarah's son, John D. Johnston, his wife, and their two boys. In 1840 John and Thomas built another cabin, moved their existing 16-by-18-foot building to the new 16-by-16-foot structure, and joined them together.[6]

Two Pathways to the Past

But this placid life was soon to change at Goosenest Prairie. As the years slipped by, Thomas died in 1851, and Sarah passed in 1869. During those years, Illinois, like much of the northern part of the United States, was becoming more industrialized and urbanized. Railroads were built in the state, and Chicago, its largest city, grew at an astounding pace. By 1870 nearly three hundred thousand people lived there, many of them newly arrived immigrants. Reflecting Chicago's significance in this transformation was its selection as the site of the Columbian Exposition. These changes wrought by the Industrial Revolution also made themselves evident, even if slowly, in the countryside of rural Illinois. By the 1870s, the subsistence farming practiced by Thomas Lincoln was becoming a thing of the past, and a market economy began to dominate.

Within a few years of the Lincolns' deaths, their cabin home fell into disrepair. In 1891 John J. Hall, a grandson of Sarah Lincoln by her first marriage, sold the cabin to James W. Craig. Craig later sold it to the Abraham Lincoln Log Cabin Association, a group of Chicago entrepreneurs who intended to exhibit it at the upcoming 1893 Columbian Exposition.[7] In early 1892 the association disassembled the building and removed it from Goosenest Prairie to Chicago. The cabin was apparently exhibited at the 1893 Exposition but vanished thereafter. Although there have been many accounts of the cabin's fate, none has satisfactorily explained its disappearance.[8]

Lincoln Log Cabin Historic Site Today

The Lincoln Log Cabin State Historic Site replicates the rural existence experienced by Stephen Sargent, Thomas Lincoln, and their families. In recognition of the historical value of Lincoln's association with this place, the State of Illinois purchased the land here in 1929 and 1930 and dedicated it as a state park in August 1936.[9] In 1935 and 1936, Civilian Conservation Corps members, using photographs and affidavits from those who had seen the cabin firsthand, rebuilt it as part of a New Deal project.[10] Later, when the Stephen Sargent Home was moved nearby, the site offered two pathways to the past—both to 1845 but to two distinct aspects of that time. Today a modern, welcoming visitor center houses meticulously prepared exhibits of the world of Thomas and Sarah Bush Lincoln, Stephen Sargent, and their neighbors. The exhibits include lifelike mannequins depicting pioneer farmers at work, women at a spinning wheel, and a clerk in Byrd Monroe's 1845 store, once located in nearby Charleston. Informative labels explain much about mid-nineteenth-century life here.

Domestic animals, similar to those familiar to the Lincolns, the Sargents, and their 1845 neighbors, are in a rustic barn, moved to the site in 1981. Authentically clad and well-prepared volunteer interpreters portray accurately the people who lived in the Goosenest Prairie neighborhood a decade and a half before the Civil War.

Standing amid the rustic buildings in this pastoral setting, a visitor needs only a little imagination to become immersed in that long-ago time. The sounds and sights and smells of almost two centuries past—the soft Southern Upland accent of a woman tending a fire, the thud of a pounding hammer, the pleasing aroma of wood smoke carried lightly on the morning breeze, the sharp odor of a barnyard—all help transport a visitor back in time to 1845.

The reconstructed Goosenest Prairie residence of Thomas and Sarah Lincoln sits on the site of the original building. It consists of two structures, joined to form two rooms, a bedroom and a kitchen. In the center wall a brick fireplace opens onto each room. The boards of the cabin's floor are dark and rough, and, as was likely the case in the earlier cabin, the inside walls are coarsely plastered and thinly whitewashed.

The east part of the cabin is the kitchen. The whitewashed bricks of the fireplace's surround are soot stained, and a blackened kettle hangs from an iron chimney crane. The building's interior is scented with the smell of wood smoke from the many fires built here. Above a well-used kitchen table with its benches and cane-seat chair, dried okra and peppers hang from the heavy, hewn beams that support the loft overhead, accessed by a crude ladder. In the original building, this room must have been a welcoming place, and it remains so today during the summer season as volunteer interpreters, garbed in 1845 attire, prepare meals.

In the cabin's west half, a simple rope bed is snugged against a wall. A trundle bed is tucked beneath the bed frame. Thomas Lincoln was a skilled cabinet maker and carpenter, but none of the pieces he crafted are found here. Although the furniture in the cabin did not belong to the Lincolns, it is authentically reflective of the kind of items they would almost certainly have owned. Nearby the cabin are a root cellar and well. Both have been reconstructed, though they are original below the ground level.

Two hundred yards to the northwest, beyond the site's modern visitor center, the Stephen Sargent farmhouse presents a sharp contrast to the Lincoln cabin. Moved here in 1985, the Sargent house was originally located about nine miles away. It provides a key to understanding the different approaches to farming found in east central Illinois in the mid-nineteenth century. Sargent was a more "progressive" farmer than Thomas Lincoln and more attuned to new agricultural approaches and practices.

Sargent's home reflects his different lifestyle. On the porch, four steps lead to the upstairs, and a door opens to a first-floor room. Inside, the walls are mustard yellow, and the woodwork around the doors and windows is gray. The room is floored with claret-colored boards. A bricked fireplace with black andirons on its hearth perhaps kept this room moderately warm on winter days. Four doors lead from the room, three to the outside and one to an additional room. The house clearly indicates that even though Stephen Sargent was a man of the mid-nineteenth century, his vision was toward the future.

Thomas Lincoln's farming method, aimed at growing his crops only for the use of his family or to trade with nearby neighbors, was fading into the past. Sargent, in line with his outlook, was oriented more toward the market, a trend that increased in Illinois, especially after the arrival of the railroad in the state. Change was inevitable in the countryside of Illinois, and Sargent more readily adapted to it than did Thomas Lincoln.

Despite their differences, however, the farms of both Lincoln and Sargent tell much about rural life in the Prairie State in the middle of the nineteenth century. They offer a view of two contrasting lifestyles. As such, these sites provide a unique view of an interesting period in the history of both Illinois and America.

Bishop Hill

Henry County

Under an expansive blue sky, the gently rolling prairieland of Henry County in northwestern Illinois sweeps off toward a distant horizon. Dotted now with the giant towers of wind turbines, this is a productive agricultural region where in summer months emerald rows of corn and soybeans border the roads and highways. Henry County is also home to Bishop Hill, a charming, pleasant village founded in 1846 by the religious mystic Eric Jansson following his flight from Sweden after conflict with church authorities there. This small, captivating community has played an uncommon role in Illinois history, one similar to that of only a few of the state's other towns and cities.[1]

Many of Bishop Hill's residents are conscious of this special past, and they have conserved much of it in the form of buildings, furniture, and other artifacts from the Janssonist period. Several structures from those busy years nearly two centuries ago when Jansson and his followers hoped to plant a utopian Zion here are still present. Some have been restored; others are yet in need of preservation, but all provide tangible links to this town's unique history.

One of the oldest buildings from the years when hundreds of Jansson's followers were gathered here is the Colony Church, built in 1848 and owned

Old Colony Church, where Eric Jansson's followers once worshipped. *Illustration by Phil Glosser.*

today by the Historic Preservation Division of the Illinois Department of Natural Resources.[2] The building appears much as it must have well over a century and a half ago. A gambrel-roofed, frame structure sided with white, wooden clapboards, it is on the west side of Bishop Hill Street, just south of Maiden Lane. A boardwalk leads to twin exterior stairways on the building's front. These ascend to a balcony where two doors admit to a narthex that gives access to the sanctuary, open today to the public.

The sanctuary, with walls and pulpit of white, can seat a thousand worshipers in its polished walnut pews. Each pew has an elegantly turned spindle-backed rail of maple. In the daytime sunrays sift through the windows and onto the pews, and a dim, velvet light fills this sacred place. At night candles in five chandeliers must have cast a soft, flickering illumination on evening services. Women and children were seated on one side of a center rail and men on the other while Jansson ministered to his followers.

Beneath the sanctuary, the church's first floor is also open to visitors. A long corridor bisects the building. Ten rooms, five on either side, open onto the corridor. Filled today with dozens of pieces of original furniture and household objects, these served as one-room apartments where colonists lived. The church's brick basement holds yet another ten rooms, also once used as living quarters.[3]

Two blocks south of the Colony Church is the Steeple Building, another striking structure from the town's Janssonist period. Constructed in 1854 and extensively renovated in 2013, it is used today as the Bishop Hill Heritage Association's administrative center. A museum and archive are also located here.[4] The building, which fronts on quiet, tree-shaded Bishop Hill Street, is three stories tall, and its buttercream exterior is accented by white trim. Centered on the building's front is a white-columned portico, and directly above is a balcony with a railing of gracefully crafted balusters.

The Doric columns and pediments here are of Greek Revival style. An octagonal clock tower rises above the third floor, topped in turn with a brick-red roof and an arrow weathervane. A dark-green railing surrounds the tower. The clock's faces, fifty inches in diameter, are black with gold numerals. These unusual clocks have only a single, white hour hand, leaving a viewer to estimate the minutes.

Inside, artifacts from the early days of the town fill the rooms. The first floor features an array of furniture and period tools. On the second floor a room is devoted to spinning, an important activity during the colonial period at Bishop Hill. The Janssonists used the flax grown near here to produce high-quality linen that they sold.[5]

The Colony Store, 101 West Main Street, is a two-story building of Greek Revival style, built in 1853.[6] It was extensively repaired in 2013 through private contributions to the Bishop Hill Heritage Association. Built of red brick, the store's white-trimmed pediment features a sunburst painted on a background of light blue. Several shelves and display cases here date from the store's early years. Once used to show the merchandise of a general store, they today hold books, candy, clothing, candles, coffee, and other souvenirs, many associated with the village's Swedish heritage.

Another building from the Janssonist period is the Bjorklund Hotel at Main and Park Streets. Built in 1852 as a residential facility, it was converted

Bjorklund Hotel in Bishop Hill. *Photo courtesy of Illinois Department of Natural Resources.*

in "about 1855" to a hotel.[7] The three-story, tan stucco exterior is somewhat stained. A white, two-story tower, surrounded by a railing and surmounted by a black weathervane of an eagle on a sphere, extends above the lower three stories. The hotel, owned by the Historic Preservation Division of the Illinois Department of Natural Resources, remains in need of restoration. There is much evidence of its age, and the blemished exterior and other signs of disrepair mar this once-stately structure, casting an air of melancholy over it. But inside, signs of the hotel's former grandeur can yet be found in its expansive rooms and several pieces of original furniture on the first floor, now open to the public.

On the south edge of Bishop Hill, a modern museum, operated by the Historic Preservation Division, houses a large collection of paintings by the artist Olaf Krans. Krans arrived in Jansson's utopia as a twelve-year-old boy with his parents in 1850.[8] In 1875 he began painting from memory portraits of many village residents as well as scenes of everyday life there. Some of the paintings are of agricultural activities—planting corn, harvesting grain—and vividly convey the communitarian nature of life in the colony. The square, Swedish faces that peer from Krans's pictures are serious and often creased and careworn from time and work. Looking into their eyes, even in the climate-controlled atmosphere of this contemporary gallery and at a distance into the past of more than a century, a viewer feels the deeply human dimension of this place.

Much of the effort to preserve the memory of these people and the old buildings they once used has been by the Bishop Hill Heritage Association and the Historic Preservation Division. Some public funding and much private help through contributions and volunteer work have returned some of the town's structures to their original appearance. Like the artifacts and paintings in the museums here, they help us understand how the early residents of this unique place lived, and why they came to this tranquil spot in Illinois.

The stories of Bishop Hill and of Jansson and his dream of a religious utopia on the Illinois prairie are similar to those of the other communitarian experiments that are a part of American history. Janssonists and Shakers, Owenites and the Oneida colonists all participated in the colorful pageant of our past. Parts of their histories, as unusual as they may sometimes seem today, in many ways reflect the larger story of America.

A Prophet's Vision

The journey that brought Jansson to Bishop Hill in 1846 began fifteen years earlier near his home in Sweden, when he underwent a striking religious experience. That experience, through which Jansson said he was healed of a debilitating illness, made him a visionary who believed he was at the very least a chosen prophet of God. Jansson also later said he believed God had chosen him to "come in Christ's place to bring grace."[9]

With light-brown hair, blue eyes, and what contemporary accounts called an "ordinary build," Jansson, except for unusually large front teeth, was unremarkable in appearance.[10] He must have emanated a kind of charisma, though, for he shortly acquired several zealous followers. Jansson soon began preaching his vision of Christianity, and as his influence spread across parts of Sweden, his ideas eventually set him at odds with the country's established church. When his unorthodox views and participation in the burning of religious books finally made him intolerable to Swedish ecclesiastical authorities, Jansson escaped to America in 1846.[11]

A year earlier Jansson had sent an associate, Olof Olsson, to the United States to find a location for what was to be the Janssonists' Zion. Olsson traveled to Henry County where he bought "sixty acres of land for $250 out of the colonists' common fund."[12] Encouraged by Olsson's glowing reports of the area's promise, Jansson and four hundred devoted disciples combined their resources and departed Sweden for their "new Jerusalem" the next year.

After an arduous and uncomfortable passage, Jansson and his flock arrived in Chicago in the summer of 1846.[13] From there they angled their way 160 miles southwestward across the flatness of Illinois's Grand Prairie toward Henry County. When they arrived, however, they quickly saw that life in their new Eden would be difficult. .

An autumn chill soon edged the air. The settlers found only limited shelter from the rapidly approaching rigors of a harsh Illinois winter. Faced with bitter cold, the colonists dug caves into the banks of a ravine that ran through the future village site.

Descriptions of these crude accommodations offer a bleak glimpse of the first months in Jansson's new prairie Jerusalem. By nearly every reckoning, the first year in the colony was without question daunting. The caves, thirty feet long by eighteen feet wide, with a log front of a door and two windows were by some accounts tolerable, by others they were dark, damp, and miserable.[14] That life in them must have been at the very least challenging is evident from the fact that of the first four hundred settlers who arrived in the fall of 1846, ninety-six did not survive to see the spring of 1847.[15]

Utopian Hopes

But life improved. Permanent structures rapidly replaced the crude caves of that first terrible winter as the Janssonists began an ambitious building program. The colonists worked together in this first phase of a tightly knit collective effort that was to characterize nearly every aspect of Bishop Hill for almost all its existence. Communitarian life was similar to that in several other nineteenth-century utopian experiments, and Jansson's disciples ate, lived, and labored together. In that shared work, including planting, harvesting, and bridge building, men and women toiled side by side.

As more buildings arose and new arrivals appeared, Bishop Hill became a thriving hub of activity. The town's enterprises included both manufacturing and agriculture. There were wagon shops, carpenter shops, grain mills, sawmills, a brickyard, and a tannery. Women working at looms produced the high-quality linen cloth that became for a time a specialty of Bishop Hill. In 1851 the colonists began growing broom corn and shortly afterward produced and sold thousands of brooms.

The Janssonists also became efficient farmers, and the colony soon acquired several thousand acres of rich farmland nearby.[16] Charles Wilson, visiting Bishop Hill in 1854, described in a letter home a busy, prosperous place with fruit orchards and expansive fields of winter wheat, barley, oats, and flax.[17]

But in the midst of this prosperity, a cloud shadowed Bishop Hill. Cholera, a disease that appears again and again in the story of frontier America, swept like a scythe through the village in the summer of 1849. The illness took the lives of well over a hundred inhabitants.[18]

Bishop Hill recovered and began to return to normal. But this prospering town all too quickly experienced an especially devastating loss. On May 13, 1850, Jansson met a sudden and violent death when John Root, a disaffected former resident of the colony, killed him in the nearby village of Cambridge.

Root, who was married to Jansson's cousin Charlotta, had earlier taken his wife, apparently in opposition to her own wishes, to Chicago. Contrary to Root's hopes, Charlotte and her son were soon returned to Bishop Hill.[19] Enraged, Root swore vengeance.

Jansson temporarily left the community to avoid Root but encountered him on a spring day in a second-floor courtroom in Cambridge, the county seat of Henry County. Jansson was in court dealing with lawsuits related to the colony. Root, who was in the building on an unrelated matter, accosted Jansson during the noon recess. The pair exchanged heated words, and Root pulled a pistol and shot Jansson to death.[20] Like the Mormons at Nauvoo, the Janssonists had now abruptly lost their prophet and inspirational leader.

Following Jansson's death, Jonas Olson took control of the colony. An energetic and gifted disciple of Jansson, he had been the founder's close associate since their days in Sweden. Olson orchestrated the legal incorporation of the town, and due largely to his initiative, the State of Illinois issued Bishop Hill a charter in 1853.[21] In accordance with the charter's terms, seven trustees governed the village and its adjacent lands. Under Olson's leadership, Bishop Hill continued for a time to prosper. Workshops, where colonists produced wagons, shoes, harnesses, carriages, brooms, and other products, hummed with activity. Twelve new brick buildings went up in town, along with several frame structures.[22]

By 1857, though, Bishop Hill was in difficulty. Unwise investments and overexpansion by the trustees, the nationwide Panic of 1857, and disagreements among the residents all contributed to the colony's financial instability.[23] Within three years it was clear that Bishop Hill was unsustainable. In 1861 the colonists agreed to divide the property and to end the colony that had once been Eric Jansson's utopian dream. Some residents remained, others moved away, and in time the town drifted into a quiescence not unlike that found in many small towns across the state.

Bishop Hill Today

Jansson's dream of a utopia on the Illinois prairie did indeed end, and his name today is remembered mostly at the village that he did so much to shape. Jansson's hope was one example of a larger movement in America in the first third of the nineteenth century, a movement that saw everyday people embarked upon an earnest pursuit for the perfect, a quest for a place where they could live in harmony with those of like minds. Bishop Hill today is emblematic of Illinois's role in this important and unique part of American history, and a sense of that history remains palpable here. It is present in what historians and sociologists like to call material culture—the buildings, tools, furniture, and other objects that reveal the ordinary life of a people and a place. In this small village, where utopian hopes briefly blossomed, those things impose themselves immediately upon the visitor's senses. It is in this way that Bishop Hill, like other places where failed dreams once flourished, can help visitors understand one part of the American story.

On the east edge of Bishop Hill an expansive, well-tended cemetery is bordered by the rural countryside. The graveyard is filled with headstones bearing Swedish names that mark the ethnicity of many of those who rest here. About three-quarters of the distance down a narrow, rocked lane, the cemetery's groomed lawn surrounds an obelisk marker. Standing stark-white against the green grass, the stone is well-kept but effaced by time. Shaded by a giant evergreen, the stone marks the final resting place of Eric Jansson, who with theological visions, idealistic dreams, and a captivating personality, began a utopia on the Illinois prairie so long ago. Jansson's perfect society in the end failed, but his story and those of the other pioneers who lived at Bishop Hill are colorful pieces in the mosaic of the state's past.

Reuben Moore Home and the Thomas Lincoln (Shiloh) Cemetery

South Lincoln Highway Road, Coles County

Seven miles southwest of the university town of Charleston, in east central Illinois, the two blacktopped lanes of Lincoln Highway Road pass through the tiny community of Campbell. Originally known as Farmington, Campbell today is a cluster of a few houses and mobile homes standing hard by a sturdy, red-brick church. Located just north of Goosenest Prairie, near where Abraham Lincoln's father and stepmother once lived in a rough log cabin, Campbell is in an area imbued with Lincoln lore. Campbell's connection to the Lincoln story is a building near the north end of the village, the historic Reuben Moore Home, a small frame structure where Lincoln's stepmother temporarily resided with her daughter, Matilda "Tildy" Moore.

During a sentimental visit to Mrs. Moore's home on January 31, 1861, a buggy carrying two men moved slowly through the chill air of an Illinois

Moore Home, where Lincoln visited with his stepmother, Sarah Bush Lincoln, before leaving Illinois for Washington, DC, and the presidency. *Photo by the author.*

winter. Crossing the ice-choked Kickapoo Creek, the buggy continued south on the road, past the fields and dark woods of southern Coles County. One of the men in the buggy was Abraham Lincoln, president-elect of the United States; the other was Augustus H. Chapman, married to the daughter of Lincoln's stepsister Tildy.[1]

During the crowded days before he left for Washington following his election, Tildy's home became one of the last places Lincoln visited in Illinois. A presidency dominated by the great crisis of the Civil War and tragically ended by his assassination prevented Lincoln from seeing again this part of Illinois where he had long had family, friends, and associates.

Soon after his arrival, Lincoln, Chapman, and possibly Lincoln's first cousin once removed John Hanks made a trip to the unmarked grave of Lincoln's father, Thomas.[2] The older Lincoln had died in January 1851, but

Abraham was unable to attend his funeral. Thomas had been buried in what was then known as the Gordon Cemetery, a rural graveyard a little more than a mile northwest of his Goosenest Prairie cabin. Now, a decade later while standing at his father's grave, Abraham stated that he would provide a stone so that the place could be properly marked. However, as president, Lincoln was focused on meeting the unrelenting demands of the Civil War, and this never occurred.[3]

Among Friends and Family

As news of Lincoln's presence spread, excitement rippled through the normally quiet village. A crowd from the Goosenest Prairie area assembled to see the president-elect, and for a time the Moore residence was filled with acquaintances and well-wishers. The rural school nearby was dismissed, and the students congregated close by the small building for a glimpse of Lincoln. Mrs. Moore, assisted by some of the neighboring women in Farmington, prepared a dinner for her stepbrother. After Lincoln returned from the cemetery, she and her friends served the special meal they had made, and several people joined Lincoln at the table.[4]

At some point Sarah worriedly expressed to her stepson her fear that she would not see him again and told him she was afraid he would never return from Washington, DC, alive. Lincoln gently tried to assure her that this would not be the case. This tender exchange between them may have occurred at the Moore Home, but it is also possible that it took place at Chapman's residence after Lincoln and his stepmother returned to Charleston.[5] The following day Lincoln left Charleston for Springfield to get ready to travel to Washington.

Thomas Lincoln (Shiloh) Cemetery

The cemetery that Lincoln visited on that cold, damp January day now also holds the grave of his stepmother, who died in the spring of 1869, eight years after she last saw her stepson. A peaceful place of final repose, the burial ground is now called the Thomas Lincoln Cemetery. Sometimes also referred to as Shiloh Cemetery, it is about a mile and a half distant from and slightly to the southwest of the Moore Home. The graves are near the Shiloh

Presbyterian Church, a red-brick building with a gray, shingled roof, white trim, and stained-glass windows.[6]

The church and the graveyard are on the north side of Lincoln Highway Road, which, about a half-mile south of Campbell, curves sharply to the west. The burial ground is shaded by large cedar, walnut, and locust trees and surrounded by neighboring farms. A small stream, bordered by a narrow band of elm, walnut, locust, and mulberry trees, trickles along the cemetery's north edge. Many of the headstones here are clearly very old. They are thin, and the faces of some are so worn by weather and the passing of the years that the names of the dead are no longer legible.

The graves of Abraham Lincoln's father and stepmother are enclosed by a black iron fence. Their resting places are marked by two small stones, gray and plain. Etched into these are Thomas's and Sarah's names, birth and death dates, and an inscription stating that the stones were emplaced by the Danville Kiwanis Club in 1925. Also enclosed by the fence is a large dedicatory marker etched with their names, the dates of their births and deaths, and the following inscription:

FATHER AND STEP MOTHER

OF OUR MARTYRED PRESIDENT

THEIR HUMBLE BUT WORTHY HOME

GAVE TO THE WORLD

ABRAHAM LINCOLN

A small etched line at the bottom of this marker states that it was placed here by the Lions Clubs of Illinois.

A few yards northeast of this more recent commemorative stands another gravestone for Thomas Lincoln. A white sandstone obelisk, it is dappled with patches of moss and lichens. Placed in the cemetery in 1880, it was relocated from the Lincolns' actual graves to its present site in 1926. This second monument, also enclosed by a black iron paling, is badly effaced by time and scarred by vandals who have chipped away pieces of it.[7]

A marker honoring Thomas and Sarah Lincoln in Thomas Lincoln (Shiloh) Cemetery. *Photo by the author.*

Moore Home and the Cemetery Today

The house where Lincoln visited his stepmother in that troubled January 1861 is two miles north of his father's Goosenest Prairie cabin. Constructed during the 1850s, it became the property of the State of Illinois in 1925. It sits on the west side of a road near the north end of the now almost vanished hamlet of Campbell. The house of four downstairs rooms and a loft is a plain, rectangular building with a steeply pitched roof of dark wooden shingles. It is covered with clapboard siding, tan-colored and weather-beaten. The window frames and doors are deep maroon. The building's architectural style, with its clapboard siding and balloon framed construction, reflects the more affluent status of its builder and original owner, Reuben Moore. Extending to the west behind the house is a large lawn, shaded in summer by maple and walnut trees. The Moore Home is easily reached by taking the Lincoln Highway Road south from Charleston. Informative signs describing the home's history are close to a small parking lot nearby.

Like the Moore Home, the Thomas Lincoln Cemetery (or Shiloh Cemetery) is quiet on most days, though there is from time to time a burial here, for the graveyard remains in use. Sometimes visitors interested in Lincoln view this place associated with the president's family. But much of the time the cemetery and the churchyard are undisturbed. Although the cemetery, like the Moore Home, is secluded in a rural part of the state, both are worth visiting.[8] The appearance of the area where they are located changes dramatically with the seasons. When winter's hand lies heavily on the landscape, the brown fields are empty, and the woods stand gray and bare. A chilling wind sweeps out of the west and cuts across the prairie. Snowflakes often dust the cemetery's gravestones and swirl around the eaves of Matilda Moore's home. On those days the discomforts and difficulties so common to life in rural America nearly two centuries ago are starkly apparent, and a modern sightseer is happy to hurry to the comfort of a waiting automobile.

But in warm-weather months, when the wildflowers bloom and the trees and the grass show the life of a new season, the Goosenest Prairie area is transformed. The golden sunlight of an Illinois summer day gives the countryside an almost luminous glow. A green patina covers the fields, and a cornflower-blue sky arcs overhead. On those days a kind of tranquility is present here that is now sometimes too rare, and the visitor wants to linger. But at any season these places can help us understand the family and the background that surely helped to shape one of America's greatest presidents.

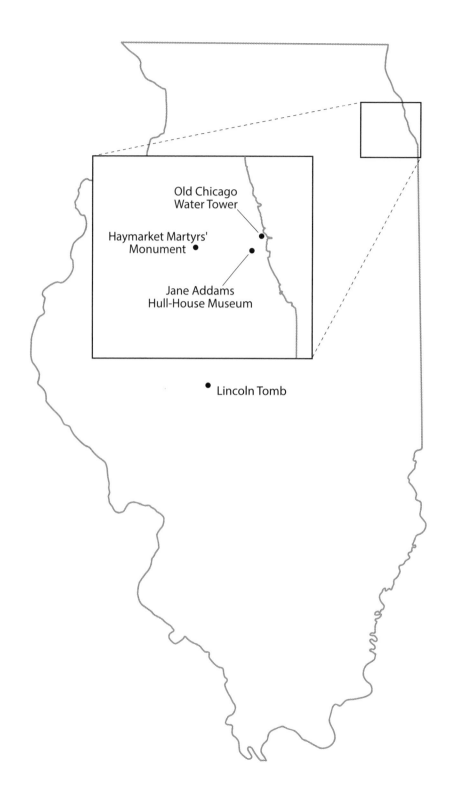

Old Chicago
Water Tower

Haymarket Martyrs'
Monument

Jane Addams
Hull-House Museum

Lincoln Tomb

Part 4

AT THE TURN OF THE CENTURY

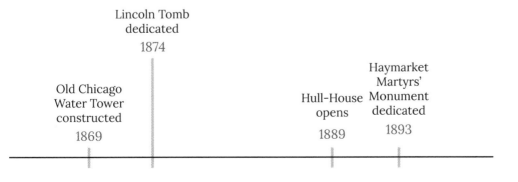

Lincoln Tomb
dedicated
1874

Haymarket
Martyrs'
Old Chicago   Hull-House Monument
Water Tower   opens   dedicated
constructed   1893
1869   1889

Prologue

Like much of the rest of America, Illinois during the last three decades of the nineteenth century was undergoing enormous change. In the aftermath of the Civil War, new forces were unleashed that would alter forever the fabric of the nation. By the year 1900, the innovations of the Second Industrial Revolution had done much to transform life in the Prairie State. One of the places where this could readily be seen was in Chicago, which had grown greatly between 1870 and 1900.

Chicago's growth was accompanied by several challenges, including that of providing adequate water for the city. To meet this daunting task, the city government in 1869 constructed a new water system that included a 182-foot-tall limestone structure known today as the **Old Chicago Water Tower**. In an ironic twist of events, the water tower played almost no role in combatting the Great Chicago Fire when it swept across the city in 1871. The water tower survived the fire almost unscathed, however, and stands today in its original location in Jane Byrne Plaza on North Michigan Avenue.

Abraham Lincoln, who was assassinated in 1865, did not witness the astounding cascade of postwar change that inundated the state he had served. His name, however, remained lodged in the state's public memory because of his wartime presidency and martyr's death. Almost immediately after his assassination, Lincoln's associates and family planned to have his remains interred in Illinois. Those plans were realized with the construction in Springfield's Oak Ridge Cemetery of the **Lincoln Tomb**, dedicated in 1874 and now a state historic site.

The closing decades of the nineteenth century were rife, too, with labor unrest. Workers, burdened by long hours of poorly paid, difficult, and dangerous toil, often went on strike or held rallies in attempts to improve their conditions. A meeting of workers near Chicago's Haymarket Square in 1886 turned unexpectedly violent when a homemade bomb exploded, killing several police officers and civilians. The individual who threw the bomb was never identified, but eight Chicago radicals were arrested. After an irregular trial, four were executed. They were buried in Forest Park's Forest Home Cemetery, where their graves are marked by the **Haymarket Martyrs' Monument**.

The mechanization and mass production of the Second Industrial Revolution required a massive urban workforce. Many of those laboring in Chicago's factories and stockyards were recently arrived immigrants, large numbers of whom were found in the ramshackle tenements and rundown cottages of Chicago's Near West Side. In 1889 two remarkable young women, Jane Addams and Ellen Gates Starr, hoped in some small way to improve the lives of those living in such conditions when they established **Hull-House**, one of the nation's first settlement houses, at 800 South Halsted Street in Chicago.

Though some of the Prairie State's history at the end of the nineteenth century is stamped by the disorder and dislocation associated with almost all periods of rapid societal change, it was for many, nonetheless, a time of progress. Exciting new developments transformed Illinois. The Old Chicago Water Tower is one emblem of that transformation. So, too, is Hull-House, which sought to address some of the myriad problems of the city. The Haymarket Martyrs' Monument is another symbol of the era, commemorating the victims of the period's unfortunate disorder. Yet, as technology altered society in new and unforeseen ways, interest remained in the state's past and in those who had helped to shape it. That interest was realized in the Lincoln Tomb, which honors a president who had acquired a status of near-mythic proportion and who had guided the nation during its greatest crisis.

Old Chicago Water Tower

806 North Michigan Avenue, Chicago

Michigan Avenue is one of the most famous streets in Chicago. Stretching north from 127th Street, it becomes, in the middle of the city, a sparkling strand of stylish shops, chic restaurants, upscale hotels, and historic buildings. A few blocks south of where Michigan merges finally with Lake Shore Drive, it intersects with East Chicago Avenue, a street that cuts an arrow-straight course west to the north branch of the Chicago River and beyond into the western suburbs. Here, where Michigan and Chicago Avenues meet, near a small patch of greenery called Jane Byrne Plaza, the tan castellated walls of the Old Chicago Water Tower rise incongruously amid its fashionable surroundings.

Marvels of Engineering

Chicago's rapid growth in the 1860s had made providing clean water to its residents a significant challenge. Raw sewage and liquid waste from the city's many industries made their way into the Chicago River, a smelly, polluted stream consisting of three branches that cut through the city and drained into Lake Michigan. There, because the water system's intake facility was close to the shoreline, contaminated water often entered the some-

The old and the new: the Old Chicago Water Tower among the city's modern buildings. *Photo by the author.*

The ornate Old Chicago Water Tower. *Illustration by Phil Glosser.*

what-rudimentary water-distribution system that served some residents.[1] Disease, including cholera and typhoid, resulting in part from the unclean water, was common.

To solve the problem, Chicago's engineer of public works, Ellis S. Chesbrough, suggested the construction of an intake station much farther offshore. Two miles out, this so-called crib was connected by a tunnel beneath Lake Michigan to a new pumping station near the lake shore. The pumping station pumped the water to the top of a standpipe inside the water tower to help stabilize the pressure in the city's distribution system.[2]

Chesbrough's plan was finalized when the water tower was finished in 1869. The water tower and pumping station are both nineteenth-century marvels of engineering.

The water tower was designed by architect William W. Boyington. A native of Massachusetts, Boyington came to Chicago in 1853 and in the years just after the Civil War became one the city's best-known architects.[3] Originally constructed to conceal the 138-foot-tall standpipe, the water tower was an integral part for several years of the city's efforts to supply water to its residents until it became obsolete and ceased to be used in the municipal water system. The nearby pumping station, however, remains in use today in its original role to help supply the city with water from Lake Michigan.

The water tower was constructed in 1869 to improve Chicago's drinking water. A vital component of the city's water system, it also had the obvious role of providing water to the city fire department for fighting fires. In a case of historical irony, however, the water tower, although it survived the ravages of the Great Chicago Fire of 1871, played almost no role in combatting this most devastating blaze in the city's history.

The Great Chicago Fire

That a fire was a real possibility was evident on the warm autumn evening of Sunday, October 8, 1871, when Chicago's residents gathered as usual around dining-room or kitchen tables for their meal. It was the close of yet another day of the wilting heat that had plagued the city throughout the summer and early fall. There had been few cool days and almost no rain for more than two months, and whether one lived in the expensive homes of Chicago's well-to-do or in the squalid slums of the city's poor neighborhoods, there was little escape from the unremitting misery the weather inflicted.

The population of Chicago in 1871 was booming, and builders hastily constructed many new structures, residential and commercial, from wood. Shipped from Wisconsin's forests or elsewhere and shaped in one of Chicago's many planing mills, wood became an integral part of this raw, restless city crowding Lake Michigan's shore. Abundant and relatively inexpensive, wood, especially pine, was the construction material of choice.

Frame buildings, fronted by sidewalks of wooden planks, soon character-ized many parts of the city. Some streets were paved with wooden blocks. Grain elevators, lumber yards, hay-filled stables, and block after block of cheap, wooden houses all heightened the chances for a fire that was almost certain to have disastrous consequences.[4]

The possibility of an accidental blaze grew during the last days of September, and harbingers of the catastrophe to come were two large fires that flared on the city's Southwest Side. One was extensive enough that it left a scar of four square blocks of blackened ruins. Firefighters had, with considerable difficulty, extinguished both blazes, but the firemen were exhausted, and some of their equipment was damaged.[5] The terrifying threat of a future citywide blaze became even more apparent to some Chicagoans.

At approximately 9:30 p.m. on October 8, 1871, that threat became a reali-ty when Patrick and Catherine O'Leary's barn near 137 West De Koven Street in a shabby, Southwest Side neighborhood, somehow caught fire.[6] Within a few hours that single burning barn fire spread with stunning speed to the north and east, becoming the Great Chicago Fire, a massive conflagration that devoured an enormous part of the city.

Driven by a capricious wind generated in part by convection whirls (pil-lars of very hot air that ascend and cause cooler air to enter the fire), the fire quickly ignited buildings east of the Chicago River's south branch.[7] The wind and the astounding power of the convection whirls lifted pieces of burning debris high above and sent them sailing far ahead of the fire front itself. The flaming pieces dropped onto buildings and ignited new fires beyond the main blaze.

Flames sometimes reached a hundred feet high, and the fire relent-lessly seared its way east to Lake Michigan and, turning north, crossed the Chicago River's main channel. As it swept north, the fire was heading for the municipal water tower and pumping station.[8]

In the early morning of October 9, one of these pieces of flaming mate-rial carried overhead by the wind or a convection whirl fell on the pump-ing-station roof. Despite efforts to put out the flames, the roof caught fire and soon caved into the building.[9] Waterworks employees shut down the pumping mechanisms to avoid an explosion of the steam boilers.[10] The city's water-distribution system was no longer of use. The only water accessible to the firemen was in the distribution system's pipes and in the water tower—not nearly enough to effectively fight the fire. Even if a fire engine was near the Chicago River or the lake, it was nearly impossible to quench the flames.[11]

At Fullerton Avenue (about six miles from De Koven Street and about two miles from the water tower) and about thirty hours later early on Tuesday morning, October 10, rain and a scarcity of readily available fuel finally ended the fire. The water tower itself was almost unscathed.

The Old Chicago Water Tower Today

Jane Byrne Plaza is really a courtyard of sorts, paved with large cement squares. Concrete lampposts with round globes stand at various places, and on the west side of the courtyard is a circular concrete fountain. Park benches are arranged in a semi-circle west of the water tower. Large trees and mulch-covered beds of cultivated flowers make this in summertime a shady, verdant island set amidst the gray cement of the urban cityscape.

As can be expected in the middle of an urban area, this is a bustling, busy place. The plaza is filled with the clamor of traffic: the blaring of horns, the rumble of buses, the sound of endlessly passing automobiles. Pedestrians walk through the small park constantly, and the ever-present pigeons swoop to land on the courtyard or to perch on one of the water tower's many ledges.

The tower is dwarfed by nearby skyscrapers, including, about two blocks north, one of Chicago's tallest, the 875 North Michigan Avenue (formerly the John Hancock Center). The water tower is constructed of yellow-tan limestone, quarried near Joliet, Illinois. Boyington favored the Gothic Revival design, and he used it for both the water tower and the pumping station. The water tower's first story is a rectangle with castle-like walls. Turreted towers are at each corner and next to the four entry ways, one located on each side. Window and door frames, along with the building's other wooden trim, are painted a creamy tan.

The second story is very nearly a smaller, though slightly taller, version of the base, inset several feet from the first story's walls. The third story is also adorned with turrets and battlements. The tower's topmost part extends upward from this third portion, is octagonal, with small, slot-like windows, and is topped with a dark-gray octagonal cap. Just below the cap, small castellated turrets again surround the tower.

The entrance to the water tower is on its west side, off the courtyard. Inside, hallways form a rectangle around the building's center, which once contained the standpipe this structure was built to conceal. On the walls of the north and south hallways are small water fountains with ornate sculptures of lion heads. No longer functional, they are decorative reminders of the quaint Victorian origins of this place. The hallway's walls now serve as an art gallery—the City Gallery in the Historic Water Tower. The gallery was established in 1999 and features the work of Chicago artists.

The Chicago Pumping Station, constructed at the same time as the water tower, is directly across Michigan Avenue (known at the time of the fire as Pine Street). It is of the same architectural style and fashioned from the same sort of limestone as the tower. It remains in use not only as an electrified pumping station but also as the home of the Lookingglass Theatre Company.

The Old Chicago Water Tower, with its busy exterior of rugged battlements and castle-like stone walls, stands in sharp contrast to its sleek, twenty-first-century surroundings. Located at a key point on the Magnificent Mile in the heart of the gleaming sophistication of what is, perhaps, Chicago's premier mercantile area, this unusual, intriguing structure is an artifact of another time. One historian has observed that the water tower was "a monument to the hubris of Chicagoans who thought that such a water system could save their city from a disastrous fire."[12] Still, it is here one can sense the continuity and change that so many historic sites impart. And, as one of the few public buildings to survive the Great Chicago Fire almost undamaged, it serves as an enduring emblem of Chicago's ongoing, irrepressible spirit and vitality.

Lincoln Tomb
State Historic Site

Oak Ridge Cemetery,
1500 Monument Avenue, Springfield

Places of Remembrance

Cemeteries are a part of almost all communities. They vary from well-maintained burial grounds amidst the cityscapes of large urban areas to clusters of graves in village churchyards to tiny, weedy, nearly forgotten plots accessible only by the remote backroads and narrow country lanes of rural America. These places of remembrance evoke a variety of emotions from their visitors. Sometimes this may be merely a curiosity about the tombstones seen in nearly any graveyard. In some instances, it might be a simple respect for the deceased. In still other cases there is the deep feeling of loss for family members or friends interred there. And for many, perhaps, there is the unwelcome and unsettling sense of the brevity of all life.

Some cemeteries, however, assume a broader significance. They stir the same emotions prompted by almost all burial grounds and yet transcend them. One of these is Arlington National Cemetery with its verdant lawns and precisely ordered white stones that reveal where thousands who have served the nation are now in eternal sleep. Another is Gettysburg National Cemetery. There, seemingly endless rows of markers attest to the terrible, tragic cost of the American Civil War. A third, perhaps, is Boston's Granary Burying Ground and the ancient, time-effaced stones that disclose the final resting places of Revolutionary patriots Samuel Adams, John Hancock, and Paul Revere.

Another such place is in the Prairie State. Located on 365 acres of gently rolling hills, it is in Springfield, the state's capital city. This is Oak Ridge Cemetery, which since 1865 has held the remains of President Abraham Lincoln and several members of his family. Seventy-five thousand graves are in Oak Ridge, including those of many prominent citizens of the state.[1] On the cemetery's tranquil, tree-shaded grounds are memorials, too, that recognize the Illinois dead from several of the country's conflicts—the Civil War, World War II, the Korean War, and the Vietnam War—and the Illinois Purple Heart Memorial that commemorates those awarded a Purple Heart during service in any of America's wars.

Commemoration of a President

It is the Lincoln Tomb and the enduring mystique of Abraham Lincoln that especially draw many of those who visit Oak Ridge Cemetery each year. Although it has been over 150 years since America's sixteenth president was murdered on an April day in Washington, DC, his name remains deeply fixed in the nation's collective memory. Lincoln, who had emerged from a difficult and impoverished backwoods youth, was a remarkable example of how ability, wit, and effort can overcome a host of obstacles imposed by a life lacking in privilege. His rise from rural poverty to the presidency mirrored what was once an archetypal myth for American political success. Consistently rated as one of America's greatest chief executives, his prominence in the presidential pantheon is akin only to George Washington or Franklin D. Roosevelt.

Like many who moved to Illinois in the early nineteenth century, Lincoln was born in Kentucky and spent much of his early youth in southern Indiana. But it was his years at New Salem, Illinois, his lengthy career as an Illinois attorney, his prominence in the state's new Republican Party during

President Abraham Lincoln's Tomb in Oak Ridge Cemetery, Springfield. *Illustration by Phil Glosser.*

the troubled years of the late 1850s, and, of course, his presidency that have embedded him in Illinois and American history and placed him at the forefront of notables from the Prairie State.

Lincoln's remarkable capacity as president during the great national crisis of the Civil War, his authorship of the Emancipation Proclamation, and his untimely and tragic death remain familiar to many Americans as well as to people from other nations. Vachel Lindsay's elegiac depiction of Lincoln as "a bronzed lank man" attired in "his suit of ancient black, a famous high-top hat and plain worn shawl" evokes yet a commonly held image of the extraordinary man who rests here. The tomb that holds Lincoln's remains sits at the top of a moderate slope and is fronted by a trimmed greensward that sweeps toward a low, abbreviated, semi-circular granite wall. Beyond the wall is a cement plaza, accessible by broad walkways that lead from a parking lot a short distance to the west. Here one encounters the familiar bronze rendering of Lincoln's head, the nose rubbed shiny by the touching of countless hands. Resting on a tall pedestal, the work is a reproduction of a marble piece created by Gutzon Borglum, perhaps best known as the artist who carved the enormous likenesses of four presidents into the face of Mount Rushmore. Just beyond Borglum's iconic sculpture, steps ascend to a second plaza and the tomb's entrance.

The Lincoln Tomb is a square, gray structure made of smooth Quincy granite. It is surrounded by a cement walkway, with semi-circular edifices extending from the front and back of the building.[2] Large shields, each representing a state of the Union and linked to each other to indicate national solidarity, adorn the exterior walls. The door to the tomb's interior is in the center of the southern extension, and just above the door is a bronze plaque of Lincoln's Gettysburg Address. Granite bannisters guard stone stairs that ascend to the top of the tomb, where two balconies and a base for the obelisk rise above it. At the corners of the base are plinths holding sculpted bronze figures signifying the military forces under Lincoln's command during the Civil War. Extending skyward 117 feet from the monument's center is the obelisk that forms the striking focal point of the tomb.[3]

At the obelisk's foot is a sculpture of the martyred president. Holding the Emancipation Proclamation in his left hand, a careworn Lincoln gazes to the southeast. This piece, as well as the rest of the statuary here (except for Borglum's sculpture of the president's head), was created by the American artist Larkin Goldsmith Mead, who also designed the tomb itself.

A movement to create a special burial place honoring Lincoln emerged shortly after his assassination. A group of prominent Illinois political leaders, along with some of the late president's friends, formed the National Lincoln Monument Association on April 24, nine days following Lincoln's death on April 15, 1865, to perpetuate Lincoln's memory with a monument marking his grave in Springfield, and they soon began a widespread effort to solicit funds to build it.[4] The association aimed to construct the monument at the Mather Block, the highest plot of land in Springfield and not far from the current state Capitol.[5]

The association's plans, however, conflicted with those of the president's widow, Mary, and the Lincolns' son Robert. After first considering an interment in Chicago or Washington, DC, Mary decided that the burial should be in Oak Ridge Cemetery.[6] When members of the association persisted in their hopes for the Mather Block site, Mary told them that she would arrange to have her husband interred either in Chicago or in a crypt in the national Capitol that was originally intended for George Washington.[7] The association reluctantly agreed to Mary's demand and began plans for a tomb and memorial at Oak Ridge.[8] In 1868 the National Lincoln Monument Association accepted a design by sculptor Mead, one of more than thirty people who had submitted plans.[9] A Vermont artist who resided for much of his life in Italy, he worked mostly in the neoclassical style.

Construction of the Lincoln Tomb, following Mead's plan, began in 1868. On October 15, 1874, the association dedicated Lincoln's final resting place. Ulysses S. Grant, who a decade earlier during the Civil War had been one of President Lincoln's key army commanders and who now as president was himself commander in chief, was present.[10] In 1895 the association relinquished ownership to the State of Illinois.[11]

A Family Resting Place

Mary Lincoln died in 1882, and her remains were placed in the tomb in July of that year.[12] The three Lincoln sons who had died earlier, Edward in 1850, William in 1862, and Thomas in 1871, were also buried in the tomb. The remaining son, Robert Lincoln, died in 1926 but is buried in Arlington National Cemetery. When his son, Abraham Lincoln II (known as Jack) died in 1890, he was placed in the Oak Ridge tomb, but in 1930 Robert's widow had Jack's remains transferred from the tomb and interred near his father at Arlington.

Mary's hope that her husband's grave would be in a place of quiet repose did not materialize. Hundreds of people visited the site, disturbing the tomb's tranquility. In 1876, just two years after the monument's dedication, a band of counterfeiters hatched a bizarre plan to steal Lincoln's body and hold it for ransom until one of the gang's members, who was confined in a state prison, was released. Although the grave robbers gained entry to the tomb, their scheme was discovered before they could carry it to completion.[13]

And the tomb itself soon presented problems. Because of flaws in the initial construction, the state had to begin rebuilding it in 1900.[14] Robert Lincoln had been troubled by the earlier attempt to rob the grave. Understandably concerned about the security of his father's remains, he specified during the renovation a detailed plan to ensure that Lincoln's body could never be disturbed again. A coffin holding the late president was enclosed inside a cage of steel bars. The cage was placed at the bottom of a ten-foot-deep pit under the floor of the chamber at the monument's north end.[15] Workers then filled the pit with cement and relaid the tomb's floor over it. Although the problem of how to protect Lincoln's body had been solved, the tomb by the late 1920s once more displayed signs that it needed repair. In 1930 the state began a massive restoration of the monument. When the work was finished, the Lincoln Tomb had assumed much of its contemporary appearance.

The Lincoln Tomb Today

Today a dark-bronze door on the south side of the monument opens to the interior. Visitors enter an oval-shaped rotunda, in the center of which is a small bronze replica of Daniel Chester French's familiar marble sculpture in the Lincoln Memorial in Washington, DC. The rotunda's floor is made of marble. The walls are composed of sixteen column-like panels. At the sides of each of these are dark-brown columns, each topped with a small star representing the states of the Union at Lincoln's death in 1865. The rotunda is discreetly lit by concealed LED lighting. and it is here, in the hushed, solemn atmosphere of the monument's interior that, as would be expected, the essence of the sixteenth president is somehow manifest.[16]

Four corridors, also illuminated by indirect light, form a square around the center of the monument. Alcoves in the corridors' corners hold sculptures by several artists portraying Lincoln at various stages of his life. On one wall, light gleams faintly from a plaque featuring Lincoln's biography. Similar markers on other hallway walls display his 1861 farewell address, the Gettysburg Address, and a portion of his second inaugural address.

Abraham Lincoln's dark-red marble marker. *Photo courtesy of Illinois Department of Natural Resources.*

In the center of the rear east–west hall, a reddish-brown marker, massive and polished, designates the martyred president's burial place. Made of red ark fossil marble, the marker is inscribed with only his name and the years of his birth and death. The American flag, a presidential flag, and flags of the states in which Lincoln or his ancestors resided hang from staffs arranged in a semi-circle around the stone. In gilt letters on the curving frieze of the wall beyond are the words spoken by secretary of war Edwin M. Stanton moments after Lincoln's death: "Now he belongs to the ages."[17] On the wall of this same hallway and facing Lincoln's stone are inscriptions marking the crypts for Mary and for three of the Lincolns' sons, Edward (Eddie), Thomas (Tad), and William (Willie). Another crypt for Robert T. Lincoln, never used, is also here.

Each day individuals and small clusters of people arrive at this place that memorializes an almost mythic Lincoln, a Lincoln who to many is a kind of archetype that represents an idealized American national ethos. Despite this near-constant stream of visitors, the tomb and its grounds are for the most part quiet, and the tranquility is disturbed only by the soft murmur of voices or sometimes the muffled sound of an automobile in the parking lot not far to the west. The atmosphere here resembles the almost reverential ambiance characteristic of other historic sites, such as the Lincoln Memorial or Washington's tomb at Mount Vernon, or those quiet rooms with their green-draped tables found behind the old red-brick walls of Independence Hall in Philadelphia. In these places, what William Manchester once called "the haze of tribal sentiment" still lingers, even if it is perhaps not as thick as it once was.[18] Lincoln's Tomb, honoring as it does a truly remarkable American, can tell us much—not only about Lincoln the president but also about the flaws, challenges, and successes of the United States of America.

Haymarket Martyrs' Monument

Forest Home Cemetery,
863 Des Plaines Avenue, Forest Park

Chicago, the largest metropolis in Illinois and the third-largest city in the United States, is the heir of a rich and important history. From its origin two centuries ago as a trading post and army fort, it has grown into a vast metropolis, a center of industry, commerce, and innovation. In many ways the economic hub of the Midwest, it is a place of great museums and famous universities, of impressive buildings and stunning centers for the arts.

By the late nineteenth century, Chicago was well launched on this trajectory that would lead to its prominence in American life. A magnet to newcomers from abroad as well as from its own hinterland, the city provided seemingly unbounded opportunities for those seeking new prospects in their lives. And the opportunities did, indeed, appear limitless, for the marvels of the Second Industrial Revolution were everywhere in Chicago. The railroads, the stockyards, the meat-packing plants of Gustavus F. Swift and Philip D. Armour, the farm-machinery factory of Cyrus H. McCormick—all these and hundreds of other companies large and small provided employment for the thousands who were drawn to this busy, brawling city by the lake.

The innovative architectural genius of Daniel Hudson Burnham, Louis Sullivan, John Root, and William Le Baron Jenney was fast reshaping the cityscape. A sheen of sophistication, too, was visible in the presence of the Art Institute, established in 1879. The downtown streets were lined with new stores and fashionable eateries. Prairie Avenue, where the wealthy were beginning to construct their imposing gray-stone mansions, was a ribbon of elegance on the city's South Side. Even the young men and women employed as salesclerks and office workers in establishments that daily buzzed with the city's business prospered to an extent rarely known in an earlier day.

But just beneath this shining surface, all was not well. Not far from the hum and hurry of the commercial district was another Chicago. Though it was only a few blocks distant, it was in all ways other than proximity infinitely removed from the comfortable neighborhoods of the upper and middle classes. In this Chicago hundreds of thousands of men, women, and children experienced lives burdened by almost unrelieved toil and unceasing care. Huddled in the foul warrens of the Near West Side and other slum areas, they endured unclean water and polluted air. They labored daily at jobs frequently difficult and too often unsafe. Ten-hour days and the whirling hazards of factory machines were common for those earning wages barely adequate for marginal shelter and meager food.

A Smoldering Discontent

Unsurprisingly, among some who experienced life in this Chicago was a smoldering discontent. This dissatisfaction had grown during the first half of the 1880s and by mid-decade had produced a small, intense group of anarchists, socialists, and other radicals who were angrily demanding change. The dissatisfaction had also pushed large numbers of working people into several of the less extreme "white bread" labor unions. The call for the eight-hour day, one of labor's persistent demands, had grown in intensity in the early months of 1886.[1]

To draw attention to their situation, thousands of laboring men and women marched peacefully in a parade along Michigan Avenue on Saturday, May 1, 1886. The following Monday, however, matters turned violent. Two workers were killed in a vicious clash between strikers and strikebreakers at the McCormick Harvesting Machine Co. plant on the city's West Side.

August Spies, a leader in Chicago's anarchist community and editor of the anarchist newspaper *Arbeiter Zeitung*, saw the chaos. Shocked, Spies penned an emotionally charged flyer demanding that workers resist those he believed were responsible for not only the events he had just witnessed but also for the oppression of all the city's working people.[2]

The evening of May 3 a group of anarchists met at Greif's Hall, a narrow, four-story building on Lake Street, about a block north and three blocks east of a spot soon to be burned forever into the city's history: Haymarket Square. Though this meeting had nothing to do with the McCormick tragedy, it did result in another handbill, written by a radical anarchist named Adolph Fischer. The handbill urged attendance at a protest rally the next evening, May 4, in Haymarket Square.[3] With the printing of Spies's flyer and Fischer's circular, threads leading to the Chicago Haymarket Affair were being rapidly drawn together.

Scheduled to begin at 7:30 p.m., the poorly planned gathering did not start until almost 8:30. The crowd, at perhaps just over two thousand, was disappointingly small, and the meeting was moved up Des Plaines Street, just north of the Haymarket. Standing on an empty freight wagon, Spies and another anarchist, Albert Parsons, spoke to a waning audience. Parsons and Spies were followed by Samuel Fielden, a self-employed teamster also involved in the labor struggle. At approximately 10:30 p.m., as a strong breeze started to blow and a spring rain threatened, Fielden was finishing his speech to a fast-decreasing crowd.

Standing on the wagon, he was surprised to see a formation of policemen moving quickly toward him. Police Captain William Ward, the officer in charge, demanded that the meeting disband peacefully. A puzzled Fielden responded that the meeting was peaceful and then agreed to end his talk.[4] Just as he stepped from the wagon, someone standing close to a nearby alleyway tossed a small, sparking, crackling object toward the police. It was a crudely manufactured bomb, and it detonated with astonishing force near the wagon and among the police. A few seconds of stunned silence followed the explosion, and then the meeting became a chaos of gunfire, screams, and fleeing people.[5]

Thrown by a person still unidentified, the bomb killed Officer Mathias Degan almost at once. Seven other policemen ultimately died. It is unknown how many members of the crowd died, but perhaps as many as eight civilians were killed. The number wounded is also unclear but perhaps reached forty.[6]

In the aftermath of the bloodshed in Haymarket, suspicion, fear, and anxiety surged across Chicago. Within a few days, authorities had arrested numerous people they believed were linked to the bombing, most of whom were known to be associated with the city's anarchist community. Among these were seven who became the Haymarket defendants: George Engle, Fielden, Fischer, Louis Lingg, Oscar Neebe, Michael Schwab, and Spies. An eighth suspect, Albert Parsons, had fled to Wisconsin but voluntarily surrendered on June 21.

As shock at the bombing and hatred of the accused spread, authorities convened a grand jury on May 17. Ten days later, it indicted the eight suspects and two others.[7] A few days afterwards, the primary suspects were charged with murder and conspiracy. One of those indicted was later released; another, a radical named Rudolph Schnaubelt, vanished before he could be apprehended.[8] In the weeks before the trial, the city was awash with anger against anyone faintly suspected of radicalism.

The trial itself, conducted by Judge Joseph E. Gary, was highly irregular and included the seating of prejudiced jurors, use of improperly obtained evidence, and the trampling by the prosecution of several other constitutional rights. It was obvious that the bomb had been thrown by neither Spies nor Fielden, both of whom who had been standing near where it detonated. Witnesses agreed that none of the others on trial were present when the explosion took place. No credible person testified to actually seeing who threw the bomb, nor was it proved that any of the accused had planned the bombing. Yet, all were convicted, and the jury sentenced Engle, Fielden, Fischer, Lingg, Parsons, Schwab, and Spies to death by hanging. Neebe received a sentence of fifteen years' confinement. In an appeal to the Illinois Supreme Court, the convictions were upheld, and the US Supreme Court declined to hear the case.

During the appeal process, an effort to secure reconsideration of the death sentences emerged. Friends and family members of the convicted men, along with some labor leaders as well as others who sensed the trial had been less than fair, sent letters and petitions to Governor Richard J.

Judge Joseph E. Gary, presiding, the Haymarket trial. *Photo courtesy of the University of Illinois at Urbana–Champaign Library.*

Oglesby.[9] But support for the verdict remained strong. Two of the sentenced, Fielden and Schwab, asked the governor for mercy. Oglesby commuted their sentences to life in prison. The remaining defendants did not appeal to the governor, nor did he change their sentences. The day before the executions, Lingg committed suicide in his cell.

Just before noon on Friday, November 11, 1887, Engle, Fischer, Parsons, and Spies, all in ankle-length white shrouds, stood on the platform of a wooden gallows in the Cook County Jail. Deputies placed a rope around each man's neck and slipped a white hood over the head of each. Seconds before the trapdoor on which he stood opened, Spies spoke: "The time will come when our silence will be more powerful than the voices you strangle today." Spies's words were followed by shouts of "Hurrah for anarchy!" from Engle and Fischer. Then as Parsons tried to ask to be allowed to speak, the trapdoors were released, and the condemned men fell beneath the platform.[10]

The funeral for the four men took place on Sunday, November 13. A crowd that grew to several thousand watched as a funeral procession with its black, horse-drawn hearses moved slowly through the city from the various homes where the dead men had been taken after their execution. The deceased were then placed on a special train that took them and their mourners to Waldheim Cemetery, in what is now the West Chicago suburb of Forest Park. There, as an autumn sun slipped below the horizon, the four were lowered into a temporary crypt. Nearly a month later, on the chill Sunday of December 18, the four men were reburied in a permanent grave.[11]

On June 25, 1893, just over seven years following the Haymarket tragedy, several thousand people gathered near the burial site in Waldheim Cemetery.[12] As they watched, Albert Parsons Jr. removed a red covering from a striking statue fashioned to honor the memory of his father and the others buried there. The sculpture, now known as the Haymarket Martyrs' Monument, was crafted by Albert Weinert. It was paid for by donations to the Pioneer Aid and Support Association, a group formed by Parsons's widow and others to help support the families of the dead men.[13] The following day Governor John P. Altgeld pardoned Fielden, Neebe, and Schwab.

The Haymarket Martyrs' Monument Today

The monument unveiled on that solemn summer day is in what is now called Forest Home Cemetery and is near the edge of a blacktop drive leading into the burial ground from the cemetery's Des Plaines Avenue entrance. The monument, which faces east, is a hundred yards or so directly west of the street. A short concrete walk leads from the drive to the monument and then forms a square around it.

About sixteen feet tall, the monument's base is made of smooth, light-gray granite. It is a two-tier square, on top of which is the die, a slightly tapering obelisk-like shaft capped by a carved pyramid. Weinert's bronze sculpture is positioned on a step-like ledge on the front (or east) side of the monument. The sculpture, coated with a dark, gray-green patina, is of the life-size figure of a hooded woman standing in front of a supine male laborer. Beneath the cowl of her cloak the woman's attractive face displays a strong, clean-cut femininity. The cloak billows to the south, as if a north wind is whipping it away. She grasps the cloak's folds across her chest with her right hand; she extends her bare left arm downward; in her left hand, she holds a laurel wreath just above the brow of the full-bearded worker, well-muscled and ruggedly handsome. Below the two figures are bronze-sculpted, classical flowers and fronds.[14]

In front of the monument, a bronze tablet states that in 1997 the Haymarket Martyrs' Monument was designated a National Historical Landmark. Inscribed in a time-darkened tablet mounted on the west side is an excerpt from Altgeld's pardon for the remaining Haymarket defendants. Beneath this the names of the five men first buried here are chiseled into the granite.

On the front and in the center of the stone base on which the sculptor has positioned the two figures, the date 1887 stands in relief on the smooth granite. Carved also into the granite step-like extension at the bottom of the marker are the words spoken by August Spies just before his execution.

The Haymarket Martyrs' Monument has become a sort of shrine for anarchists, socialists, and some persons in organized labor. Several of those associated with radical movements of the past are buried nearby, including Lucy Parsons, Emma Goldman, William Z. Foster, and Elizabeth Gurley

Photo by David A. Sonnenfeld. *Wikimedia Commons*, CC-BY-SA-4.0.

Flynn. Oftentimes, bouquets of red flowers can be found cradled in the woman's right arm or at the foot of the statue, along with other objects in memory of those buried here or in recognition of the causes they represented.

The cemetery's groomed lawn is accented here and there by small bushes, dark green and trimmed. The thousands of headstones stretch away in all directions, and especially when looking to the west from the monument, they appear countless. Large oaks, maples, and catalpas shade the markers. Tall locust trees nearby cast their feathery shadows on the bronze features of the woman and the worker she shields.

Like most cemeteries, Forest Home is a peaceful place, with a stillness born of respect for the many who rest here. Only a low rumble from the traffic on Interstate 290 to the north sometimes filters into the tranquility. And yet the stillness here is not complete, for it seems in some undefined way to be disturbed by those last moving words of August Spies.

Jane Addams
Hull-House Museum

800 South Halsted Street, Chicago

As on many other streets in Chicago, the traffic on South Halsted Street is heavy and brisk. Cars and trucks and busses rumble busily along its four broad lanes as they pass an aged but elegant two-story house that sits near where an abbreviated strip of Polk Street meets Halsted. Just over a mile northeast of here and a little past where the Chicago River's gray-green water cuts through the city, the familiar shapes of the Willis Tower and the 875 North Michigan Avenue building (formerly the John Hancock Center) press the urban sky. High overhead a silver jet, gaining altitude from O'Hare International Airport, becomes smaller as it arcs higher above the city. These aspects of modern life, so familiar in Chicago today, contrast sharply with the stately, mid-nineteenth-century home at 800 South Halsted.

This finely crafted old building is Hull-House, where, in the last decade of the nineteenth century, Jane Addams and Ellen Gates Starr began the first settlement house in Chicago, an undertaking that quickly became an emblem of the growing Progressive movement in America. Now a part of the Jane Addams Hull-House Museum, it sits on the east edge of the University

Charles Hull's mansion, where in 1889 Jane Addams and Ellen Starr began one of the country's best-known settlement houses. *Illustration by Phil Glosser.*

of Illinois at Chicago campus. The house is nearly two centuries old, but the broad porch is welcoming, and the impressive Italianate exterior still projects an air of substance. The Halsted Street neighborhood, however, once in the center of one of the poorest, most congested parts of the city, is greatly changed from that which Addams and Starr saw when they moved into Charles Hull's old mansion on an autumn day in 1889.

That year the city was the second largest in the nation, a noisy, malodorous, growing metropolis with clattering trains, smoke-darkened skies, and a population of approximately a million people.[1] Chicago was a busy railroad hub and a thriving industrial center, and its manufacturing plants and meatpacking stockyards placed it at the pulsating center of America's Second Industrial Revolution. Striking new structures, such as architect William Le Baron Jenney's Home Insurance Building, often considered the country's first iron-frame skyscraper, put the city at the vanguard of American architectural innovation. Downtown, Marshall Field's department store, sparkling and smart on State Street, and the fashionable grandeur of Potter Palmer's hotel presented an air of sophistication, as did the imposing mansions of Chicago's wealthy in the city's upper-class neighborhoods.[2]

But only a few blocks from State Street's stylish elegance were the filthy sidewalks and garbage-strewn alleys of the Near West Side. Here were the rotting cottages and crowded tenements of some of the worst slums in the city. Here were many of the 856,754 immigrants who made Chicago their home.[3] And here, on September 18, 1889, Addams and Starr moved into the rundown old home they would make the most prominent settlement house in America.[4]

Two Members of a New Subculture

The two young women who took up residence amid the squalor of Chicago's Nineteenth Ward had been close friends since their college days at Rockford Female Seminary (now Rockford University). Following college Addams and Starr entered a newly emerged, late nineteenth-century subculture of unmarried, college-educated young women who found themselves with only limited opportunities to use their abilities in America's larger society.[5]

Teaching was one of the few vocations open to such women, and Starr left Rockford Female Seminary after a year to work as a teacher, first in Mt. Morris, Illinois, and then at the private and exclusive Kirkland School for Girls in Chicago.[6] Addams continued at Rockford until she graduated in 1881, but she and Starr remained in close contact while Addams finished her education.

Addams, even before her college years, had expressed a growing desire to lead a useful life, perhaps as a physician.[7] After Rockford, motivated by a deeply seated wish to be of service, she began medical school in Philadelphia but soon became almost incapacitated by a spinal condition that had troubled her for years. Although frustrated in her attempt to enter the medical profession and distressed for a time by her illness, the persistent hope she held for a meaningful life did not dim.

In 1883, like many young women of her class, she traveled to Europe. A second trip followed in 1887, this time with Starr. Addams had heard

Jane Addams, ca. 1900. Bain News Service, publisher. *Photo courtesy US Library of Congress, Prints and Photographs Division, LC-DIG-ggbain-12065. George Grantham Bain Collection. https://www.loc.gov/item/2014691661/.*

of Toynbee Hall, a social settlement established in 1884 by the Reverend Samuel Barnett and his wife, Henrietta, in London's Whitechapel area, one of that city's foulest slums. Addams visited Toynbee Hall and soon after considered the idea of founding a similar place in Chicago. She shortly shared her dream with Starr, who agreed to join her.[8]

When Addams and Starr returned to the United States in 1888, the two began plans to put what they called their "scheme" into place. Starr had con-

Ellen Starr, cofounder of Hull-House, ca. 1917. Bain News Service, publisher. *Photo courtesy of US Library of Congress, Prints and Photographs Division, LC-DIG-ggbain-23460. George Grantham Bain Collection. https://www.loc.gov/item/2014703410/.*

tacts with several wealthy Chicago women, including those in the Chicago Woman's Club, an influential group of well-to-do women interested in civic improvement. She and Addams successfully used these contacts to secure support—financial and otherwise—for their endeavor.[9] The two women wanted to locate their settlement on the Near West Side, in the congested, heavily immigrant area where Halsted and Harrison Streets intersected with Blue Island Avenue.[10] Their search for a proper location took several months, but finally in the spring of 1889 they found, tucked between a saloon and a funeral home, the former country residence of Charles J. Hull, a Chicago millionaire who had died earlier that year.

Since Hull had vacated the once-grand mansion years before, it had been used as a home for the aged, a store that sold used furniture, and a warehouse.[11] Hull had willed his fortune, including the house at what was then 335 South Halsted Street, to his cousin Helen Culver, who owned much other property on the Near West Side. Addams and Starr approached her about renting the house, and she agreed to lease the vacant part of it to them.[12] When Addams, Starr, and their housekeeper, Mary Keyser, moved into the old mansion on an autumn day, they were able to occupy only the upstairs rooms and the spacious drawing room on the first floor. The remainder of the downstairs was in use by the Sherwood Desk Co., a Chicago school-furniture firm.[13]

After years of misuse, Hull's old home needed attention, and even before they moved in, Addams and Starr began to make it an attractive and cultured place. They hired workmen who repaired the floors and painted the interior in ivory and gold. The upstairs dining room was painted in tones of terracotta, its floor covered with a fine carpet, and furnished with an oak table, an oak sideboard, and bentwood chairs. On the walls Addams and Starr hung the copies of European art they had collected during their travels.[14] The elegant interior, the expensive furniture, the fine paintings—all reflected the belief Addams and Starr held in the early months at Hull-House that if these elements of upper-class culture were shared with the disadvantaged, they would then be uplifted and enriched.[15]

And their efforts soon resulted in a successful endeavor, though not precisely in the way the two had envisioned. Although some neighborhood residents were at first mystified by why two educated and well-dressed young ladies had chosen to live in the Halsted Street area, Addams's and Starr's warm and welcoming approach shortly drew a number of women from the neighborhood to Hull-House, many of whom brought their children. In less than a month Jenny Dow, a young woman who traveled each day from the North Side home of her well-to-do parents, was teaching a kindergarten class in the mansion's drawing room. Addams and Starr held receptions, taught classes, and gave talks on art and literature. They sometimes watched children and assisted sick neighbors, and Addams and another resident even helped a mother deliver her baby.[16]

Growth and a Change of Approach

In the spring of 1890, Culver leased the remainder of the house to Addams and Starr, and they soon put the rest of the downstairs rooms to use. But the activities at Hull-House grew quickly, and yet more space was required. By 1895, after six years at their settlement, Addams, Starr, and the residents assisting them also changed their approach. Instead of only providing elements of culture to people they believed were deprived of them, they began to attack the actual causes of the problems affecting those who lived nearby. The art appreciation lectures and literature classes continued, but Hull-House residents now often worked in campaigns against child labor, tried to get the city to collect the trash and clean up the filthy streets, and offered classes aimed at helping their immigrant clientele thread their way through an often confusing and intimidating new culture.[17]

With the continued assistance of well-to-do supporters, including Culver, several new buildings were constructed, and within a decade the old Hull mansion had nearly been engulfed by other structures. Ultimately, Hull-House grew into a complex of thirteen buildings, including an art gallery, bakery, coffee shop, residents' dining hall, and several other structures.

By the early part of the twentieth century, Hull-House was, perhaps, the most celebrated settlement house in America. Addams's renown as a social reformer grew as well far beyond Halsted Street and Chicago, through her books, articles, and addresses to groups working for various reforms. Early on, John Dewey, Henry Demarest Lloyd, Albion Small, and other well-known intellectual luminaries were drawn to Hull-House. Later, however, because of her involvement in the peace movement during World War I and the

1920s, the luster of her previous popularity dimmed. In these years she was occasionally accused of being a socialist or even a communist sympathizer.[18]

But in the early 1930s, as the Great Depression descended on America and as Addams continued her efforts to aid the growing numbers of the unemployed and destitute in the Halsted Street neighborhood, she regained much of her former standing. Though some people continued to demean her, the attacks were much fewer than earlier. She received honorary degrees and appeared on lists of "great women" and "outstanding Americans."[19] In 1931 Addams, along with Nicholas Murray Butler, received the Nobel Peace Prize.

In the later years of her life, Addams suffered from several health problems. In the middle of May 1935, surgery revealed she was afflicted with inoperable cancer. She died on May 21. She was seventy-four years old. Thousands of people attended her funeral, held at Hull-House on May 24. She was buried alongside her father in the family plot in a mossy, tree-shaded cemetery in Cedarville.

Starr, who over time became less prominent than Addams, continued to focus on arts and crafts, learned and taught bookbinding, actively supported the labor-union movement, and even entered politics as a socialist candidate for alderman. After searching for spiritual fulfillment for much of her life, she became a member of the Roman Catholic Church in 1920. She remained at Hull-House until 1929, the same year she became paralyzed below the waist and needed spinal surgery. Following the operation, however, she remained unable to walk. She moved to a New York convent, where she died in February 1940 at age eighty.[20]

Hull-House continued after the passing of its founders. Although their spirit remained present, the place was in some ways an artifact from another time. The progressivism of the late nineteenth century, which had been at the core of Hull-House and the settlement movement, had receded into what seemed, after two world wars and the Great Depression, a quaint and distant past. The world had changed greatly since the September day when Addams and Starr had begun their work.

In 1946 the University of Illinois opened a branch campus at Navy Pier in Chicago. Enrollment grew, and the university sought a new location for an expanded campus. In 1961 the university and the City of Chicago agreed to relocate the university to the Near West Side, much of it on the site of the Hull-House complex. Despite protests, lawsuits, and demonstrations by Hull-House residents and citizens of the neighborhood, the plan went forward. The university finally agreed to preserve two buildings, the original Hull mansion and the residents' dining hall, in recognition of Addams and the settlement she and Starr had established. But by 1963 the remainder of the Hull-House complex was gone, its buildings demolished, and its grounds cleared to make way for the new campus.

Hull-House Today

Charles Hull's old Italianate mansion is now part of the Jane Addams Hull-House Museum. It stands in the shadow of a large and modern university building just a few feet away. When the Hull-House complex was razed, the house was substantially reconstructed to appear as it did when Hull built it in 1856. However, it still resembles in some ways the home Addams excitedly glimpsed on a spring day in 1889.

The mansion, of course, no longer bears the scars and blemishes it did then, nor is it crowded between two less-elegant buildings amid a squalid, sprawling slum as it was when Addams and Starr moved into it on that September day so long ago. The cupola that sits atop the building was likely not there when Addams first viewed it, and the color of the brick exterior differs slightly from that of the original in 1889. But graceful Corinthian columns like those Addams describes in her memoir *Twenty Years at Hull-House* support the roof of the wide veranda. The tall, beautifully arched windows and the double front doors, now painted a very dark green, impart a genteel, welcoming, and refined character to this historic place.

Inside, the first-floor walls that Addams and Starr had once painted ivory and gold are light gray.[21] The ornate molding that trims the doorways is painted white and retains its heavy, braided rope motif. Marble fireplaces and the ornamented Italianate shelf brackets above the windows and doors still tastefully bespeak the mansion's classic style, once so admired by Addams and Starr.

The drawing room, used in those first full days in the fall of 1889 for Jenny Dow's kindergarten, is now a venue for exhibits. On a wall hangs a portrait by Alice Kellogg Tyler of Dow, who died in 1905. In the library, furnished with period authentic furniture, the walls are painted in warm, terracotta colors.

The mansion's central stairway, carpeted now with a green runner and flanked by a black bannister with tastefully turned balustrades, ascends to the second floor of Hull-House. There, a doorway on the south side of the landing leads to Addams's bedroom, where the walls are covered with colorful William Morris wallpaper. The room holds a marble fireplace, Addams's double-sided writing desk, a twin-size bed with a dark wooden headboard, and an enormous grandfather clock. A large portrait of Addams's close friend Mary Rozet Smith, also painted by Tyler, hangs on one wall. On another is a painting of a somber Tolstoy, dressed in a white peasant blouse. The remaining second-floor rooms are used to house various exhibits of the museum.

The Jane Addams Hull-House Museum also includes a second building, the residents' dining hall. Located just south of the Hull mansion, it is a large, two-story, red-brick structure with windowed gables adorning its second floor. Designed by architects Allen Pond and Irving Pond, it was built in 1905, and here the residents of the settlement gathered for meals. When the Hull-House complex was razed, the dining hall was moved about two hundred feet closer to the mansion. The downstairs holds a large meeting room; the upstairs contains a gift shop.

Hull-House, Addams, and Starr have intrigued people for well over a century. From the immigrant neighbors who on an autumn day in 1889 were puzzled by why these two young, college-educated women chose to live where they did to the latest historian focused on the relationships among those who resided or worked here, the mystique of Hull-House and its two founders endures. The Jane Addams Hull-House Museum is one avenue to understanding what Addams and Starr were about in those busy, hectic days at Hull-House.

To stand now in the drawing room once filled with the happy sounds of Dow's kindergarten or to step into Addams's bedroom, where she surely found a welcome, peaceful, and private silence, is a moving experience. It is an act that brings one at least a little closer to that long-ago time when two idealistic women moved into a rundown old house on Halsted Street where they hoped, as Addams had written during her student days at Rockford, to somehow change a small corner of the world.

The Eternal Indian
(Black Hawk) Statue

South Side Community
Art Center

Vachel Lindsay Home

Part 5

ONLY YESTERDAY

The Eternal
Indian statue
dedicated
1911

Vachel Lindsay
returns to live in
family home
1929

Eleanor Roosevelt
dedicates South
Side Community
Art Center
1941

Prologue

As the final years of the nineteenth century spun into the past and the twentieth century dawned, the cascade of change released during the forty years following the Civil War continued undiminished. The first decade of the new century was an unparalleled period of growth, and America—and the Prairie State—became even more urbanized and industrialized.

This era was also one of originality in the fine arts and architecture. One of the best-known artists of the time was Lorado Taft, who created many notable pieces of sculpture, including the haunting *Eternal Silence* in Chicago's Graceland Cemetery and his *Alma Mater* on the University of Illinois at Urbana-Champaign campus. Perhaps, the most unusual of Taft's works, however, is the **The Eternal Indian Statue** (sometimes called the **Black Hawk Statue**). Though it was dedicated in 1911, its sculptor looked backward, this time through a sentimental lens to a long-vanished and never-to-be-recaptured past. Taft's statue of poured concrete, now totally refurbished, stands today on a wooded bluff overlooking the Rock River in Lowden State Park in Oregon.

A decade or so after the dedication of Taft's sculpture, a period of excellence in literature also appeared in the Prairie State. Known as the Chicago Renaissance, it included an important collection of writers and poets who made lasting contributions to the body of American letters. Prominent members are Sherwood Anderson, Carl Sandburg, Floyd Dell, Theodore

Dreiser, and Edgar Lee Masters. The group also includes the poet Vachel Lindsay, a native of Springfield, whose poetry was nationally recognized during the 1920s. The **Vachel Lindsay Home**, the house where Lindsay was born, wrote some of his verse, and tragically ended his own life still stands in the Prairie State's capital as a memorial to an unusual and creative figure in the nation's literary past.

Another notable sign of the blossoming of the fine arts in Illinois was evident in Chicago's Bronzeville area in the 1930s. There, even while the Great Depression shadowed America, a vibrant expression of painting, drawing, and sculpture emerged in this historic African American neighborhood. Many of the artists from the area, several of whom later became well known on the nation's art scene, first displayed their work at the **South Side Community Art Center**. Founded as part of the New Deal's Federal Art Program and dedicated in 1941 by first lady Eleanor Roosevelt, the **SSCAC** continues its mission of promoting African American art at 3831 South Michigan Avenue.

In the first half of the twentieth century, Illinois witnessed a period remarkably rich in artistic expression. Despite war twice bringing widespread disruption to everyday life and though economic dislocation clouded the nation's skies between those wars, rays of optimism and confidence from the people of the Prairie State, nonetheless, pierced those clouds with Taft's lofty *Eternal Indian* sculpture, Lindsay's powerful and unusual verse, and the creativity found at the South Side Community Art Center.

The Eternal Indian
(or Black Hawk) Statue

Lowden State Park, 1411 North River Road, Oregon

From north of the community of Oregon, the Rock River traces its way through a wide and pleasant valley and flows beneath a 125-foot-tall, tree-masked cliff. Located in Lowden State Park, the cliff's face is, perhaps, a hundred yards from the water's edge and ascends sharply to a forested summit. The scenic prospect here is pleasing, as the Rock's silver-green water ripples around the elongated and wooded shores of Margaret Fuller Island, which briefly splits the river into two channels. Like so many other places in Illinois, the bluff and the woods at its top are changed greatly by the seasons. In early spring the trees display a soft, gauzy green and in summer a deep emerald. Autumn reveals a patchwork of crimson and gold and russet. In winter, the bluff, edifice-like, is somber and gray.

Amid this striking display of natural beauty and tucked into a niche in the trees just below the bluff's summit is an enormous sculpture, a monumental representation of an American Indian. The figure was crafted more than a century ago as an eloquent, imposing remembrance of the people who once lived in this valley and nearby forests. This is *The Eternal Indian*, by Lorado

A relaxed moment for Lorado Taft, sculptor of *The Eternal Indian* (Black Hawk) statue. Special Collections Research Center, University of Chicago Library.

Taft, a sculptor who at the turn of the twentieth century was one of Illinois's best-known artists.

An Artist of Uncommon Gifts

The uncommonly gifted man whose artistic genius was responsible for this colossal piece of art was born in 1860 in Elmwood, Illinois, and grew up in Champaign, the son of a geology professor at the University of Illinois. After his graduation from the university, Taft spent several years in Paris, France, including time at the Ecole des Beaux-Arts, where he studied sculpture.[1]

Upon his return to the United States, the twenty-five-year-old artist resided briefly in St. Louis but moved to Chicago in 1886.[2] There, within a few years, he became one of the most celebrated sculptors in the city and by the time of his death in 1936 was a nationally recognized artist. From his Chicago studio Taft produced an extraordinary amount of work, much of which, especially in the late nineteenth century, honored Civil War soldiers. His oeuvre also includes such notable pieces as the monumental *Fountain of Time*, in Washington Park, Chicago; the haunting, disquieting *Eternal Silence*, in Chicago's Graceland Cemetery; and *Alma Mater*, on the University of Illinois at Urbana-Champaign campus.[3]

In 1898 Taft and a few other artists, writers, and musicians began spending summers on a bluff above the Rock River, at a colony they called the Eagle's Nest.[4] The camp was on the estate of Chicago attorney Wallace Heckman, and Taft and his associates valued it as a kind of refuge where during the summer months they could distance themselves at least for a time from a crowded Chicago.[5] On the night of their very first visit as guests at Heckman's estate, Taft and his wife were captivated by the rustic beauty of the place, and they and several friends began to stay at the colony each summer.[6]

During one such summer at Eagle's Nest, Taft conceptualized his colossal sculpture. He related the experience at the statue's unveiling ceremony in 1911, explaining that the idea for *The Eternal Indian* came to him late one day while walking along the bluff toward Heckman's house. Stopping briefly at a certain spot when the evening's shadows were draped across the landscape, the artist was struck by the moment. Recalling how he and his friends admired the view, he said, "We involuntarily fold our arms and the pose is

The Eternal Indian (Black Hawk statue) gazing westward across the Rock River. Photo by IG-2000. Wikimedia Commons.

that of my Indian—restful, reverent. It came over me that generations of men have done the same thing right here. And so the figure grew out of the attitude, as we stood and looked on these beautiful scenes."[7]

When he envisioned *The Eternal Indian*, Taft surely believed he was honoring the state's native people. At the sculpture's unveiling, he expressed, too, an esthetic appreciation for the natural setting where those people once lived. It is somewhat ironic that he said nothing about the tragic fate of many of those his statue represented. Perhaps, Taft did not see this as an appropriate topic for his remarks. Or perhaps, like many people at the time, he was captured by a kind of "noble savage" mindset and was not fully aware of the heartbreaking conditions facing those who had, by the time his statue was completed in 1911, been mostly consigned to reservations often found in remote areas of the country.

The American Indians' plight, however, was recognized, at least implicitly, by two of Taft's associates. Heckman, who wrote the foreword to the booklet recounting the unveiling ceremony, believed Taft did understand the conditions that had led to the Indians' dilemma. He saw Taft as a "strong, ready champion of every victim of injustice" who viewed Black Hawk as "a lingering representative" of the "individuate race" that Taft attempted to honor through his sculpture.[8] Frank O. Lowden, a wealthy lawyer soon to be the state's governor and who spoke at the unveiling, saw in Black Hawk a tragic figure who in defeat asked only that his former home be respected. Lowden quoted a moving passage from Black Hawk's autobiography in which the great chief asked the white people who had driven him from the ancestral land he loved to treat it only as he and his people once had.[9]

A Challenging Undertaking

Bringing the statue from conceptual inspiration to reality proved to be a challenging undertaking. Taft had earlier seen a new chimney of reinforced concrete under construction at Chicago's Art Institute.[10] Workers constantly poured liquid cement into a form. As the cement solidified, the form was slid upward, and cement again was poured into it, a process that was repeated until the project was completed. This "slip form" technique, later extensively used in the construction of many concrete grain elevators, struck the artist as a possible approach to creating *The Eternal Indian*. Although an accomplished sculptor, Taft had never worked with cement as a medium and was unfamiliar with specifics about how it might be used in sculpture.[11]

From his studio in Chicago, Taft first crafted an eight-inch-tall maquette. This was followed by a six-foot model that served as a prototype for the proposed work. To begin the actual statue, he turned to John Prasuhn, a student in his Chicago studio who was familiar with cement construction.[12]

The logistics were daunting, and if it had been undertaken by someone with less than Taft's drive and influence, it may never have been completed. A staggering amount of material went into *The Eternal Indian*, including more than two hundred yards of concrete, dozens of steel bars used to reinforce the cement, chicken wire and plaster to create the mold into which the concrete would be poured, and lumber used for the frame and scaffolding.[13]

The project encountered a setback when a storm destroyed the first set of scaffolding, but during ten days in December 1910, workers were pouring cement into Prasuhn's mold. For the slip-form technique to be successful, it was necessary to pour the cement twenty-four hours a day. When the pour was finished, Taft and Prasuhn let the concrete set for several months and then removed the mold to reveal their stunning achievement.[14]

Following Lorado Taft's death in 1936, members of the colony continued their annual outings there until World War II began. After the Eagle's Nest was no longer used, area residents worked to purchase the area where it once stood. Assisted by the Illinois Department of Natural Resources, they raised funds to match a state appropriation for a memorial for Governor Lowden, the state's chief executive from 1917 to 1921 and who owned a farm nearby. The area became Lowden State Park in 1945.[15]

The Eternal Indian Today

Today Lorado Taft's *Eternal Indian* is the focal point of a lovely 273-acre park that preserves an important part of the rustic beauty of the Rock River region. The gray, cement statue sits not far from the edge of the tree-shaded bluff that falls sharply away to the river below. It is readily accessible by automobile via a hard-surfaced drive that winds pleasantly through the park to an asphalt parking lot adjacent to the sculpture.

The statue, on a large base, depicts an American Indian, handsome and dignified, standing with arms crossed, draped in the folds of a blanket.

Although it is often called the Black Hawk Statue, the figure here has no resemblance to the historical man of that name, and Taft did not intend it to be an accurate likeness of the famous Sauk leader.

The artist has portrayed the Indian's hair as falling in two heavy braids, one over the front of each shoulder. A strong and attractive though solemn face conveys a sense of self-reliance and pride. The figure gazes to the west, looking beyond the river and into the far distance across the valley, as if in contemplation of the untamed and now-vanished wilderness.

Although the statue is seen to best advantage in its larger setting from a pull-off on Illinois Route 2, just across the Rock River, the view from near the statue itself, in Lowden State Park, is spectacular. Looking west from near the low, stone retaining wall that runs north and south a few feet in front of Taft's monumental work, a visitor sees the natural beauty of this spot: the thick woods that descend sharply from the bluff to sweep away toward the river, the shimmer of sunlight off the water of the Rock, the view to the distant horizon.

Over time the statue's condition began to alarmingly deteriorate. Citizens of the area who hoped to see the sculpture preserved consulted with state officials and raised money, but for several years, the statue was draped with a thick plastic shroud while progress was sporadic. Eventually enough money from private contributions, combined with a grant from the state, resulted in the completion of the statue's restoration in early 2020.

Vachel Lindsay Home

603 South Fifth Street, Springfield

The Prairie State's capital city, Springfield, is a thriving, bustling place. With a population of nearly 116,000, it is a modern, midsized metropolis. The tower of a large hotel and other tall buildings jut skyward, and the storefronts of commercial establishments line the spacious streets. The capitol, with its lofty silver dome, sits amid a cluster of government offices that house the many agencies necessary to administer a state that has seen enormous change since it entered the Union more than two centuries ago.

Scattered among these contemporary buildings are structures that reveal another Springfield. These are the architectural artifacts from an earlier and simpler era. Abraham Lincoln's two-story home, painted in beige, brown, and green; the striking Dana-Thomas House, reflecting Frank Lloyd Wright's signature prairie-style design; the cinnamon-colored façade of the Old State Capitol; and the red-brick, Greek-revival Lincoln-Herndon Law Office all provide evidence of the historical significance of this place.

Tucked amidst this remarkable treasure trove of important old buildings is an ofttimes overlooked jewel: the Vachel Lindsay Home. This charming and beautifully maintained building, across the street from the Illinois Governor's Mansion, was once the residence of one of America's best-known poets of the first third of the twentieth century. Here Nicholas Vachel Lindsay was born, wrote some of the poetry for which he became famous, and, at age fifty-two, met a tragic and untimely end.

At the peak of his popularity, Lindsay was a recognized figure among the American literary establishment. He was acquainted with Carl Sandburg and Edgar Lee Masters, and his work was praised by the novelist William Dean Howells. He was friends with Harriet Monroe, the founder of *Poetry* magazine, and had a brief romantic relationship with the prize-winning poet Sara Teasdale. Lindsay lectured widely, including at Oxford University, where he became acquainted with John Masefield, who was named poet laureate of Britain in 1930. A prolific writer, Lindsay was the author of more than a dozen volumes of verse, many of which were issued by major publishing companies.

Lindsay's house is at 603 South Fifth Street, on the southwest corner of the intersection of Fifth and East Edwards. Fifth Street is a wide, heavily traveled one-way thoroughfare for southbound traffic. Lindsay's two-story frame home sits on a raised parcel of ground on the west side. Two large trees, one of which likely stood when Lindsay lived here, shade the small front lawn, planted now in a green ground cover with a few bushes to the side. A red-brick walk, set in a herringbone pattern, leads from the front walk around the south side of the house, and then to the back of the building.

Though it is best known for Lindsay's connection with it, this place had historical significance even before his parents bought it in 1878. Constructed sometime in the 1840s, it was, beginning in 1853, the home of Ann Todd Smith and her husband, Clark. Ann was the sister of Mary Todd Lincoln, Abraham Lincoln's wife, and the future president visited here.[1]

Born on November 10, 1879, Nicholas Vachel Lindsay was the son of a physician, Vachel Thomas Lindsay, and his wife, Esther Catherine Frazee.[2] Doted on as a child by his mother, he attended the local schools in Springfield, a city that was to hold a lifelong, almost mystical grip on him. After completing the elementary grades, he enrolled in Springfield High School, graduating in 1897. While there one of his favorite faculty members was Susan Wilcox, a popular and inspirational English teacher. Wilcox, who offered reassurance and support for Lindsay's artistic and literary aspirations, "became a guiding light for the rest of his life."[3]

Vachel Lindsay's family home in Springfield. *Photo by the author.*

Lindsay's father hoped Vachel would become a doctor, and for three years he pursued premedical studies at Ohio's Hiram College with only moderate success. His own inclinations lay toward poetry and art, and he finally left Hiram to study at the Art Institute of Chicago.[4] There, he wrote in his diary, he hoped to become " a Caesar in the world of art, conquering every sort, every language and people."[5]

Though his artwork reveals a passing resemblance to that of the English illustrator Aubrey Beardsley, Lindsay's ambition exceeded his artistic ability; and his studies at the Art Institute, as was the case with an additional period spent at the New York School of Art (now the Parsons School of Design), were largely unsuccessful. While at the School of Art, Lindsay asked one of his teachers, the painter Robert Henri, whether he should perhaps pursue poetry rather than art. When Lindsay gave an animated and vigorous recitation of his poem "The Tree of Laughing Bells," an astonished Henri counseled him to switch from art to poetry.[6] Although his talent as an artist was limited, he apparently, according to the editor of a collection of Lindsay's letters, "never renounced that preoccupation," and his art "turned into the creative, inspirational source of his poems."[7]

The Artist Becomes a Poet

Lindsay had written poetry since his time at Springfield High School, and while in New York, he continued to write verse, attempting on two nights in March 1905 to sell leaflets of his poetry on the city's streets.[8] Though he had little luck with street sales in New York, he did have two of his poems published there.[9] It was when Vachel decided, as Henri had suggested, to pursue poetry rather than art that he turned in earnest to the work that was to propel him, at least for a time, to a place among the country's better-known writers.

Lindsay left New York in March 1906, traveling by boat with a friend to Florida.[10] Once there he undertook a six-hundred-mile hike from Jacksonville to Kentucky, where he paused near Louisville at the home of an aunt.[11] This was the first of several "tramps" from which he later became known as "a self-fashioned troubadour or wandering poet."[12] During these trips Lindsay offered his poetry in exchange for a place to sleep and something to eat, though he frequently found this a challenge.

Lindsay's verse first gained national attention and critical praise in early 1913 when his poem "General Booth Enters into Heaven" appeared in *Poetry* magazine, a Chicago publication founded and edited by Harriet Monroe.[13] For the next several years, Lindsay was associated with the Chicago Renaissance, a period during the early part of the twentieth century when an exceptionally talented group of writers emerged in the city, helping to lift it to a prominent place in the development of American letters. Others active at the time include Theodore Dreiser, Floyd Dell, Sherwood Anderson, and Lindsay's fellow poets Carl Sandburg and Edgar Lee Masters. Like the New York artists of the Ashcan School whose paintings during this same period illustrated the stark realism of their surroundings, the novelists, poets, and journalists of the Chicago Renaissance depicted the unvarnished reality of Chicago and the rural Midwest.

Lindsay to some extent shared this bleak view of urban life, but he, along with Sandburg and Masters, saw rural Illinois in a different light. All three viewed pastoral Illinois almost "as if it were an Eden," a luminous, idealistic land seated in the heart of the nation.[14] Though Masters believed this "paradise" had largely vanished due to the massive changes wrought by industrialism, Lindsay remained optimistic.[15] His vision of the Midwest, and of Illinois, as a mostly unspoiled garden is visible in much of his writing and remained with him throughout his life.[16]

Lindsay held a special admiration for Lincoln, who, in Lindsay's view, seemed an almost mythic figure who emerged from Springfield to assume the burden of leading the nation at the time of its greatest crisis—the Civil War. His appreciation of both Springfield and Lincoln is evident in two of his better-known poems: "Abraham Lincoln Walks at Midnight in Springfield, Illinois" and "On the Building of Springfield."

Imbued from childhood with a deep vein of religious feeling acquired from his devout parents, much of Lindsay's writing has a religious motif.[17] "General Booth Enters into Heaven" is one example; "The Soul of the City Receives the Gift of the Holy Spirit," written about Springfield, is another. And the image of Lincoln as portrayed in "Abraham Lincoln Walks at Midnight in Springfield, Illinois" is very nearly Christ-like. In the poem, written in 1914, an arisen Lincoln, walking the streets of Lindsay's hometown, is carrying "on his shawl-wrapped shoulders . . . the bitterness, the folly, and the pain" of a war-torn world.

But Lindsay's verse also addressed places far from the Prairie State. One of his best-known poems is "The Congo," written after he heard a sermon in which his pastor mentioned a missionary who drowned in the Congo River.[18] In the poem Lindsay offers imagined scenes of tribal life along the Congo River, but his knowledge of Africa was limited, and the images in his poem are drawn from caricature and ignorance. The piece depicts a place dominated by "skull faced witch men lean" who rule through "hoo doo" until white Christianity finally triumphs. It was this poem and, to a lesser extent, his "Modest Jazz Bird" that caused some critics to accuse Lindsay of racist views.[19]

Other poems, such as "I Heard Immanuel Singing" and "I Went Down into the Desert," are permeated with unusual and haunting religious imagery. Lindsay's verse focused on additional topics as well, often social or political. His "Bryan, Bryan, Bryan, Bryan" and "Factory Windows Are Always Broken" reflect his sympathy for the Progressive movement, while "A Curse for Kings" and "The Unpardonable Sin" display the poet's strong, often graphic, antiwar sentiments.

By 1920 Lindsay was at the apex of his career. He traveled extensively and made several appearances where he recited his verse. He traveled internationally, and at Oxford his work gained popular acknowledgment among his English audiences.[20] By the early 1920s he had become a nationally known poet through the publication of several books of verse and frequent public readings. Yet, he was facing personal challenges, and within a few years his star began to decline, imperceptibly at first, then steeply and tragically by the end of the decade.

That decline seems likely to have started in late 1922 when during a recitation tour, he fell ill. Lindsay was sick enough that at times he was nearly bedridden. During this period he also began to exhibit outward signs of emotional distress, often losing his temper and engaging in angry outbursts against friends, including his manager, A. Joseph Armstrong.[21] These behaviors continued with increasing severity until Lindsay's death in 1931.

Following a recitation at Gulf Park Community College, Gulfport, Mississippi, Lindsay became so ill that Dr. Richard Cox, the college's president and a friend from Lindsay's days at Hiram College, insisted that the poet rest in Cox's home. A few months later, while still in Gulfport, Vachel endured sinus operations. The surgery, according to one of his biographers, seemed to initially improve his spirits though his difficulties ultimately continued.[22]

After Lindsay's recovery, Cox offered him a position on the Gulf Park faculty. He spent close to an academic year there, mostly teaching poetry. Yet, he remained restless and came to think that the school did not appreciate his work. His discontent worsened until in what can only be described as delusional behavior, he believed he was being watched and that he was a victim of persecution by the college. His brother-in-law, Dr. Paul Wakefield, visited him and was alarmed by his behavior. After spending time with Vachel, he urged him to visit the Mayo Clinic. The visit revealed that Lindsay was epileptic.[23]

Lindsay's unhappiness deepened. Frustrated, he moved to Spokane, Washington, in 1924. Lindsay had visited Spokane earlier. He was drawn again to the city by its proximity to one of the country's national parks and by the tug of what he called the "west-going heart." He took up residence in the city's Davenport Hotel and continued to write and make public presentations. Lindsay was initially well received in Spokane, where he mingled with the city's artistic community. It was also in Spokane that Lindsay fell in love with Elizabeth Conner, and the two were married on May 19, 1925.[24] The marriage was apparently a happy one initially, and Vachel and Elizabeth became the parents of two children, Susan and Nicholas.

But as had been the case in Gulfport, Vachel grew dissatisfied in Spokane. The powerful attraction of Springfield once again pulled him toward the city of his youth. Feeling the need to return there, Lindsay and his family left Spokane in April 1929 and moved into his parents' old house on Fifth Street.[25]

The house, which Vachel and Elizabeth rented from his family for $500 per year, had deteriorated since his parents' deaths, and it required repair to restore it to a condition that Vachel found suitable.[26] The rent, the repairs, and other expenses were significant, and Lindsay had to resume making presentations on the road to meet them.

Though these appearances were successful, the family's finances remained precarious. The necessity to increase his income, the diminishing sales of his books, a fear that his reputation as a major poet was declining, and the strange alterations in his personality apparently contributed to a further deterioration in his emotional state. He was sometimes delusional, believing at one point that his father-in-law wanted to kill him.[27] At one moment he would become angry and verbally abusive toward Elizabeth and at the next tearfully proclaim a deep and undying love for her. His behavior and some of the letters he wrote became so bizarre that his brother-in-law believed he should be institutionalized.[28] Yet, at other times, Vachel appeared calm, even buoyant; but this, in the end, was deceptive.

On the evening of November 30, he appeared at Springfield's First Christian Church to recite his poetry to an admiring audience. But his illness was exerting an increasingly powerful pull on him. Four days after his success at the church, after dinner at home, Lindsay began a tirade against what he perceived to be the injustices and misfortunes that had befallen him since his years as a child. He blamed Elizabeth for some of these. Apparently exhausted, he retired to bed.[29] But, shortly afterward he arose and went downstairs, where he arranged a display of photographs of his wife and their children on a table in the dining room. He lit two candles and placed them on the table with the pictures. Then, in the final, fatal grip of his sickness, he drank a glass of Lysol. He died what surely was an agonizing death a brief time later, early in the morning of December 5, 1931, in the bedroom above the room in which he had been born.

By the time of his death, the audience for Lindsay's poetry had started to slip away. Following the stock market crash of 1929, the shadows of the Great Depression began to deepen, and the hectic, exuberant years of post–World War I America faded into the past. Lindsay's verse, parts of which had always been rather opaque, now seemed removed from the concerns of the new decade. And yet, some of Lindsay's work has endured. His "Abraham Lincoln Walks at Midnight in Springfield, Illinois" remains a poignant tribute to the sixteenth president, and Lindsay's antiwar verse carries a powerful message that yet resonates with the contemporary world.

A Lovely Place of Remembrance

The Vachel Lindsay Home is administered as a state historic site by the Historic Preservation Division of the Illinois Department of Natural Resources with assistance from the Vachel Lindsay Association. Guided tours of the building are available through advance arrangement.[30] Almost all the furniture and other items in the house are original and were returned by members of the Lindsay family. These artifacts would have been familiar to Vachel as a youth and later as an adult. Their presence provides an ambience to this place where an enormously talented and deeply troubled man lived and died.

This lovely, meticulously maintained house is two stories tall and sided with light-gray weatherboarding. A shallow front porch supported by four columns extends across the middle two-thirds of the lower story. The building's front projects a Greek-revival style and is dominated by four tall windows with gray shutters, two on either side of the front door. This doorway, which has a Victorian appearance, is flanked by narrow sidelights and topped by transom windows.

Through the doorway is a vestibule, or foyer. The room immediately to the right or north of the entryway was the bedroom for Lindsay's parents

Vachel Lindsay's boyhood bedroom. *Photo by Elda Ueleke.*

and is where the poet was born. Later used by Vachel and his wife, Elizabeth, as a front room, it features a large fireplace on the north wall. Behind this room is the dining room and then the kitchen. The room to the left of the entryway is the parlor, and beyond it is the library, which holds a case filled with some of Lindsay's books.

A stairway with a highly polished wooden newel post, bannister, and ornately turned balustrades leads to the second floor, where Vachel and Elizabeth's bedroom is directly above the room where he was born and is where he died. Immediately behind this is a small bedroom used by Vachel when he was a boy and later was his study. The room contains a narrow bed and a dark, wooden nightstand. One wall holds a framed photograph of Susan Wilcox, Lindsay's high school English teacher, who encouraged him in his writing and who remained a lifelong friend.

This is the place where Vachel composed some of his poetry. The small table where he did his writing is here, with its wooden armchair. An old Oliver typewriter sits on the table, and a floor lamp stands adjacent to it. Another small table here is where Lindsay drew the illustrations that sometimes accompanied his work.

Lindsay's verse is not as popular as it once was, but it can still be found in many anthologies and in collections of the writings of American poets. Lindsay's work is often unusual, even at times hauntingly mysterious. Still it remains as an important if sometimes controversial part of the early twentieth-century American literature canon.

South Side
Community Art Center
3831 South Michigan Avenue, Chicago

Chicago's Michigan Avenue is one of the city's storied streets. Twelve miles long, it runs, with occasional interruptions, from Lake Shore Drive at its northern end to 127th Street in Harvey, a south suburb of the city. North of the Chicago River, Michigan Avenue quickly becomes a glamorous and sparkling stretch of commercial establishments known as the Magnificent Mile; south of the river it extends deep into the city's South Side. Michigan Avenue passes the Art Institute and Millennium Park, the Symphony Center and Mercy Hospital until near Thirty-First Street, where it reaches an area of the city called Bronzeville.

In the middle of one of Chicago's most historic neighborhoods, the South Side Community Art Center (SSCAC) stands as an emblem of the vibrant African American culture that has been present here since the Great Migration of the early twentieth century. Appearing during the artistic and literary flowering of the Chicago Black Renaissance, the center, at 3831 South Michigan, is housed in an impressive Georgian Revival mansion that once belonged to wealthy Chicago grain-dealer George Seaverns Jr.[1]

The idea for the South Side Community Art Center emerged from a group of black artists who were connected through the Arts Crafts Guild, an influential member of which was South Side artist George E. Neal.[2] Members of the guild included several artists who later attained national reputations, such as Margaret Goss Burroughs, Eldzier Cortor, and Charles White.[3] This thriving art community flourished in Bronzeville, but its members, because of Chicago's persistent Jim Crowism, all too often found only a few places to exhibit their work.[4] In addition to the artists, an energetic group of Bronzeville residents saw the need for a place that would bring the arts to the neighborhood.[5]

Interest in creating a Bronzeville venue for the arts grew, but the Great Depression still held America stubbornly in its grip. Across the nation, millions of workers in business, the construction trades, and industry lost their jobs, and Americans in nearly every part of the economy faced bleak futures, including writers, artists, actors, directors, and others in the arts. Breadlines and soup kitchens were common, and "Hoovervilles" (makeshift communities where the unemployed lived in huts and shacks made of cast-off materials) still dotted the cityscapes of many metropolitan areas.

President Franklin D. Roosevelt, committed to the belief that all Americans should be gainfully employed, worked with Congress to fight the country's economic ills through the "alphabet agencies" of the New Deal. One of the most prominent of these was the Works Progress Administration (WPA), established in 1935 with the goal that, rather than provide relief payments to those the Great Depression displaced, the WPA would put people to work. To attack joblessness in the fine arts, Congress established the Federal Art Project (FAP) as a part of the WPA. Writer and art curator Holger Cahill served as FAP national director, and through his efforts and those of the state art project directors, many out-of-work artists were employed, largely as painters of murals in public buildings but also as easel artists, illustrators, and sculptors.[6]

The stunning success of North Carolina FAP official Daniel S. Defenbacher in launching several community art centers there shortly came to Cahill's attention. Cahill at once saw their value and encouraged the establishment of centers in other states—places where the wider public could gain a deeper appreciation of and knowledge about art through gallery exhibits, lectures, art classes, and other activities.[7]

The community art center idea soon made its way to the Prairie State. Peter Pollack, a Chicago art gallery owner, was the community art center director for the Illinois Art Project (IAP), the state's division of the FAP. Pollack had exhibited work by African American artists in his downtown gallery and so was aware of the vibrant arts community in Bronzeville. In 1938 Pauline Kligh Reed and four other community-minded African American women from the South Side met with Pollack and George Thorpe, Illinois Art Project director, to explore the intriguing possibility of an art center.[8]

Under FAP policy, the government would pay the salaries of center staff members, but the cost of acquiring and maintaining a facility fell to the community.[9] Following a series of meetings, neighborhood residents formed a committee that rapidly began work to find the dollars to buy a location for the center. Through energetic and innovative fund-raising techniques, such as the Mile of Dimes Campaign and the Artists and Models Ball, enough money was collected to purchase a dilapidated old mansion on the east side of South Michigan Avenue, not far north of East Pershing Road.[10]

An enthusiastic group of artists and other community volunteers from the Bronzeville area worked to modernize the aged building, converting it to its new life as an art center.[11] The interior of the building was refurbished in the New Bauhaus style, a modernistic design concept with antecedents in the original Bauhaus in post–World War I Germany.[12] An important member among those working on the renovation was Burroughs, an artist, poet, and educator, who was closely associated with nearly every facet of the center in its early years. A dynamic personality, she worked to celebrate the value of African American culture as expressed through art.

The First Lady Dedicates the SSCAC

By late 1940 a variety of exhibitions, classes, and other activities were underway in the recently renovated mansion. First Lady Eleanor Roosevelt, a strong advocate for the FAP and the formation of community art centers, formally dedicated the center at a May 17, 1941, ceremony. Others involved in the dedication included Reed; Pollack, the center's first director; and Alain Locke, a distinguished African American author and Howard University professor. The center has been in continuous operation since 1940, remain-

Ausbra Ford's *Move On Up a Little Higher*, front lawn, South Side Community Art Center. *Photo by the author.*

ing open even during World War II. Following the war, SSCAC continued to bring art in a variety of forms to the Bronzeville area, and its exhibits often featured the work of many well-known artists.

However, as was the case with other FAP community art centers, the SSCAC faced challenges, especially during its first fifteen years. Like many other programs funded by New Deal agencies, it wrestled with financial difficulties after the Roosevelt administration ended the WPA in 1943.In the early 1950s, the center had to deal with problems of a different sort. As McCarthyism (a near-hysterical campaign against communism) and the Second Red Scare (fear of communist power) spread across America, the members of the House Un-American Activities Committee of the US Congress suspected that some of the center's artists during its early years had been associated with the Communist Party. Burroughs and other artists, such as Charles White, who, during the grim days of the Great Depression, had seen art as a means of confronting social injustice and racial discrimination, were now the subject of government investigation.[13]

Setting for the Arts

Despite these challenges and others that beset the South Side Community Art Center from time to time, it today remains one of Chicago's most important and inspiring settings for the celebration of African American art. From its beginning during the anxious years of the Great Depression, the SSCAC has continuously featured exhibits of many well-known African American artists, held art auctions, and offered hundreds of art classes. Named a Chicago Historic Landmark in 1994, the center "conserves, preserves, and promotes the legacy and future of African American art and artists while educating the community on the value of art and culture."[14]

The center occupies its original location at 3831 South Michigan. The house of three-and-one-half stories, built in 1892, was designed by Chicago architect L. Gustav Hallberg. Added to the National Register of Historic Places in 2018, the home sits a short distance back from the street, behind a black, wrought-iron fence that encloses a diminutive green lawn shaded by a large locust tree. On the lawn, mounted on a cement base, is a striking steel sculpture, *Move On Up a Little Higher*, by the African American artist Ausbra Ford.

The Georgian-style structure of reddish-brown brick is seated on a base of limestone. Reflecting its origin as the home of one of Chicago's turn-of-the-century elites, the building's first and second stories have large bays, each with three tall windows separated by brick columns with Ionic capitals. The crossheads and sills of the windows and the building's other trim also are made of limestone.

Six wide steps ascend to the center's front entrance under an impressive Greek revival–style limestone portico that extends across a third of the building's front. Under this portico, brown double doors with tall glass panes provide a welcoming entry to the building. From the foyer, where artwork adorns the walls, another doorway immediately to the right leads to the expansive main gallery, where paintings hang on walls of cinnamon-colored, vertical wooden paneling. At one end of this room is a fireplace; nestled near the room's bay window at the opposite end is a baby grand piano.

South Side Community Art Center, 3831 South Michigan Avenue, Chicago. *Photo by Alan Scott Walker. Wikimedia Commons, CC-BY-SA-4.0.*

Beyond the foyer a staircase, with wide, graceful handrails reflecting the flowing New Bauhaus look employed when the SSCAC was remodeled in 1940, leads to a second-floor corridor with African sculptures and paintings. One end of the corridor takes art lovers to a sunny, yellow room designated the Eldzier Cortor Gallery in honor of the African American painter. A staircase from the gallery to the center's third floor takes visitors to a large room sometimes used for classes, sometimes used by aspiring artists to pursue their work. All these rooms recognize not only the importance of African American art but also the importance of sharing that art with all the public.

In this exciting home for the arts, visitors can view exhibits, attend Artist Talks presentations, and purchase artwork at annual art auctions. In these ways the South Side Community Art Center clearly continues to fulfill today, as it has for over eight decades, the vision of Burroughs, Kligh Reed, Carter Cole, Pollack, and others who spent so much time, energy, and effort to bring it about. This is a place that assuredly speaks to the better nature of the human spirit and that, as its founders hoped, brings joy.

Acknowledgments

The years spent writing *Exploring the Land of Lincoln* have taken me on an exciting, rewarding, demanding, and enjoyable journey into the state's past. That journey, however, was not taken alone, and it is with deep appreciation that I recognize those who helped make it possible.

I thank Phil Glosser, who drew the pen-and-ink illustrations for this book and who worked closely with me in the project's early stages. Acknowledgment goes also to Dan Hockman and Robert Sterling, members emeritus of the history department at Eastern Illinois University, who read many of the chapters and provided important counsel.

Many thanks are due to James Quivey, chair emeritus of EIU's department of English, who reviewed nearly every chapter. His astute suggestions were important contributions. I am grateful also to the late Ken Hesler, who retired as director of university relations at Eastern and provided insightful comments on the introduction and other parts of the manuscript. Appreciation also goes to John Hoffmann, curator emeritus of the Illinois History and Lincoln Collections of the University of Illinois Library at Urbana-Champaign, who offered valuable thoughts on early chapters.

Thanks goes to several others who generously took time from their work to critique parts of the manuscript: Timothy Pauketat of the department of anthropology, University of Illinois at Urbana-Champaign, who has extensively studied the Cahokia settlement; archeologist William Iseminger, retired assistant site manager at Cahokia Mounds State Historic Site; David Schultz, site supervisor at Fort de Chartres State Historic Site; Masequa Myers, former executive director, South Side Community Art Center; Mary Cole, former site superintendent at Vandalia State House; John Winterbaur at the Vachel Lindsay Home; and Tom Vance, retired site superintendent at Lincoln Log Cabin State Historic Site.

I also send appreciation to Mary Lou Kowaleski for her meticulous editing of the manuscript; Roberta Fairburn of the Abraham Lincoln Presidential Library for her valuable assistance with acquiring illustrations; and to Bob Appleman at the Illinois Department of Natural Resources, who made available many of the photographs. Christine Colburn at the University of Chicago Library's Special Collections Research Center provided helpful assistance with the image of Lorado Taft. Bill Nelson's careful cartographic expertise produced the maps. I thank, too, the staff at Booth Library at Eastern Illinois University for their assistance.

An especially significant debt of thanks goes to James Engelhardt, formerly at the University of Illinois Press, for his insightful comments, invaluable advice, and unending patience.

My deepest gratitude goes to my partner, Elda Ueleke, whose unwavering support and assistance have been central to helping this book take shape. Her enthusiasm, cheerfulness, optimism, and encouragement, as well as her technological ability to shoo the gremlins out of my laptop, have made this project immeasurably easier.

Any errors or omissions are mine alone.

Charles Titus
Charleston, Illinois

Appendix

Additional Sites of Interest

In addition to this book's twenty selected historic sites, dozens of additional locations with historical significance are scattered across the Prairie State. Each can be a valuable resource for learning more about the events and people that have made up the colorful pageant of Illinois history. Listed below by geographical region are seventeen such places you may wish to visit.

NORTHERN ILLINOIS

Mary Ann "Mother" Bickerdyke Monument, lawn of the Knox County Courthouse, Galesburg

Mary Ann "Mother" Bickerdyke, a resident of Galesburg, Knox County, when the Civil War began, earned a place in the hearts of hundreds of Union Army soldiers whom she tended as they languished ill or wounded in military hospitals during the war. A native of Ohio, Bickerdyke moved to Galesburg in 1856. Because of her experience as a nurse, she was entrusted by Knox County residents to take a shipment of clothing and medical supplies to their soldiers at the Cairo, Illinois, hospital. She remained with the army and nursed the ill and wounded at the Battles of Shiloh, Atlanta, and several other places, where those soldiers gave her the title of Mother. Following the war, she continued to assist veterans of the Union army. Mother Bickerdyke died in 1901, and in 1906 a monument honoring her was placed near the Knox County Courthouse in Galesburg. The bronze sculpture, atop a large granite base, depicts Bickerdyke holding up a wounded or ill soldier against her knee while offering him a drink of water.

Owen Lovejoy Homestead, 905 East Peru Street, Princeton

Owen Lovejoy, born in Maine in 1811, was the younger brother of Elijah Parish Lovejoy, an abolitionist minister and editor murdered in 1837 in Alton, Illinois. Owen, also a minister, served for nearly twenty years as pastor of the Congregational Church in Princeton, Illinois. Later elected to the Illinois legislature and then to the US House of Representatives, he was a friend of Abraham Lincoln. Lovejoy was a fervent abolitionist, and as escaped slaves made their way north to freedom, he sheltered them in this house, making it a stop on the Underground Railroad. The Owen Lovejoy Homestead is open for tours Friday, Saturday, and Sunday, May through September or by appointment by calling 815–879–9151.

Adlai Stevenson Historic Home, 25200 North Saint Mary's Road, Mettawa

Adlai Stevenson was governor of Illinois from 1949 to 1953 and a two-time Democratic presidential candidate in the 1950s. He also served as President John F. Kennedy's ambassador to the United Nations during the Cuban missile crisis. Important people visited Stevenson at his Mettawa residence, and it is where he did much of his writing and campaign preparation. Stevenson's home is a National Historic Landmark and is on the National Register of Historic Places. The service building, near the main house, is a museum and is open from April through October daily.

CHICAGO AREA

Ida B. Wells-Barnett House, 3624 S. Dr. Martin Luther King Drive, Chicago

Ida B. Wells was an influential African American journalist, educator, and reformer who became prominent in the late nineteenth and early twentieth centuries. Born into slavery in Mississippi in 1862, she worked throughout her life for civil rights for black Americans and especially attacked the prevalence of lynching that frequently occurred in the Jim Crow south in which she spent the first thirty years of her life. She and her husband, Ferdinand Lee Barnett, resided in this impressive three-story home between 1919 and 1930. The Wells-Barnett House is a private residence and is not open to visitors.

Ebenezer Missionary Baptist Church, 4501 South Vincennes Avenue, Chicago

Ebenezer Missionary Baptist Church has played a significant role in the religious experience of residents of Chicago's Bronzeville neighborhood for well over a hundred years. During the Great Migration in the early part of the twentieth century, the church was a religious refuge for many of the thousands of African Americans who moved to Chicago to escape the oppression of the Jim Crow laws then found in many southern states. Over the years since its founding in 1904, notable figures such as Mahalia Jackson, Dr. Martin Luther King Jr., and Ralph Metcalf, among others, have been guests at the church. Religious services at Ebenezer Missionary Baptist Church are offered on Sunday.

Grant Park, 337 East Randolph Street, Chicago

Grant Park is one of Chicago's premier parks, perhaps best known for Buckingham Fountain. The park was one of the principal sites of conflict between antiwar demonstrators and the Chicago Police Department during the Democratic Presidential Nominating Convention of 1968. A statue of General John A. Logan, a Union army Civil War hero from Southern Illinois, is a prominent feature of the park. Sculpted by Augustus Saint-Gaudens and Alexander Phimister Proctor, the sculpture was a kind of rallying point for the protestors. Grant Park is also near other prominent Chicago landmarks and is where President Barack Obama spoke when elected on November 4, 2008. Grant Park is open daily.

Pullman Factory and Hotel Florence, 1114 South Forrestville Avenue, Chicago

George Pullman was a well-known entrepreneur during the last part of the nineteenth century. Pullman's Palace Car, an early version of a railroad sleeper car, was enormously successful and became the mainstay of

Pullman's business. In 1880, in a move unusual at the time, Pullman built a model community for his factory employees. Originally a separate town that included housing for plant workers, a park, and a hotel, it has now been incorporated into the city of Chicago. One of the most famous labor disputes in Illinois history occurred during an economic downturn in 1894 when Pullman reduced his workers' salaries by 6 percent but made no reduction in their rent in the town. A strike resulted that soon spread across several states when the American Railway Union became involved. The strike was finally broken by a federal injunction and President Grover Cleveland's authorization to use federal troops to restore order. The Pullman Historic District includes the Pullman factory building, the Hotel Florence, a visitor center, and other buildings. The visitor center is open Tuesday through Sunday. However, the site is closed for part of the winter season. Visitors should call 773–785–8901 for information about when the site is open.

CENTRAL ILLINOIS

Beecher Hall, Illinois College, 1101 West College Avenue, Jacksonville

Illinois College was a center of antislavery sentiment and activism in the years before the Civil War. The college's president, Edward Beecher, was a member of the famous Beecher family, which included Henry Ward Beecher and Harriet Beecher Stowe. Because of the actions of the faculty and students at the college in assisting escaped enslaved persons, Beecher Hall, constructed in 1829, was an important part of the Underground Railroad in Illinois. The building is currently used by student organizations at the college. Visits can be scheduled in advance by calling 217–245–3000.

Center for American Archeology Museum, 101 North Broadway, Kampsville

The Center for American Archeology pursues a range of activities related to the archeology of the lower Illinois River Valley, focusing largely on prehistoric Native Americans. Exhibits in the center's museum address both the prehistorical and historical periods of the Illinois past. The museum does not charge admission but does accept contributions. It is open from the last Tuesday in April until the Sunday prior to Thanksgiving and is closed on Mondays. Unscheduled closings are posted on the museum's Facebook page and on the center's website.

Clover Lawn, David Davis Mansion, 1000 Monroe Drive, Bloomington

David Davis, an Illinois attorney, politician, US Supreme Court Justice, and US Senator who was a friend of Abraham Lincoln, began construction on this three-story, Victorian-style mansion in 1870. Davis and his wife, Sarah, shared the home until her death in 1879. Davis lived here until his death in 1886. Clover Lawn, a National Historic Landmark, has a notable flower garden and offers an array of activities throughout the year. The building is open Wednesday through Saturday.

Dana-Thomas House, 301 East Lawrence Avenue, Springfield

Susan Lawrence Dana, who was born in 1862 and died in 1946, was an affluent and well-known socialite in Springfield. A world traveler who was a fervent women's rights activist, she was associated with the National Woman's Party and served for a time as its legislative chairperson in Illinois. In 1902 she commissioned architect Frank Lloyd Wright to design this house, which Susan used to entertain her friends and associates. Wright, often considered among America's great architects, worked early in his career for one of Chicago's premier architectural firms of the late nineteenth century, Adler and Sullivan. During his lengthy career, he designed hundreds of structures. The striking twelve-thousand-square-foot, thirty-five-room Dana-Thomas House is an exemplar of Wright's unique prairie-style architecture. It holds a stunning collection of furniture and other items that showcase Wright's unusual architectural concepts. The Dana-Thomas House can be visited every day of the week.

Dickson Mounds Museum, 10956 North Dickson Mounds Road, Lewistown

The museum is highly regarded for its dedication to increasing knowledge about and understanding of Native American culture and life in the Illinois River Valley. Permanent and temporary exhibits relate the rich and fascinating story of some of the state's earliest residents. The museum is open each day except for New Year's Day, Thanksgiving Day, and Christmas Day.

Everett McKinley Dirksen Statue, across from Mineral Springs Park, Pekin

Everett McKinley Dirksen, a native of Pekin, was a well-known and popular Illinois politician. A Republican, he served in the US House of Representatives from 1933 to 1949 and as a US Senator from 1950 to 1969. Dirksen was celebrated for his eloquence and good humor. He supported the Civil Rights Act of 1964 and during his time in office was considered one of the most powerful members of the Senate. The seven-foot-tall statue was sculpted by Carl Topol.

Ronald Reagan Museum, Donald B. Cerf Center, Eureka College, Eureka

President Ronald Reagan, who graduated from Eureka College in 1932, gave most of the objects in the Reagan museum's large collection. Except for holidays, the museum is open to the public.

SOUTHERN ILLINOIS

Governor Edward Coles Memorial, Valley View Cemetery, 1564 Lewis Road, Edwardsville

Edward Coles, who served as the state's second governor, was born into an elite Virginia family in 1786. For a time, he was President James Madison's private secretary and was sent by Madison on a diplomatic mission to Russia. A member of a slaveholding family, Coles was repelled by what he termed "the curse of slavery." He relocated to Illinois in 1818, courageously freeing his slaves en route. Elected governor in 1822, he worked to defeat a call for a constitutional convention, which, had it been held, would very likely have crafted a new frame of government converting Illinois into a slave state. Coles later left Illinois for Philadelphia where he died in 1868.

Mary Harris "Mother" Jones and Martyrs of the Progressive Miners of America Monument, Union Miners Cemetery, Mt. Olive

Mary Harris "Mother" Jones was a central figure in many labor disputes in the late nineteenth and early twentieth centuries, especially those in the coal-mining industry. A fierce advocate for improvements in miners' working conditions, she became a prominent voice in the labor movement in Illinois and elsewhere. At her request Mother Jones, who died in 1930, was buried in the Union Miners Cemetery in Mt. Olive. A twenty-two-foot-high monument commemorating her was constructed in 1936.

Pierre Menard Home, 4230 Kaskaskia Street, Ellis Grove

This striking home built perhaps around 1802 was the home of Pierre Menard, the first lieutenant governor of Illinois. Menard, who was originally from Canada, was a Kaskaskia businessman who was active in territorial politics before Illinois entered the Union. He was also a partner in the Missouri Fur Company with explorer and fur trader Manuel Lisa and was one of the leaders of an 1809 expedition up the Missouri River to the Yellowstone region. Menard's two-story home reflects the French colonial–style architecture once common in the area. The Pierre Menard Home, a state historic site, is open from May through October, Wednesday through Sunday, and closed during the winter.

Notes

INTRODUCTION

1. David A. Kyvig and Myron A. Marty, *Nearby History: Exploring the Past around You*, 2nd ed. (Walnut Creek, CA: AltaMira, 2000), 7.

CAHOKIA MOUNDS STATE HISTORIC SITE

1. William Iseminger, *Cahokia Mounds: America's First City* (Charleston, SC: History Press, 2010), 18; Claudia Gellman Mink, *Cahokia: City of the Sun*, ed. William Iseminger, rev. ed. (Collinsville, IL: Cahokia Mounds Museum Society, 1999), 8; George Milner, *The Cahokia Chiefdom: The Archaeology of a Mississippian Society* (Washington, DC: Smithsonian, 1998), 14.

2. Iseminger, *Cahokia Mounds*, 22–26. An excellent table displaying the cultural traditions, the Cahokian archaeological phases, and other chronological data is on page 21.

3. Gemma Tarlach, "Earliest American Genome Proves Siberian Origins of Native Peoples," Discover D-Brief, February 12, 2014, http://blogs.discovermagazine.com/d-brief/2014/02/12/earliest-american-genome-proves-siberian-origins-for-native-peoples. See also Andrew Curry, "Ancient Migration: Coming to America," *Nature* 485, May 3, 2012, 31, https://www.nature.com/, and Mink, *Cahokia*, 10–11.

4. Iseminger, *Cahokia Mounds*, 22; Roger Biles, *Illinois: A History of the Land and Its People* (DeKalb: Northern Illinois University Press, 2005), 5.

5. Iseminger, *Cahokia Mounds*, 23–24; Mink, *Cahokia*, 11.

6. Iseminger, *Cahokia Mounds*, 24–25.

7. For an examination of settlements in the Illinois River Valley region, see Kenneth B. Farnsworth, Thomas E. Emerson, and Rebecca Miller Glenn, "Patterns of Late Woodland/Mississippian Interaction in the Lower Illinois Valley Drainage: A View from Starr Village," in *Cahokia and the Hinterlands: Middle Mississippian Cultures of the Midwest*, ed. Thomas

E. Emerson and R. Barry Lewis (Urbana: University of Illinois Press, 1991), 83–118. See also Robert P. Howard, *Illinois: A History of the Prairie State* (Grand Rapids, MI: Eerdmans, 1972), 12; Biles, *Illinois*, 5–6.

8. Iseminger, *Cahokia Mounds*, 26.

9. Thomas E. Emerson, "An Introduction to Cahokia 2002: Diversity, Complexity, and History," *Midcontinental Journal of Archaeology* 27, no. 2 (2002): 127–48, JSTOR. Emerson suggests that rather than seeing Cahokia solely as "a typical fortified Mississippian town" or "as simply 'a big village,'" we should view it as "more a regional system than a settlement" (129).

10. An explanation of "alternative sociopolitical models" at Cahokia is in Milner, *Cahokia Chiefdom*, 10–14.

11. Milner, *Cahokia Chiefdom*, 10–13; Timothy R. Pauketat and Thomas E. Emerson, eds., *Cahokia: Domination and Ideology in the Mississippian World* (Lincoln: University of Nebraska Press, 1997), 3–4; Mink, *Cahokia*, 44–45.

12. A. Martin Byers, *Cahokia: A World Renewal Cult Heterarchy* (Gainesville: University Press of Florida, 2006), 22–28. See Milner, *Cahokia Chiefdom*, 13–14, for a discussion of alternative views of Cahokia's relationship to outlying communities.

13. Robert L. Hall, "Cahokia Identity and Interaction Models of Cahokia Mississippian," in Emerson and Lewis, *Cahokia and the Hinterlands*, 8–18.

14. For more on Cahokia's "big bang," see Timothy R. Pauketat, *Cahokia: Ancient America's Great City on the Mississippi* (New York: Viking, 2009), 4, esp. chap. 2, "Supernova," 11–24. He offers an intriguing account of the remarkable appearance of a bright star that was visible at about the time when (he and others think) Cahokia began its rapid growth. See also Iseminger, *Cahokia Mounds*, 27–28, 30–31.

15. Iseminger, *Cahokia Mounds*, 32.

16. Iseminger, *Cahokia Mounds*, 84–95; Pauketat, *Cahokia*, 34–35.

17. A fascinating account of the game is in Pauketat, *Cahokia*, chap. 4, "The Original Rolling Stones," 36–50.

18. Iseminger, *Cahokia Mounds*, 38.

19. Iseminger, *Cahokia Mounds*, 55.

20. Iseminger, *Cahokia Mounds*, 42–43.

21. Mikels Skele, *The Great Knob: Interpretations of Monks Mound*, Studies in Illinois Archaeology no. 4 (Springfield: Illinois Historic Preservation Agency, 1988), 89; Iseminger, *Cahokia Mounds*, 41; Pauketat, *Cahokia*, 35.

22. Iseminger, *Cahokia Mounds*, 58.

23. Skele, *Great Knob*, 102. Though archeologists have often used a time frame of two to three centuries for the construction of Monks Mound, recent analysis of vegetation taken from Monks Mound indicates that it could have been built much more quickly, perhaps over several decades. See Neal H. Lopinot, Timothy Schilling, Gayle J. Fritz,

and John E. Kelly, "Implications of Plant Remains from the East Face of Monks Mound," *Midcontinental Journal of Archaeology* 40, no. 3 (2015): 209–30.

24. Mink, *Cahokia*, 25; Iseminger, *Cahokia Mounds*, 44.

25. For a detailed explanation of this analysis of the Beaded Burial at Mound 72, see Thomas E. Emerson, Kristin M. Hedman, and Eve A. Hargrave, "Paradigms Lost: Reconfiguring Cahokia's Mound 72 Beaded Burial," *American Antiquity* 81, no. 3 (2016): 405–25.

26. Much has been written about Mound 72, including Pauketat, *Cahokia*, 69–84; Iseminger, *Cahokia Mounds*, 66–83; Mink, *Cahokia*, 36; Byers, *Cahokia*, 325–72; R. L. Hall, "Cahokia Identity," 11.

27. See Timothy R. Pauketat, *An Archeology of the Cosmos: Rethinking Agency and Religion in Ancient America* (New York: Routledge, 2013), esp. 70–80.

28. Pauketat, *Archeology*, 73, 105, fig. 6.8, 144, 148–52.

29. Iseminger, *Cahokia Mounds*, 131; also see Pauketat, *Archeology*, fig. 6.8.

30. Iseminger, *Cahokia Mounds*, 149–56; Mink, *Cahokia*, 66–67.

STARVED ROCK STATE PARK

1. Extensive geographical, geological, and botanical descriptions of Starved Rock are found in Carl O. Sauer, Gilbert H. Cady, and Henry C. Cowles, *Starved Rock and Its Environs*, Geographic Society of Chicago, bulletin 6 (Chicago: University of Chicago Press, 1918). See also Illinois Department of Natural Resources (IDNR), *Starved Rock State Park* (Springfield: IDNR, 2006).

2. Francis Borgia Steck, *The Jolliet-Marquette Expedition, 1673* (Glendale, CA: Clark, 1928), 143. For more about French colonial affairs in New France, see James J. Cooke, "France, the New World, and Colonial Expansion," and Glenn R. Conrad, "Reluctant Imperialist: France in North America," in *La Salle and His Legacy: Frenchmen and Indians in the Lower Mississippi Valley*, ed. Patricia K. Galloway (Jackson: University Press of Mississippi, 1982), 81–92, 93–105, respectively.

3. Several accounts of French authorities' interest in the Mississippi and their ideas about where they believed the river led are in Steck, *Jolliet-Marquette Expedition*, 109–15; Robert P. Howard, *Illinois: A History of the Prairie State* (Grand Rapids, MI: Eerdmans, 1972), 26; and Roger Biles, *Illinois: A History of the Land and Its People* (DeKalb: Northern Illinois University Press, 2005), 8.

4. A brief but detailed description of the Jolliet-Marquette expedition is in chapter 2 of Charles J. Balesi, *The Time of the French in the Heart of North America 1673–1818* (Chicago: Alliance Française, 1992), 12–25. For an earlier, book-length treatment of the journey, see Steck, *Joliet-Marquette Expedition*.

5. For Marquette's own explanation of the party's decision to return to New France, see Louis De Vorsey Jr., "The Impact of the La Salle Expedition of 1682 on European Cartography," in Galloway, *La Salle and His Legacy*, 65. Marquette noted that they left the Mississippi "about the 38th degree" and entered the Illinois. See John Gilmary Shea, *Discovery and Exploration of the Mississippi Valley: With the Original Narratives of Marquette, Allouez, Membre, Hennepin, and Anastase Douay* (Clinton Hall, NJ: Redfield, 1852), 50–51.

6. La Salle's concept of a large mercantile enterprise is described in Timothy Severin, *Explorers of the Mississippi* (New York: Knopf, 1968), 114–16. For an overview of how historians have considered La Salle over time, see Carl A. Brasseaux, "The Image of La Salle in North American Historiography," in Galloway, *La Salle and His Legacy*, 3–10.

7. Anka Muhlstein, *La Salle: Explorer of the North American Frontier*, trans. Willard Wood (New York: Arcade, 1994), 46–47, 57.

8. Muhlstein, *La Salle*, 156–57.

9. Balesi, *Time of the French*, 58.

10. A description of the place by La Salle himself is found in Robert L. Hall, "The Archaeology of La Salle's Fort St. Louis on Starved Rock and the Problem of the Newell Fort," in *French Colonial Archaeology: The Illinois Country and the Western Great Lakes*, ed. John A. Walthall (Urbana: University of Illinois Press, 1991), 18. See also Muhlstein, *La Salle*, 162; Balesi, *Time of the French*, 60; and IDNR, *Starved Rock State Park*, "History."

11. Muhlstein, *La Salle*, 210. A similar but slightly different account of La Salle's assassination is in L. V. Jacks, *La Salle* (New York: Scribner's, 1931), 250–51, a much-older biography.

12. Edmund Robert Murphy, *Henry de Tonty: Fur Trader of the Mississippi* (Baltimore: Johns Hopkins Press, 1941), 67.

13. Murphy, *Henry de Tonty*, 87. According to the "History" panel in the IDNR brochure *Starved Rock State Park*, "the French abandoned the fort by the early 1700s."

14. A detailed account of the archeological evidence, including that of burned structures, discovered during excavations at the site of Fort St. Louis on Starved Rock's summit, is found in R. L. Hall, "Archaeology," 14–28. J. H. Goodell also refers to charred remains at the site of Fort St. Louis on Starved Rock. "Some Evidences of the Route from the Lakes to the Gulf," *Journal of the Illinois State Historical Society* 5, no. 2 (1912): 227.

15. The legend of Native American warfare during which a group of Illinois Indians sought safety at the old French fort and then succumbed to starvation there is mentioned in many accounts of Illinois history. See Howard, *Illinois*, 33n9; Biles, *Illinois*, 12; Murphy, *Henry de Tonty*, 17n19. In an extensive and thorough study of the incident, Mark Walczynski has concluded that the episode did not occur, and he believes the story may have its origins in an earlier confrontation between Peoria and Fox Indians in 1722. "The

Starved Rock Massacre of 1769: Fact or Fiction," *Journal of the Illinois State Historical Society* 100, no. 3 (2007): 215–36.

16. William Steinbacher-Kemp, "The Establishment of Starved Rock State Park," *Journal of Illinois History* 2, no. 2 (1999): 125, 132, 136–40.

FORT DE CHARTRES STATE HISTORIC SITE

1. James E. Davis, *Frontier Illinois* (Bloomington: Indiana University Press, 1998), 48–50.

2. Robert P. Howard, *Illinois: A History of the Prairie State* (Grand Rapids, MI: Eerdmans, 1972), 36.

3. Howard, *Illinois*, 37; Roger Biles, *Illinois: A History of the Land and Its People* (DeKalb: Northern Illinois University Press, 2005), 12–13.

4. Biles, *Illinois*, 13; Anna Price, "French Outpost on the Mississippi," *Historic Illinois*, 3, no. 1 (1980): 1.

5. For an account of John Law's involvement in the Illinois Country, see Clarence Walworth Alvord, *The Illinois Country 1673–1818*, vol. 1 of *The Centennial History of Illinois* (Springfield: Illinois Centennial Commission, 1920), 1:149–52.

6. Illinois Historic Preservation Agency (IHPA), *Fort de Chartres State Historic Site* (Springfield: IHPA, 1996).

7. Alvord, *Illinois Country*, 151.

8. Alvord, *Illinois Country*, 154; Biles, *Illinois*, 13.

9. J. E. Davis, *Frontier Illinois*, 48.

10. IHPA, *Fort de Chartres*; Margaret Brown, "Uncovering the Mystery of the Three Forts de Chartres," *Illinois Magazine* 16, no. 9 (1977): 23; David Keene, "Fort de Chartres: Archaeology in the Illinois Country," in *French Colonial Archaeology: The Illinois Country and the Western Great Lakes*, ed. John A. Walthall (Urbana: University of Illinois Press, 1991), 30–31.

11. IHPA, *Fort de Chartres*.

12. Price, "French Outpost," 2–3; Brown, "Uncovering the Mystery," 24; Keene, "Fort de Chartres," 31.

13. IHPA, *Fort de Chartres*.

14. IHPA, *Fort de Chartres*; Price, "French Outpost," 3–4.

15. Recent archeological research indicates a third wooden fort may have been built prior to the current, reconstructed stone fort. David Schultz, site services specialist, Fort de Chartres, Fort Kaskaskia, and Pierre Menard Home State Historic Sites, conversation with author, February 18, 2016.

16. Alvord, *Illinois Country*, 237.

17. See John Frances Snyder, *Captain John Baptiste Saucier at Fort Chartres in the Illinois, 1751–1763* (Springfield: Illinois State Historical Society, 1919), 228–29, accessed June 7, 2018, http://babel.hathitrust.org/. Snyder also relates that in wet weather, some of the stones for the fort were moved by boat across a lagoon between the fort and the bluffs.

18. Joseph Wallace, "Fort de Chartres: Its Origin, Growth, and Decline," in *Transactions of the Illinois State Historical Society for the Year 1903* (Springfield: Illinois State Historical Library, 1903). Wallace cites a French officer who states the fort was nearly completed by midsummer of 1756. "Fort de Chartres," 110–11.

19. J. Wallace, "Fort de Chartres"; see also Brown, "Uncovering the Mystery," 28.

20. For a highly useful illustration of Fort de Chartres and information about its buildings, see the brochure *Welcome to Fort de Chartres State Historic Site*, published by the Society of Colonial Wars in the State of Illinois. The brochure is available at the fort's museum.

21. John Francis Snyder, "The Armament of Fort Chartres," *Transactions of the Illinois State Historical Library for the Year 1906*, no. 11 (January 1906): 222.

22. Bradley T. Gericke, "To the Distant Country: The Stirling Expedition to Fort de Chartres, 1765," *Journal of the Illinois Historical Society* 2, no. 2 (1999): 99; Wallace, "Fort de Chartres," 112.

23. Alvord, *Illinois Country*, 297; Price, "French Outpost," 4.

24. IHPA, *Fort de Chartres*; Wallace, "Fort de Chartres," 113.

25. Wallace, "Fort de Chartres," 113; Darrell Duensing, "'A Splendid Ruin': Fort de Chartres as a Historic Site," *Historic Illinois* 3, no.1 (1980): 6.

26. IHPA, *Fort de Chartres*.

27. Illinois Historic Preservation Division, "Fort de Chartres State Historic Site," *Illinois Department of Natural Resources*, accessed June 5, 2018, www.fortdechartres.us/.

28. National Society Daughters of the American Colonists, "Gateway at Fort de Chartres," NSDAC, accessed June 6, 2018, http://nsdac.org/work-of-the-society/historical/markers/fort-de-chartres/.

FORT MASSAC STATE PARK

1. For an excellent account of the geography, history, and culture of Southern Illinois, see Herbert K. Russell, *The State of Southern Illinois: An Illustrated History* (Carbondale: Southern Illinois University Press, 2012).

2. John B. Fortier, "New Light on Fort Massac," in *Frenchmen and French Ways in the Mississippi Valley*, ed. John Francis McDermott (Urbana: University of Illinois Press, 1969), 59–60.

3. Fortier, "New Light," 61. See also J. E. Davis, *Frontier Illinois*, 52.

4. Bernard de Verges, the same French military engineer who had suggested twelve years earlier that a fort be built at the Massac site, describes Fort Ascension in detail, found in Fortier, "New Light," 61–62.

5. Paul Fellows, "Fort Massac," *Historic Illinois* 4, no. 1 (1981): 1; Fortier, "New Light," 62; Illinois Department of Natural Resources, *Fort Massac State Park* (Springfield: IDNR, 2015).

6. Fortier, "New Light," 63. The fort was named Massiac in honor of a high French official. For a detailed description of the early French forts based on archeological excavations by Paul J. Maynard in the late 1930s and early 1940s, see John A. Walthall, "French Colonial Fort Massac: Architecture and Ceramic Patterning," in *French Colonial Archeology: The Illinois Country and the Western Great Lakes*, ed. John A. Walthall (Urbana: University of Illinois Press, 1991), 48–55.

7. Fortier, "New Light," 68; Fellows, "Fort Massac," 2.

8. IDNR, *Fort Massac State Park*.

9. Fellows, "Fort Massac," 2. For the comments of at least one British officer who comprehended the strategic value of the fort, see Fortier, "New Light," 68–69.

10. Fellows, "Fort Massac," 2; John Bakeless, *Background to Glory: The Life of George Rogers Clark* (Lincoln: University of Nebraska Press, 1992), 67. See also Larry L. Nelson, "Clark's Kaskaskia Expedition, June 24–July 4, 1778," in *The Life of George Rogers Clark, 1752–1818: Triumphs and Tragedies*, ed. Kenneth C. Carstens and Nancy Son Carstens, Contributions in American History, 203, ed. Jon L. Wakelyn (Westport, CT: Praeger, 2004), 24.

11. Gillum Ferguson, *Illinois in the War of 1812* (Urbana: University of Illinois Press, 2012), 9–10; Norman W. Caldwell, "Fort Massac: The American Frontier Post 1778–1805," *Journal of the Illinois State Historical Society* 43, no. 4 (1950): 267–68; Fellows, "Fort Massac," 2; Reuben Gold Thwaites asserts that Genet's intrigues included consideration of the use of Fort Massac as a cache for supplies. *On the Storied Ohio: An Historical Pilgrimage of a Thousand Miles in a Skiff from Redstone to Cairo* (Chicago: McClurg, 1903), 286–87.

12. Alvord, *Illinois Country*, 411. See also Caldwell, "Fort Massac," 268–69.

13. Fortier, "New Light," 64.

14. Alvord, *Illinois Country*, 411–12; Fellows, "Fort Massac," 2.

15. National Park Service, "Preparing an Expedition," *National Park Service*, accessed March 26, 2020, https://www.nps.gov/articles/preparing-an-expedition.htm.

16. Norman W. Caldwell, "Fort Massac since 1805," *Journal of the Illinois State Historical Society* 44, no. 1 (1951): 47; Fellows, "Fort Massac," 3.

17. Caldwell, "Fort Massac since 1805," 52–53.

18. Caldwell, "Fort Massac since 1805," 56; Ferguson, *Illinois*, 117–18; IDNR, "About Fort Massac State Park," *Illinois Department of Natural Resources*, accessed March 26, 2020, https://www2.illinois.gov/dnr/Parks/About/Pages/FortMassac.aspx.

19. Fellows, "Fort Massac," 13; Fortier, "New Light," 70n60.

20. IDNR, *Fort Massac State Park* and "About Fort Massac State Park."

21. IDNR, *Fort Massac State Park*. See also Richard S. Taylor, "How Illinois Got Its First State Park," *Historic Illinois* 4, no. 1 (1981): 4–5, 13.

PART 2 PROLOGUE

1. Stephen Leonard and Melinda F. Kwedar, *The Great Migration: Transportation and Settlement in Illinois, 1800–1850* (Springfield: Illinois State Historical Society, 1989), 3.

OLD SHAWNEETOWN

1. Edward Callary, *Place Names of Illinois* (Urbana: University of Illinois Press, 2009), 318; Clarence Walworth Alvord, *The Illinois Country 1673–1818*, vol. 1 of *The Centennial History of Illinois* (Springfield: Illinois Centennial Commission, 1920), 187n38.

2. Daniel E. Bigham, *Towns and Villages of the Lower Ohio* (Lexington: University Press of Kentucky, 1998), 33.

3. James E. Davis, *Frontier Illinois* (Bloomington: Indiana University Press, 1998), 173.

4. Solon J. Buck, *Illinois in 1818*, 2nd ed. (Urbana: University of Illinois Press, 1967), 74–75.

5. For a description of settlement activities in the Shawneetown area, see Douglas K. Meyer, *Making the Heartland Quilt: A Geographical History of Settlement and Migration in Early Nineteenth-Century Illinois* (Carbondale: Southern Illinois University Press, 2000), 121.

6. Buck, *Illinois in 1818*, 54.

7. Which American Indian tribes sold the land is not specified: "In June 1803 at Fort Wayne representatives from five tribes sold over two million acres west and southwest of Vincennes, including the valuable salt springs west of Shawneetown." J. E. Davis, *Frontier Illinois*, 119.

8. Stella Pendleton Lyles, "Shawneetown," *Journal of the Illinois State Historical Society* 22, no. 1 (1929): 169–71.

9. William E. Campbell offers an account of the industrial-like process for extracting salt. John Woods, an Englishman who traveled through Shawneetown in September 1819, noted that the town was near what he calls "the United States Saline works." Campbell,

"Shawneetown, Illinois: The Early Years" (master's thesis, Eastern Illinois University, 1965), 4–5. See John Woods, "The English Settlement, the Illinois Pioneer," in *Prairie State: Impressions of Illinois, 1673–1967, by Travelers and Other Observers*, ed. Paul M. Angle (Chicago: University of Chicago Press, 1968), 77. The significance of the salt industry to Gallatin County and Shawneetown is also mentioned in Jacqueline Yvonne Blackmore, "African-Americans and Race Relations in Gallatin County, Illinois from the Eighteenth Century to 1870" (PhD diss., Northern Illinois University, 1996), 16–17; C. Scott Brooks-Miller, "Shawneetown and Its Magnificent Bank," *Historic Illinois*, 4, no. 2 (1979): 1.

10. Blackmore, "African-Americans," 17.

11. Robert P. Howard, *Illinois: A History of the Prairie State* (Grand Rapids, MI: Eerdmans, 1972), 132. See also Lyles, "Shawneetown," 164–91.

12. Roger Biles, *Illinois: A History of the Land and Its People* (DeKalb: Northern Illinois University Press, 2005), 47; Janet Cornelius, *A History of Constitution Making in Illinois* (Urbana: University of Illinois Institute of Government and Public Affairs, 1969), 9; J. E. Davis, *Frontier Illinois*, 165.

13. Joseph Larwill, "Journal of a Trip to Illinois—1823," *Journal of the Illinois State Historical Society* 34, no. 1 (1941): 136.

14. James Hall, "Shawneetown and the Salines," in *Prairie State: Impressions of Illinois, 1673–1967, by Travelers and Other Observers*, ed. Paul M. Angle (Chicago: University of Chicago Press, 1968), 89.

15. Howard, *Illinois*, 154.

16. Biles, *Illinois*, 63–64.

17. For a map of Illinois railroads at midcentury, see Howard, *Illinois*, 268.

18. J. Hall, "Shawneetown and the Salines," 89–90.

19. Brooks-Miller, "Shawneetown," 3, 15.

20. Brooks-Miller, "Shawneetown," 2–3; Lucille Lawler, *A Walking Tour of Historic Old Shawneetown* (Southern Illinois Tourism Council and Illinois Humanities Council, 1991).

21. John Drury, *Old Illinois Houses*, ed. Jay Monaghan (Springfield: Illinois State Historical Society, 1948), 13–14.

22. Lawler, *Walking Tour*.

LINCOLN'S NEW SALEM STATE HISTORIC SITE

1. For one view of changing perceptions of Lincoln, see Barry Schwartz, *Abraham Lincoln in the Post-Heroic Era: History and Memory in Late Twentieth-Century America* (Chicago: University of Chicago Press, 2008).

2. Lincoln's time in New Salem has been described in many writings about him. Lincoln's law partner William H. Herndon provides much information about the New

Salem years in William H. Herndon and Jesse W. Weik, *Herndon's Life of Lincoln: The History and Personal Recollections of Abraham Lincoln as Originally Written by William H. Herndon and Jesse Weik, with Introduction and Notes by Paul M. Angle, New Introduction by Henry Steele Commager* (New York: Da Capo, 1983). Although historians have shown Herndon's book to be inaccurate in some instances, much of it has been accepted. Another extensive account is Benjamin P. Thomas, *Lincoln's New Salem* (Springfield, IL: Abraham Lincoln Association, 1934). New Salem is also the subject in chap. 3 of Michael Burlingame's massive *Abraham Lincoln: A Life*, 2 vols. (Baltimore: Johns Hopkins University Press, 2008), 1:57–85; and in chap. 2 of David Herbert Donald, *Lincoln* (New York: Simon and Schuster, 1995).

3. Descriptions of the original New Salem can be found in Herndon and Weik, *Herndon's Life*, 64–66, and Benjamin P. Thomas, "Lincoln and New Salem," in *An Illinois Reader*, ed. Clyde C. Walton (DeKalb: Northern Illinois University Press, 1970), 113–25. For an analysis of the present site's "authenticity," as well as how those who visit it may draw meaning from it, see Edward M. Bruner, "Abraham Lincoln as Authentic Reproduction: A Critique of Post-Modernism," *American Anthropologist*, n.s., 96, no. 2 (1994): 397–415.

4. Burlingame, *Abraham Lincoln*, 52–53; Herndon and Weik, *Herndon's Life*, 61–62.

5. This incident is found in numerous Lincoln biographies, and explanations of how Lincoln freed the boat vary. See Herndon and Weik, *Herndon's Life*, 62–63; Burlingame, *Abraham Lincoln*, 56; Donald, *Lincoln*, 38–39; Thomas, *Lincoln's New Salem*, 41.

6. Burlingame, *Abraham Lincoln*, 59; Thomas, *Lincoln's New Salem*, 43.

7. Burlingame, *Abraham Lincoln*, 60.

8. In frontier vernacular, a grocery was an establishment where liquor was served by the drink.

9. As is the case with the milldam incident, this episode appears in several books. Accounts are in Herndon and Weik, *Herndon's Life*, 69–70 (who say that Lincoln defeated Armstrong); Thomas, *Lincoln's New Salem*, 45–46; Donald, *Lincoln*, 40–41. Burlingame quotes John T. Stuart, later Lincoln's law partner, as seeing the match as "the turning point in Lincoln's life." *Abraham Lincoln*, 62. This was surely something of an exaggeration by Stuart. Benjamin Thomas's observation that the contest was "an important event" is likely more accurate. *Lincoln's New Salem*, 46. For a summary of the conflicting accounts, see Douglas L. Wilson, *Lincoln before Washington: New Perspectives on the Illinois Years* (Urbana: University of Illinois Press, 1997), 92.

10. Donald, *Lincoln*, 44–45; Burlingame, *Abraham Lincoln*, 67–71.

11. Donald, *Lincoln*, 46.

12. Burlingame, *Abraham Lincoln*, 75–76; Donald, *Lincoln*, 47, 49–50.

13. Herndon and Weik state Lincoln was still paying off the debt in 1848 while serving in Congress. *Herndon's Life*, 90. Burlingame relates that Lincoln was still strapped with the debt in 1860. *Abraham Lincoln*, 76.

14. Burlingame, *Abraham Lincoln*, 78; Donald, *Lincoln*, 50; Herndon and Weik, *Herndon's Life*, 97.

15. Herndon and Weik, *Herndon's Life*, 97–98; Thomas, "Lincoln and New Salem," 122.

16. Donald, *Lincoln*, 51; Herndon and Weik, *Herndon's Life*, 99.

17. Burlingame, *Abraham Lincoln*, 85; Donald, *Lincoln*, 53; Herndon, and Weik, *Herndon's Life*, 104.

18. Burlingame, *Abraham Lincoln*, 101; Donald, *Lincoln*, 53.

19. A thoughtful analysis of the historiography of the Ann Rutledge story is in John Y. Simon, "Abraham Lincoln and Ann Rutledge," *Journal of the Abraham Lincoln Association* 11, no. 1 (1990): 13–33, accessed June 7, 2018, http://hdl.handle.net/2027/spo.2629860.0011.104. That there is still disagreement about this part of Lincoln's life is evident in Lewis Gannett, "The Ann Rutledge Story: Case Closed?" *Journal of the Abraham Lincoln Association* 31, no. 2 (2010): 21–60, accessed June 24, 2017, http://hdl.handle.net/2027/spo.2629860.0031.205. For an examination of the criticism by some historians of the validity of Herndon's evidence concerning Lincoln and Rutledge, see Wilson, "Herndon's Legacy," chap. 2, in *Lincoln before Washington*.

20. Richard S. Taylor and Mark L. Johnson, "Inventing Lincoln's New Salem: The Reconstruction of a Pioneer Village," unpublished manuscript, 14, Lincoln's New Salem State Historic Site, New Salem.

21. Illinois Historic Preservation Agency (IHPA), *Lincoln's New Salem State Historic Site* (Springfield: IHPA, n.d.); Taylor and Johnson, "Inventing Lincoln's New Salem," 26.

22. Taylor and Johnson, "Inventing Lincoln's New Salem," 34; Illinois Department of Public Works and Buildings, *New Salem: A Memorial to Abraham Lincoln*, 2nd ed. (Springfield: Illinois Department of Public Works and Buildings, 1934), 2.

23. Illinois Department of Public Works and Buildings, *Lincoln's New Salem State Historic Site*. For an extensive explanation of how New Salem came to its present configuration, including observations about the site's "historical authenticity," see Taylor and Johnson, "Inventing Lincoln's New Salem," esp. 2–4.

24. Illinois Department of Public Works and Buildings, *Lincoln's New Salem Historic Site*.

25. Taylor and Johnson, "Inventing Lincoln's New Salem," 2.

APPLE RIVER FORT STATE HISTORIC SITE

1. Patrick J. Jung, "Fire along the Mos-co-ho-co-y-nak: The Battle of Apple River Fort during the Black Hawk War, 1832," unpublished manuscript, Apple River Fort Historic Site, Elizabeth, Illinois, 3; Frank E. Stevens, *The Black Hawk War: Including a Review of Black Hawk's Life* (Chicago: Stevens, 1903), 185.

2. *Apple River Fort, Elizabeth, Illinois* (Elizabeth: Apple River Fort Historic Foundation, 2010).

3. Patrick J. Jung, *The Black Hawk War of 1832* (Norman: University of Oklahoma Press, 2007), 4, 23.

4. Jung, *Black Hawk War*, 4, 20. See also Anthony F. C. Wallace, *Prelude to Disaster: The Course of Indian-White Relations Which Led to the Black Hawk War of 1832* (Springfield: Illinois State Historical Library, 1970), 20.

5. Wallace, *Prelude to Disaster*, 37. For a critical and unflattering description of the actions of the white persons in these events, see Cecil D. Eby, *"That Disgraceful Affair,"* *the Black Hawk War* (New York: Norton, 1973), 84–90.

6. Jung, *Black Hawk War*, 73.

7. Robert P. Howard, *Illinois: A History of the Prairie State* (Grand Rapids, MI: Eerdmans, 1972), 149; Jung, *Black Hawk War*, 73.

8. Jung, *Black Hawk War*, 73; Howard, *Illinois*, 149.

9. Wallace, *Prelude to Disaster*, 49.

10. Jung, *Black Hawk War*, 83–84.

11. Accounts of this unfortunate event vary, but most generally reflect the sequence described. See Jung, *Black Hawk War*, 88–89; Howard, *Illinois*, 150; Eby, *That Disgraceful Affair*, 127–33.

12. Jung, *Black Hawk War*, 108.

13. Stevens states there were three such messengers, but most other accounts say four men triggered the attack. Jung, *Black Hawk War*, 185, 113; Kerry A. Trask, *Black Hawk: The Battle for the Heart of America* (New York: Holt, 2006), 221. For Black Hawk's description of the battle, see Black Hawk, *Black Hawk: An Autobiography*, ed. Donald Jackson (Urbana: University of Illinois Press, 1964), 129–30.

14. Accounts vary on the number of persons inside the fort. *Apple River Fort, Elizabeth, Illinois*, a brochure available at the fort, states, "about 45 men, women, and children" were present. Jung says that "forty Illinois militiamen" and "another twenty-three women and children" were in the fort. "Fire along the Mos-co-ho-co-y-nak," 4.

15. Black Hawk, *Black Hawk*, 129–30.

16. Trask, *Black Hawk*, 222; Stevens, *Black Hawk War*, 186.

17. Stevens says the fight lasted two hours, but most other sources say forty-five minutes. *Black Hawk War*, 186. Jung says, "[Black Hawk] and his warriors commenced a forty-five minute siege against the fort"; Trask says, "The attack went on for three quarters of an hour." Jung, *Black Hawk War*, 113; Trask, *Black Hawk*, 222.

18. Trask cites the June 27, 1832, issue of the *Galenian*, a Galena, Illinois, newspaper, that Harkleroad was hit in the head and died immediately. Trask, *Black Hawk*, 222. For Black Hawk's description of this incident, see Black Hawk, *Black Hawk*, 129–30.

19. Black Hawk, *Black Hawk*, 130.

20. National Park Service registration form, Apple River Fort Site, continuation sheet, sec. 7, 2–3, National Register of Historic Places, National Park Service, US Department of the Interior, October 2, 1997, *State of Illinois*, accessed June 8, 2018, http://gis.hpa.state .il.us/PDFs/201095.pdf. Reuse of parts of unneeded forts was apparently a common occurrence. Forts de Chartres and Massac met similar fates when parts of them were appropriated for other uses.

21. *Apple River Fort, Elizabeth, Illinois*.

22. *Apple River Fort, Elizabeth, Illinois*.

23. David Blanchett, "Reconstructed Apple River Fort Now a State Historic Site," *Historic Illinois* 23, no. 5 (2001): 13.

VANDALIA STATE HOUSE STATE HISTORIC SITE

1. William E. Baringer, *Lincoln's Vandalia: A Pioneer Portrait* (New Brunswick: Rutgers University Press, 1949), 12; Robert P. Howard, *Illinois: A History of the Prairie State* (Grand Rapids, MI: Eerdmans, 1972), 118–19.

2. Paul E. Stroble Jr., *High on the Okaw's Western Bank* (Urbana: University of Illinois Press, 1993), 16.

3. Detailed descriptions of the events and effort resulting in the construction of the new capitol are in Stroble, *High on the Okaw's*, 103–4, and Baringer, *Lincoln's Vandalia*, 77–79. See also Martha Jane Downey, "The Vandalia Statehouse," *Historic Illinois* 2, no. 5 (1980): 1–2; Illinois Historic Preservation Agency (IHPA), *Vandalia Statehouse State Historic Site* (Springfield: IHPA, 2006).

4. Paul Simon, *Lincoln's Preparation for Greatness: The Illinois Legislative Years* (Norman: University of Oklahoma Press, 1965), 155–57. Simon provides a great deal of information about Lincoln's efforts in these actions and others by him while in Vandalia. See also Mary Burtschi, *Vandalia: Wilderness Capital of Lincoln's Land* (Decatur, IL: Huston-Patterson, 1963), 90–95.

5. House Journal, Illinois General Assembly, 1836–37, 817–18, quoted in Simon, *Lincoln's Preparation*, 133. See also Burtschi, *Vandalia*, 93.

6. Baringer gives an account of Lincoln's actions in the legislature's successful attempt to move the capital to Springfield. *Lincoln's Vandalia*, 105–9. For other accounts of the legislature's actions, see Stroble, *High on the Okaw's*, 126–28; IHPA, *Vandalia Statehouse State Historic Site*.

7. Stroble explains, "This legend is certainly a confusion with the actual incident on December 5, 1840, when Lincoln made such a jump from the Springfield Second

Presbyterian Church, the temporary location of the house of representatives." *High on the Okaw's*, 125. Baringer also cites the Springfield incident as the origin of the legend. *Lincoln's Vandalia*, 136n78.

8. Mary Cole, site superintendent, Vandalia Statehouse State Historic Site, to author, July 2011, and an interview with the author, August 4, 2009. See also Downey, "Vandalia Statehouse," 2.

9. IHPA, *Vandalia Statehouse State Historic Site*.

10. For more about the *Madonna of the Trail* sculpture, see Burtschi, *Vandalia*, 141–44.

NAUVOO

1. One of the best accounts of Nauvoo and the Mormons is Robert Bruce Flanders, *Nauvoo: Kingdom on the Mississippi* (Urbana: University of Illinois Press, 1965). An excellent examination of the Mormon faith is Thomas F. O'Dea, *The Mormons* (Chicago: University of Chicago Press, 1957). A more recent treatment is Matthew Bowman, *The Mormon People: The Making of an American Faith* (New York: Random, 2012).

2. Much of the land that later became the site of Nauvoo was acquired from Dr. Isaac Galland, and other landowners in the area. See Flanders, *Nauvoo*, 29–37; Bowman, *Mormon People*, 64; Glen M. Leonard, *Nauvoo: A Place of Peace, a People of Promise* (Salt Lake City: Deseret, 2002), 53–58.

3. Flanders, *Nauvoo*, 41; O'Dea, *Mormons*, 50; Bowman, *Mormon People*, 65.

4. Flanders, *Nauvoo*, 39.

5. Flanders, *Nauvoo*, 38.

6. Church of Jesus Christ of Latter-day Saints, *Church History in the Fulness of Times: The History of the Church of Jesus Christ of Latter-day Saints* (Salt Lake City, UT: Church of Jesus Christ of Latter-day Saints, 1992), 243n, and "Nauvoo Temple Sunstones," Church History, *Church of Jesus Christ of Latter-day Saints*, 2018, accessed June 7, 2018, https://history.lds.org/.

7. The conflict between the Saints and the area's "gentiles" had multiple origins with religious, political, economic, and social dimensions. John E. Hallwas and Roger D. Launius state the tension was rooted in "an ideological struggle between two cultures," one an undemocratic, city-state theocracy, the other characterized by the democratic ideas of Jacksonian America. Hallwas and Launius, *Cultures in Conflict: A Documentary History of the Mormon War in Illinois* (Logan: Utah State University Press, 1995), 4.

8. See Flanders, *Nauvoo*, 308; Bowman, *Mormon People*, 88–89; O'Dea, *Mormons*, 65–66.

9. The deaths of Joseph and Hyrum are chronicled in many sources. One of the most vividly written accounts is in Fawn M. Brodie, *No Man Knows My History: The Life of*

Joseph Smith the Mormon Prophet (New York: Knopf, 1946), 389–95. See also Bowman, *Mormon People*, 89–90.

10. Robert P. Sutton, "An American Elysium: The Icarian Communities," in *America's Communal Utopias*, ed. Donald E. Pitzer (Chapel Hill: University of North Carolina Press, 1997), 281–85.

11. "Nauvoo, Illinois Temple," Newsroom, *Church of Jesus Christ of Latter-day Saints*, 2018, accessed June 6, 2018, www.mormonnewsroom.org/.

OLD STATE CAPITOL STATE HISTORIC SITE

1. Wayne C. Temple and Sunderine Wilson Temple have provided a fascinating and finely detailed account of the history of the Old State Capitol in their book *Abraham Lincoln and Illinois' Fifth Capitol*, 2nd ed. rev. (Mahomet, IL: Mayhaven, 2006). For the laying of the cornerstone, see p. 38; for the opening of the building for use, see pp. 77–78.

2. Abraham Lincoln, *Great Speeches*, with historical notes by John Grafton (New York: Dover, 1991), 25.

3. Temple and Temple, *Abraham Lincoln*, 333; Robert P. Howard, *Illinois: A History of the Prairie State* (Grand Rapids, MI: Eerdmans, 1972), 337; Illinois Secretary of State, *Illinois Blue Book 2017–2018* (Springfield: State of Illinois, 2017), 425.

4. Temple and Temple, *Abraham Lincoln*, 333–34.

5. The offices in the current capitol were occupied for the first time in 1876 although the secretary of state had moved some records there in the preceding summer. The first legislature to sit there was in 1877. See Temple and Temple, *Abraham Lincoln*, 334.

6. Temple and Temple, *Abraham Lincoln*, 334–35; Howard, *Illinois*, 337–38.

7. Howard, *Illinois*, 338.

8. Howard, *Illinois*, 338; Temple and Temple, *Abraham Lincoln*, 335.

9. Michael Burlingame, *Abraham Lincoln: A Life*, 2 vols. (Baltimore: John Hopkins University Press, 2008), 1:686; David Herbert Donald, *Lincoln* (New York: Simon and Schuster, 1995), 252.

10. An excellent description of the renovation is in Temple and Temple, *Abraham Lincoln*, 335–36 (photographs, 332, 337).

LINCOLN LOG CABIN STATE HISTORIC SITE

1. Illinois Historic Preservation Agency (IHPA), *Lincoln Log Cabin State Historic Site* (Springfield: IHPA, 1990).

2. Charles H. Coleman, *Abraham Lincoln and Coles County, Illinois* (New Brunswick, NJ: Scarecrow, 1955), 1–3; Donald, *Lincoln*, 36.

3. Coleman, *Abraham Lincoln*, 19; IHPA, *Lincoln Log Cabin State Historic Site*.

4. Donald, *Lincoln*, 37–39.

5. IHPA, *Lincoln Log Cabin State Historic Site*. For detailed information about the various locations where the Thomas Lincoln family resided in Coles County, see Coleman, *Abraham Lincoln*, 19–35.

6. Coleman, *Abraham Lincoln*, 35, 39–40.

7. Illinois Department of Conservation (IDC), *Lincoln Log Cabin Historic Site* (Springfield: IDC, 1976); Coleman, *Abraham Lincoln*, 44–45.

8. IDC, *Lincoln Log Cabin*; IHPA, *Lincoln Log Cabin State Historic Site*; Coleman attempts to trace the history of the cabin after its sale to the Abraham Lincoln Log Cabin Association. The true fate of the building, however, remains a mystery. Coleman, *Abraham Lincoln*, 46–47.

9. Coleman, *Abraham Lincoln*, 47–48; *Lincoln Log Cabin State Historic Site* (Lerna, IL: Mattoon and Charleston Tourism Boards, n.d.).

10. IHPA, *Lincoln Log Cabin State Historic Site*; Coleman, *Abraham Lincoln*, 48–49; *Lincoln Log Cabin State Historic Site*.

BISHOP HILL

1. Nauvoo and Galesburg are two other Illinois towns with origins as sectarian communities.

2. Bishop Hill Heritage Association, *Bishop Hill, Illinois: Guidebook to Buildings* (Bishop Hill: Bishop Hill Heritage Association, 2010), illus. 6; IDNR, "Bishop Hill," *Illinois.gov*, 2017, accessed June 5, 2018, https://www2.illinois.gov/dnrhistoric/.

3. Bishop Hill Heritage Association, *Bishop Hill, Illinois*, illus. 6; Olov Isaksson and Soren Hallgren, *Bishop Hill: A Utopia on the Prairie* (Stockholm: LT, 1969), 82.

4. Bishop Hill Heritage Association, *Bishop Hill, Illinois*, illus. 1.

5. By 1847, 12,000 yards of linen had been produced; in 1851 "more than 28,000 yards" of linen were woven. Paul Elmen, *Wheat Flour Messiah: Eric Jansson of Bishop Hill* (Carbondale: Southern Illinois University Press, 1997), 126; Isaksson and Hallgren, *Bishop Hill*, 107.

6. Bishop Hill Heritage Association, *Bishop Hill, Illinois*, illus. 17.

7. IHPA and Bishop Hill Heritage Association, *Bishop Hill: Colony of Faith and Freedom* (Bishop Hill: IHPA and Bishop Hill Heritage Assoc., 2003), illus. 16, "Colony Hotel"; Bishop Hill Heritage Association, *Bishop Hill, Illinois*, illus. 14.

8. Isaksson and Hallgren, *Bishop Hill*, 162–63.

9. Isaksson and Hallgren, *Bishop Hill*, 36.

10. For two descriptions of Jansson, see Isaksson and Hallgren, *Bishop Hill*, 32, 33. In addition to the unusual teeth, Jansson's "face was disfigured by a deep scar across the forehead." Michael A. Mikkelsen, *The Bishop Hill Colony: A Religious Communistic Settlement in Henry County, Illinois* (Baltimore: Johns Hopkins Press, 1892), 45.

11. For an extensive account of Eric Jansson's life as well as his conflict with the Swedish clerical establishment, see Elmen, *Wheat Flour Messiah*, chaps. 1–7. The book not only outlines Jansson's singular religious convictions but also reveals that although he was a deeply religious man, he was in many ways an all-too-human person who was challenged by worldly temptations.

12. Linda O'Neill, *History, Memory, and Ethnic Identification: Rediscovering Community in Bishop Hill, Illinois* (DeKalb: LEPS, 1996), 11.

13. Jon Wagner, "Eric Jansson and the Bishop Hill Colony," in *America's Communal Utopias*, ed. Donald E. Pitzer (Chapel Hill: University of North Carolina Press, 1997), 301.

14. Henry L. Kiner, *History of Henry County, Illinois* (Chicago: Pioneer, 1910), 1:632. For more descriptions of the dugouts, see Elmen, *Wheat Flour Messiah*, 125, and Isaksson and Hallgren, *Bishop Hill*, 79.

15. O'Neill, *History, Memory*, 12; Wagner, "Eric Jansson," 301. O'Neill states, "[M]ore than one-third of the four hundred perished before spring" (12). Some of the deaths may have also been due to effects of the lengthy and difficult voyage to Illinois. Isaksson and Hallgren, *Bishop Hill*, 80.

16. Isaksson and Hallgren, *Bishop Hill*, 103.

17. Mark Johnson, "Bishop Hill: An 1854 Description by Charles Wilson," trans. John E. Norton *Journal of Illinois History* 4, no. 1 (2001): 41–54, esp. 48.

18. Elmen, *Wheat Flour Messiah*, 141–43; Wagner, "Eric Jansson," 304–5.

19. Wagner, "Eric Jansson," 306; Elmen, *Wheat Flour Messiah*, 154.

20. Wagner, "Eric Jansson," 306–7; Elmen, *Wheat Flour Messiah*, 160.

21. Mikkelsen, *Bishop Hill Colony*, 48–49.

22. Mikkelsen, *Bishop Hill Colony*, 52–53.

23. Wagner, "Eric Jansson," 309–10.

REUBEN MOORE HOME AND THE THOMAS LINCOLN (SHILOH) CEMETERY

1. Coleman, *Abraham Lincoln*, 199.

2. It is possible that John Hanks was with Lincoln and Chapman during the visit to the grave. There are conflicting accounts of Lincoln's journey and of who was with him at various points during that time. Historian Charles Coleman extensively examined the

visit and concluded that Hanks possibly accompanied Lincoln and Chapman although this remains unclear. Coleman, *Abraham Lincoln*, 191–210.

3. Donald, *Lincoln*, 271. Coleman provides a detailed account of the older Lincoln's death and of Abraham's visit to his grave in his chapter "The Death of Thomas Lincoln," *Abraham Lincoln*, 128–41.

4. Coleman, *Abraham* Lincoln, 203–4.

5. Like many other aspects of the visit, accounts are conflicting about this famous event, and it is more likely that it happened at the Chapman home. Coleman, *Abraham Lincoln*, 206–8.

6. Built in 1877, the church was remodeled in 1921 when the original clapboard siding was faced with brick, a bell tower was constructed, a basement was dug, and stained-glass windows were installed. Robert Martin, "Sacred by Association: The Lincolns and Shiloh Church," *Midwest Open Air Museums Magazine* 29, no. 1 (2008), 13–14.

7. For an explanation of the events leading to the marker's installation, see Coleman, *Abraham Lincoln*, 138–41. According to this account, the money for Thomas Lincoln's gravestone was acquired through voluntary donations and a contribution from Abraham Lincoln's son Robert Todd Lincoln.

8. At this writing, two murals about Lincoln's 1861 trip to Coles County can be found in Charleston. One of these, "Lincoln's Last Journey to Charleston," by Diann Graham, is on a building at Fifth Street and Monroe Avenue. It portrays Lincoln striding along the railroad track toward the Charleston station platform from the caboose of the Terre Haute, Alton, and St. Louis freight train, which he rode from Mattoon to Charleston on January 30. A second mural, "Lincoln Saying Goodbye to Sarah Bush Lincoln," by Glen C. Davies, is on the west wall of the Charleston Area Chamber of Commerce building, 501 Jackson Avenue.

OLD CHICAGO WATER TOWER

1. For detailed explanations of how Chicago's municipal leaders attempted to deal with these issues, see Dominic A. Pacyga, *Chicago: A Biography* (Chicago: University of Chicago Press, 2009), 44–46; Bessie Louise Pierce, *From Town to City, 1848–1871*, vol. 2 of *A History of Chicago*, 3 vols. (Chicago: University of Chicago Press, 1940), 329–34.

2. A fascinating account of this complex and impressive construction project is found in Donald L. Miller, *City of the Century: The Epic of Chicago and the Making of America* (New York: Simon and Schuster, 1996), 126–28.

3. City of Chicago, "Chicago Landmarks," accessed July 2, 2020, https://webapps1 .chicago.gov/landmarksweb/web/listings.htm. See also National Park Service, "Chicago Avenue Water Tower and Pumping Station," Chicago: A National Register of Historic Places

Travel Itinerary, *National Park Service*, accessed June 6, 2018, https://www.nps.gov/nr/travel/chicago/c4.htm.

4. For an account of the widespread use of wood in Chicago construction, see Robert Cromie, *The Great Chicago Fire* (New York: McGraw, 1958), 5–6.

5. Robert P. Howard, *Illinois: A History of the Prairie State* (Grand Rapids, MI: Eerdmans, 1972), 347–48.

6. Among the many explanations for how the barn, which belonged to Patrick and Catherine O'Leary, caught fire, the most common is that in some way a cow in the barn kicked over a kerosene lantern, which set hay and other combustibles ablaze. As many historians who have investigated the Great Chicago Fire have concluded, the actual cause of the calamity remains unknown. See Richard F. Bales, *The Great Chicago Fire and the Myth of Mrs. O'Leary's Cow* (Jefferson, NC: McFarland, 2002), esp. chap. 2; Carl Smith, *Urban Disorder and the Shape of Belief: The Great Chicago Fire, the Haymarket Bomb, and the Model Town of Pullman* (Chicago: University of Chicago Press, 1995), 19–20; and Cromie, *Great Chicago Fire*, 25–31.

7. For explanations of convection whirl, see Miller, *City of the Century*, 152, and Bales, *Great Chicago Fire*, 20.

8. Cromie, *Great Chicago Fire*, 137–38; Smith, *Urban Disorder*, 20–21; Bales, *Great Chicago Fire*, 38–39.

9. Bales, *Great Chicago Fire*, 38–39; Miller, *City of the Century*, 152–53.

10. Cromie, *Great Chicago Fire*, 138–39.

11. Smith, *Urban Disorder*, 20–21; Miller, *City of the Century*, 153; Bales, *Great Chicago Fire*, 39; Cromie, *Great Chicago Fire*,141.

12. Ann Durkin Keating, *Chicagoland: City and Suburbs in the Railroad Age* (Chicago: University of Chicago Press, 2005), 205.

LINCOLN TOMB STATE HISTORIC SITE

1. Lashonda Fitch, "Welcome to Oak Ridge Cemetery, Springfield, Illinois," *City of Springfield, Illinois*, 2020, accessed April 7, 2020, http://www.oakridgecemetery.org/About.aspx.

2. Illinois Historical Preservation Division, "Lincoln Tomb," Illinois Department of Natural Resources, *Illinois.gov*, accessed June 6, 2018, https://www2.illinois.gov/dnrhistoric/.

3. "The Lincoln Tomb: Design & History," *Lincoln Monument Association*, 2018, accessed June 7, 2018, http://lincolntomb.org/.

4. Mary Fogleman, "The National Lincoln Monument Association," *Historic Illinois* 3, no. 4 (1980): 10–11.

5. Jason Emerson, *Giant in the Shadows: The Life of Robert T. Lincoln* (Carbondale: Southern Illinois University Press, 2012), 110–11.

6. Emerson, *Giant in the Shadows*, 111–12.

7. Emerson, *Giant in the Shadows*, 112; Michael Burlingame, *Abraham Lincoln: A Life*, vol. 2, (Baltimore: John Hopkins University Press, 2008), 826–27; Fogleman, "National Lincoln Monument Association," 10–11.

8. Sangamon County Historical Society, "Lincoln Tomb 'Battle of the Gravesite,'" *SangamonLink*, October 25, 2014, accessed June 7, 2018, http://sangamoncountyhistory .org/wp/.

9. Carol Andrews, "The Second Remodeling of Lincoln's Tomb," *Historic Illinois* 5, no. 4 (1982): 8.

10. "Lincoln Tomb: Design & History."

11. Andrews, "Second Remodeling," 8.

12. Emerson, *Giant in the Shadows*, 239–40.

13. Lincoln's son Robert played a key part in stopping the scheme. See Emerson, *Giant in the Shadows*, 189–202.

14. Andrews, "Second Remodeling," 8; "Lincoln Tomb: Design & History."

15. Emerson, *Giant in the Shadows*, 202; Nancy Hill, "The Transformation of the Lincoln Tomb," *Journal of the Abraham Lincoln Association* 27, no. 1 (2006): 48–49, accessed June 6, 2018, http://hdl.handle.net/2027/spo.2629860.0027.105.

16. For a detailed description of the monument's interior, including a listing of the various types of marble and other stone used, see Bess King, comp. and ed., *The Tomb of Abraham Lincoln* (Springfield, IL: Lincoln Souvenir and Gift Shop, 1941), accessed June 6, 2018, https://archive.org/.

17. Whether Stanton said, "Now he belongs to the ages," or "Now he belongs to the angels," has been a point of minor dispute among some historians. For an interesting examination of the question, see Adam Gopnik, "Angels and Ages: Lincoln's Language and Its Legacy," *New Yorker*, May 28, 2007, accessed June 6, 2018, https://www.newyorker. com/.

18. William Manchester, *Portrait of a President* (New York: Macfadden, 1964), 15.

HAYMARKET MARTYRS' MONUMENT

1. For an analysis of the eight-hour movement, especially during its resurgence in 1886, see Bruce C. Nelson, *Beyond the Martyrs: A Social History of Chicago's Anarchists, 1870–1900* (New Brunswick: Rutgers University Press, 1988), 177–84.

2. Miller, *City of the Century*, 474–75; Smith, *Urban Disorder*, 120.

3. Paul Avrich, *The Haymarket Tragedy* (Princeton: Princeton University Press, 1984), 191, 193. Though the meeting was planned to take place in Haymarket Square, it was actually held a short distance away up Des Plaines Street.

4. Douglas O. Linder, "Testimony of Samuel Fielden (August 6–7, 1886)," Famous Trials, UMKC *School of Law*, 1995, accessed June 6, 2018, www.famous-trials.com/haymarket/ 1193-fieldentestimony. See also Avrich, *Haymarket Tragedy*, 206; Smith, *Urban Disorder*, 121; Bessie Louise Pierce, *The Rise of a Modern City, 1871–1893*, vol. 3 of A *History of Chicago* (Chicago: University of Chicago Press, 1957), 279.

5. Douglas O. Linder, "Selected Testimony from the Haymarket Trial (June 21 to August 20, 1886)," Famous Trials, UMKC *School of Law*, 1995, accessed June 11, 2018, www.famous-trials.com/haymarket/1180-selectedtestimony. Various descriptions of the meeting and the events following the bombing can be found at Linder, "Selected Testimony."

6. Smith, *Urban Disorder*, 120–21; Avrich, *Haymarket Tragedy*, 208–10.

7. Sigmund Zeisler, *Reminiscences of the Anarchist Case* (Chicago: Chicago Literary Club, 1927), 15, 18.

8. Schnaubelt was Michael Schwab's brother-in-law and known to the police as a radical anarchist. In many accounts of the Haymarket Affair, he is often identified as the person most suspected of actually throwing the bomb, but this has never been confirmed. Schnaubelt fled the United States shortly after Haymarket and never returned. Avrich, *Haymarket Tragedy*, 234–39.

9. Details of the clemency movement are in Avrich, *Haymarket Tragedy*, chaps. 21 and 22; Pierce, *Rise*, 3:285–86.

10. Avrich, *Haymarket Tragedy*, 392–93; Miller, *City of the Century*, 478–79. Miller states Spies said, "The day will come when our silence will be more powerful than the voices *you are throttling today*"; Avrich writes that Spies shouted, "The time will come when our silence will be more powerful than the voices *you strangle* today." (emphasis added to highlight differences). The words on the base of the monument are, "The time will come when our silence will be more powerful than the voices you are throttling today."

11. Avrich, *Haymarket Tragedy*, 395–97.

12. The number of those present is uncertain. Irving Werstein writes that the number was close to ten thousand. *Strangled Voices: The Story of the Haymarket Affair* (New York: Macmillan, 1970), 109. Avrich states "more than 10,000 people" were in attendance. *Haymarket Tragedy*, 396.

13. "The Monument of the Chicago Martyrs at Waldheim Cemetery," The Dramas of Haymarket: Act V: Raising the Dead: Mourning and Memory, *Chicago History Resources*, 6, accessed May 22, 2019, chicagohistoryresources.org/.

14. The front of the bronze bottom base of the sculpted figure is inscribed on the right with the words "A. Weinart, Sculptor" and on the left "Cast by American Bronze Company, Chicago."

JANE ADDAMS HULL-HOUSE MUSEUM

1. Figures from the US Census Bureau show that Chicago's population in 1890 was 1,099,850, behind New York City's 1,515,301. United States, *Miscellaneous Documents of the House of Representatives for the Fifty-Second Congress 1891–92* (Washington, DC: Government Printing Office, 1895), clxii.

2. In the 1880s one of Chicago's premier neighborhoods for the well-to-do was along Prairie Avenue on the city's South Side. By the early 1890s, however, many of Chicago's wealthy were following the lead of Potter Palmer and moving to the Gold Coast area on the north side of the city. Harold M. Mayer and Richard C. Wade, *Chicago: Growth of a Metropolis* (Chicago: University of Chicago Press, 1969), 252; Miller, *City of the Century*, 413–14.

3. United States, *Miscellaneous Documents*, clxii.

4. Jane Addams, *Twenty Years at Hull House with Autobiographical Notes*, 15th ed. (1910; New York: Macmillan, 1951), 94–95.

5. In chapter 4, "The Snare of Preparation," in *Twenty Years at Hull House*, Jane Addams alludes to her search for a meaningful life. See also Louise W. Knight, *Citizen: Jane Addams and the Struggle for Democracy* (Chicago: University of Chicago Press, 2005), 143.

6. Jennifer L. Bosch, "The Life of Ellen Gates Starr, 1859–1940" (PhD diss., Miami University, Oxford, Ohio, 1990), 18–19, 22–24.

7. Knight, *Citizen*, 77.

8. Addams, *Twenty Years*, 87.

9. Allen F. Davis, *American Heroine: The Life and Legend of Jane Addams with a New Introduction by the Author* (Chicago: Dee, 2000), 53–55.

10. Addams, *Twenty Years*, 92–93.

11. Addams, *Twenty Years*, 93.

12. Mary Lynn McCree, "The First Year of Hull House, 1889–1890, in Letters by Jane Addams and Ellen Gates Starr," *Chicago History Magazine*, n.s., 1, no. 2 (1970): 107–8.

13. McCree, "First Year," 108.

14. Nora Marks, "Two Women's Work: The Misses Addams and Starr Astonish the West Siders," *Chicago Tribune*, May 19, 1890; Mary Lynn McCree Bryan and Allen F. Davis, eds., *100 Years at Hull-House* (Bloomington: Indiana University Press, 1990), 16–19; McCree, "First Year," 108. The ivory and gold color of the walls is described in Marks

and in Ellen Starr to Mary Blaisdell, May 18–May 22, 1890, in Bryan and Davis, *100 Years*, 19–20; the dining room is described in Jane to her sister, September 13, 1889, a portion of which is reprinted in McCree.

15. Jane Addams's explanation of this idea can in part be found in Addams, *Twenty Years*, 91, 452–53. See also Charlene Haddock Seigfried, "Cultural Contradictions: Jane Addams's Struggles with the Life of Art and the Art of Life," in *Feminist Interpretations of Jane Addams*, ed. Maurice Hamington (University Park: Pennsylvania State University Press, 2010), 55–79; Pacyga, *Chicago*, 126–29.

16. Addams describes these early experiences and others in chap. 5, "First Days at Hull House," *Twenty Years*.

17. An analysis of two major changes in Addams's views about these matters is found in Knight, *Citizen*, 354.

18. See Davis, *American Heroine*, 96–97, for the involvement of Chicago's intellectuals with Hull-House. A good account of the criticism leveled against Addams because of her work in the antiwar movement during World War I and the continuing attacks on her during the 1920s are also in Davis, *American Heroine*, chaps. 12, 13, and 14.

19. Davis, *American Heroine*, 282–84; Louise W. Knight, *Jane Addams: Spirit in Action* (New York: Norton, 2010), 255.

20. Bosch, "Life of Ellen Gates Starr," 157–58, 172.

21. This description of Hull-House is based on its appearance when the author visited there on June 4, 2015.

THE ETERNAL INDIAN (OR BLACK HAWK) STATUE

1. June Skinner Sawyers, *Chicago Portraits: Biographies of 250 Famous Chicagoans* (Chicago: Loyola University Press, 1991), 243.

2. Allen Stuart Weller, *Lorado Taft: The Chicago Years*, ed. Robert G. La France and Henry Adams with Stephen P. Thomas (Urbana: University of Illinois Press, 2014), 9, 11–12.

3. For an excellent examination of Taft's work while he lived in Chicago, see Weller, *Lorado Taft*.

4. For a description of the Eagle's Nest camp and the activities there, see Timothy J. Garvey, *Public Sculptor: Lorado Taft and the Beautification of Chicago* (Urbana: University of Illinois Press, 1988), 108–12.

5. Taft had spent time earlier at a northern Indiana camp called Bass Lake. When malaria broke out there in 1897, Taft found a new location at the Eagle's Nest. Weller, *Lorado Taft*, 97–98.

6. Weller, *Lorado Taft*, 97–98. See also Illinois Department of Natural Resources (IDNR), *Lowden State Park* (Springfield: IDNR, 1996).

7. Frank O. Lowden, ed., *Lorado Taft's Indian Statue "Black Hawk": An Account of the Unveiling Ceremonies at Eagle's Nest Bluff, Oregon, Illinois, July the First, Nineteen Hundred and Eleven, Frank O. Lowden Presiding* (Chicago: University of Chicago Press, 1912), 95–96, https://archive.org/details/loradotaftsindia00heck/page/n14/mode/2up.

8. Lowden, *Lorado Taft's Indian Statue*, 15.

9. Lowden, *Lorado Taft's Indian Statue*, 98–99.

10. Weller, *Lorado Taft*, 176; Theodore W. Hild, "A Work of Art in Concrete: The Rock River Colossus," *Historic Illinois* 32, no. 5 (2010): 4.

11. Taft describes his conception of using concrete as a medium in Lowden, *Lorado Taft's Indian Statue*, 96–97.

12. Weller, *Lorado Taft*, 176; Hild, "Work of Art," 4.

13. For accounts of the construction process, see Hild, "Work of Art," 4–5; Richard Carpenter, "The Indian Statue, near Oregon, Illinois," *Journal of the Illinois State Historical Society* 4, no. 4 (1912): 470–71; Michael Sherfy, "A Persistent Removal: Black Hawk, Commemoration, and Historic Sites in Illinois," *Journal of the Illinois State Historical Society* 100, no. 3 (2007): 257–58.

14. Sherfy, "Persistent Removal," 257; Stu Fliege, *Tales & Trails of Illinois* (Urbana: University of Illinois Press, 2002), 170. For a depiction of the statue's unveiling ceremony, see Lowden, *Lorado Taft's Indian Statue*.

15. See IDNR, *Lowden State Park*.

VACHEL LINDSAY HOME

1. "History of the Vachel Lindsay Home," *Vachel Lindsay Association*, 2012, accessed October 3, 2018, www.vachellindsay.org/history.html.

2. Edgar Lee Masters, *Vachel Lindsay: A Poet in America* (New York: Scribner's, 1934), 25; Dennis Camp, "Biography in Brief," *Vachel Lindsay Association*, 2012, accessed September 13, 2018, http://www.vachellindsay.org/bio.html.

3. Dale Kramer, *Chicago Renaissance: The Literary Life in the Midwest 1900–1930* (New York: Appleton-Century, 1966), 86; see also Camp, "Biography in Brief."

4. Eleanor Ruggles, *The West-Going Heart: A Life of Vachel Lindsay* (New York: Norton, 1959), 70.

5. Ruggles, *West-Going Heart*, 73; Kramer, *Chicago Renaissance*, 87.

6. Ruggles, *West-Going Heart*, 93–94; Kramer, *Chicago Renaissance*, 90–92.

7. Marc Chenetier, ed., *The Letters of Vachel Lindsay* (New York: Franklin, 1979), xxiv–xxv.

8. Kramer, *Chicago Renaissance*, 93; Joseph G. Kronick, "Vachel Lindsay's Life," *Modern American Poetry*, accessed April 12, 2020, http://maps-legacy.org/poets/g_l/lindsay/lindsay_life.htm.

9. "Vachel Lindsay," *Poetry Foundation*, accessed October 5, 2018, https://www.poetry foundation.org/poets/vachel-lindsay.

10. "Vachel Lindsay"; Camp, "Biography in Brief."

11. Chenetier, *Letters*, xix.

12. Kronick, "Vachel Lindsay's Life."

13. Kronick, "Vachel Lindsay's Life"; Kramer, *Chicago Renaissance*, 231.

14. Blair Whitney, "The Garden of Illinois," in *The Vision of This Land: Studies of Vachel Lindsay, Edgar Lee Masters, and Carl Sandburg*, ed. John E. Hallwas and Dennis J. Reader (Macomb: Western Illinois University, 1976), 17.

15. Whitney, "Garden of Illinois," 17.

16. For an examination of Lindsay's views toward the Midwest and rural life, in general, see Marc Chenetier, "Vachel Lindsay's American Mythocracy and Some Unpublished Sources," in Hallwas and Reader, *Vision of This Land*, 42–54.

17. Kronick, "Vachel Lindsay's Life."

18. Vachel Lindsay, *The Congo and Other Poems* (New York: Macmillan, 1933), 11n.

19. An analysis of this criticism can be found in Mark W. Van Wienen, "Vachel Lindsay [1879–1931]: Lindsay and Racism," *Modern American Poetry*, accessed April 12, 2020, http://maps-legacy.org/poets/g_l/lindsay/racism.htm.

20. Kronick, "Vachel Lindsay's Life"; Masters, *Vachel Lindsay*, 333.

21. Ruggles, *West-Going Heart*, 307.

22. Ruggles, *West-Going Heart*, 313.

23. Masters, *Vachel Lindsay*, 339–40; Ruggles, *West-Going Heart*, 322–23; Kronick, "Vachel Lindsay's Life." The time Lindsay spent at Gulf Park College following his surgery appears to be when he began to experience increasingly serious emotional struggles.

24. According to Masters, Lindsay intended to visit Spokane only for the summer but later changed his mind and remained in the city. Masters, *Vachel Lindsay*, 340. Ruggles states that Lindsay chose to reside in Spokane's Davenport Hotel because of its appealing ambience, which "had the candlelit atmosphere of an old Virginia tavern," and because he was given a special rate by the hotel. Ruggles provides accounts of Lindsay's association with Spokane's artists and writers and of the rather unusual way Lindsay became engaged to and married Elizabeth. Ruggles, *West-Going Heart*, 325–26, 329–30, 340–42.

25. Kramer, *Chicago Renaissance*, 344.

26. Ruggles, *West-Going Heart*, 394–95.

27. Ruggles, *West-Going Heart*, 424; Kramer, *Chicago Renaissance*, 344.

28. Ruggles, *West-Going Heart*, 414.

29. Ruggles, *West-Going Heart*, 430; Masters, *Vachel Lindsay*, 360–61.

30. Illinois Historic Preservation Division, "Vachel Lindsay Home," Illinois Department of Natural Resources, *Illinois.gov*, accessed October 18, 2018, https://www2.illinois.gov/ dnrhistoric/Experience/Sites/Central/pages/vachel-lindsay.aspx.

SOUTH SIDE COMMUNITY ART CENTER

1. City of Chicago, "Chicago Landmarks: South Side Community Art Center," *City of Chicago*, 2010, accessed November 30, 2018, http://webapps1.chicago.gov/landmarks web/web/listings.htm. See also Tom Pfister, "African American Art Center in Chicago Achieves National Register Status," *Forbes*, September 27, 2018, accessed November 30, 2018, https://www.forbes.com/. Anne Meis Knupfer describes the Chicago Black Renaissance as the time between 1930 and 1960 that saw "a revitalization of the black expressive arts, especially music, art, literature, theater, and dance." Knupfer demonstrates that women played a significant part in this revitalization. Anne Meis Knupfer, *The Chicago Black Renaissance and Women's Activism* (Urbana: University of Illinois Press, 2006), 1.

2. Bill V. Mullen, *Popular Fronts: Chicago and African-American Cultural Politics, 1935–46* (Urbana: University of Illinois Press, 1999), 77; Erin P. Cohn, *Art Fronts: Visual Culture and Race Politics in Mid-Twentieth-Century United States* (PhD diss., University of Pennsylvania, 2010), 104, https://repository.upenn.edu/edissertations/156.

3. Cohn, *Art Fronts*, 104; Jeffrey C. Stewart, *The New Negro: The Life of Alain Locke* (New York: Oxford University Press, 2018), 806–7.

4. Mullen, *Popular Fronts*, 77; D. A. Hardy, "And Thus We Shall Survive: The Perseverance of the South Side Community Art Center as a Counter-Narrative, 1938–1959," in *The Palgrave Handbook of Race and the Arts in Education*, ed. Amelia M. Krache, Ruben Gaztambide-Fernandez, and B. Stephen Carpenter II (New York: Palgrave, 2018), 124.

5. "About," *South Side Community Art Center*, accessed December 1, 2018, https://sscartcenter.org/.

6. Roger G. Kennedy and David Larkin, *When Art Worked* (New York: Rizzoli, 2009), 160; Don Adams and Arlene Goldbard, "New Deal Cultural Programs: Experiments in Cultural Democracy," *Institute for Cultural Democracy*, 1995, accessed December 1, 2018, http://www.wwcd.org/policy/US/newdeal.html.

7. William F. McDonald, *Federal Relief Administration and the Arts* (Columbus: Ohio State University Press, 1969), 464–65.

8. Cohn, *Art Fronts*, 106–7; Hardy, "And Thus We Shall Survive," 125; Stewart, *New Negro*, 807. Mullen explains what he calls "conflicting communal lore" concerning the center's origin. Margaret Burroughs recalled, "Thorpe and Pollack came directly to a small group of 'leading' black citizens, including poor, young artists like herself, to discuss forming the art center." However, James Graff, "in a commemorative fiftieth anniversary program," stated in 1991 that Pollack asked Metz Lochard, Chicago *Defender* editor, to set up a meeting with those who could assist with establishing the center and that Pollack, Pauline Kligh Reed, and others met through Lochard. Mullen, *Popular Fronts*, 81–82.

9. "South Side Community Art Center," National Treasures, *National Trust for Historic Preservation*, accessed December 1, 2018, https://savingplaces.org/.

10. The center is frequently misidentified as having been the home of Chicago White Sox owner Charles Comiskey. Designed by the well-known Chicago architect L. Gustave Hallberg, the building was actually the residence of George Seaverns Jr. and his family. A plaque in the center states that the building was once Seaverns's home, as does information from the City of Chicago's Commission on Chicago Landmarks.

11. Hardy, "And Thus We Shall Survive," 126.

12. "South Side Community Art Center."

13. Hardy, "And Thus We Shall Survive," 131. Cohn outlines the connections of some artists at the SSCAC, such as Margaret Burroughs and Charles White, to other Depression-era leftist members of the art community who had hoped "to link the activities of the Center to larger efforts for social justice for African Americans." Burroughs, who remained an active poet, artist, and educator throughout her life, later founded Chicago's DuSable Museum of African American History. She was appointed by President Jimmy Carter to the National Commission on African American History and Culture, and in 2010, following her death at age ninety-five, she was lauded by President Barack Obama for her achievements in the arts and education. Cohn, *Art Fronts*, 111–12.

14. "About," *South Side Community Art Center*.

Bibliography

222

Adams, Don, and Arlene Goldbard. "New Deal Cultural Programs: Experiments in Cultural Democracy." Webster's World of Cultural Democracy. *Institute for Cultural Democracy*, 1995. Accessed December 1, 2018. http://www.wwcd.org/policy/US/newdeal.html.

Addams, Jane. *Twenty Years at Hull House with Autobiographical Notes.* 1910. 15th ed. New York: Macmillan, 1951.

Alvord, Clarence Walworth. *The Illinois Country, 1673–1818.* Vol. 1 of *The Centennial History of Illinois.* Springfield: Illinois Centennial Commission, 1920.

Andrews, Carol. "The Second Remodeling of Lincoln's Tomb." *Historic Illinois* 5, no. 4 (1982): 8–10, 15.

Apple River Fort, Elizabeth, Illinois. Elizabeth: Apple River Fort Historic Foundation, 2010.

Avrich, Paul. *The Haymarket Tragedy.* Princeton: Princeton University Press, 1984.

Bakeless, John. *Background to Glory: The Life of George Rogers Clark.* Lincoln: University of Nebraska Press, 1992.

Bales, Richard F. *The Great Chicago Fire and the Myth of Mrs. O'Leary's Cow.* Jefferson, NC: McFarland, 2002.

Balesi, Charles J. *The Time of the French in the Heart of North America, 1673–1818.* Chicago: Alliance Française, 1992.

Baringer, William E. *Lincoln's Vandalia: A Pioneer Portrait.* New Brunswick: Rutgers University Press, 1949.

Bigham, Daniel E. *Towns and Villages of the Lower Ohio.* Lexington: University Press of Kentucky, 1998.

Biles, Roger. *Illinois: A History of the Land and Its People.* DeKalb: Northern Illinois University Press, 2005.

Bishop Hill Heritage Association. *Bishop Hill, Illinois: Guidebook to Buildings.* Bishop Hill: Bishop Hill Heritage Association, 2010.

Black Hawk. *Black Hawk: An Autobiography.* Edited by Donald Jackson. Urbana: University of Illinois Press, 1964.

Blackmore, Jacqueline Yvonne. "African-Americans and Race Relations in Gallatin County, Illinois from the Eighteenth Century to 1870." PhD diss., Northern Illinois University, 1996.

Blanchett, David. "Reconstructed Apple River Fort Now a State Historic Site." *Historic Illinois* 23, no. 5 (2001): 13.

Bosch, Jennifer L. "The Life of Ellen Gates Starr, 1859–1940." PhD diss., Miami University, Oxford, Ohio, 1990.

Bowman, Matthew. *The Mormon People: The Making of an American Faith.* New York: Random, 2012.

Brasseaux, Carl A. "The Image of La Salle in North American Historiography." In Galloway, *La Salle*, 3–10.

Brodie, Fawn M. *No Man Knows My History: The Life of Joseph Smith the Mormon Prophet.* New York: Knopf, 1946.

Brooks-Miller, C. Scott. "Shawneetown and Its Magnificent Bank." *Historic Illinois* 4, no. 2 (1979): 1–3, 15.

Brown, Margaret. "Uncovering the Mystery of the Three Forts de Chartres." *Illinois Magazine* 16, no. 9 (1977): 23–28.

Bruner, Edward M. "Abraham Lincoln as Authentic Reproduction: A Critique of Post-Modernism." *American Anthropologist*, n.s., 96, no. 2 (1994): 397–415.

Bryan, Mary Lynn McCree, and Allen F. Davis, eds. *100 Years at Hull-House.* Bloomington: Indiana University Press, 1990.

Buck, Solon J. *Illinois in 1818.* 2nd ed. Urbana: University of Illinois Press, 1967.

Burlingame, Michael. *Abraham Lincoln: A Life.* 2 Vols. Baltimore: Johns Hopkins University Press, 2008.

Burtschi, Mary. *Vandalia: Wilderness Capital of Lincoln's Land.* Decatur, IL: Huston-Patterson, 1963.

Byers, A. Martin. *Cahokia: A World Renewal Cult Heterarchy.* Gainesville: University Press of Florida, 2006.

Caldwell, Norman W. "Fort Massac: The American Frontier Post 1778–1805." *Journal of the Illinois State Historical Society* 43, no. 4 (1950): 265–81.

———. "Fort Massac since 1805." *Journal of the Illinois State Historical Society* 44, no. 1 (1951): 47–60.

Callary, Edward. *Place Names of Illinois.* Urbana: University of Illinois Press, 2009.

Camp, Dennis. "Biography in Brief." *Vachel Lindsay Association*, 2012. Accessed September 13, 2018. http://www.vachellindsay.org/bio.html.

Campbell, William E. "Shawneetown, Illinois: The Early Years." Master's thesis, Eastern Illinois University, 1965.

Carpenter, Richard. "The Indian Statue, near Oregon, Illinois." *Journal of the Illinois State Historical Society* 4, no. 4 (1912): 469–72.

Chenetier, Marc, ed. *The Letters of Vachel Lindsay*. New York: Franklin, 1979.

———. "Vachel Lindsay's American Mythocracy and Some Unpublished Sources." In *The Vision of This Land*, edited by John E. Hallwas and Dennis Reader, 42–54. Macomb: Western Illinois University, 1976.

Chicago Historical Society and Northwestern University. "The Dramas of Haymarket." Accessed May 22, 2019. http://www.chicagohistoryresources.org/dramas/.

Church of Jesus Christ of Latter-day Saints. *Church History in the Fulness of Times: The History of the Church of Jesus Christ of Latter-day Saints*. Salt Lake City, UT: Church of Jesus Christ of Latter-day Saints, 1992.

———. "Nauvoo Temple Sunstones." Church History. *Church of Jesus Christ of Latter-day Saints*, Accessed June 7, 2018. https://history.lds.org/article/nauvoo-temple-sunstones?lang=eng.

———."Nauvoo, Illinois Temple." Church Newsroom. *Church of Jesus Christ of Latter-day Saints*. Accessed June 6, 2018. www.mormonnewsroom.org/article/nauvoo-illinois-temple.

City of Chicago. "Chicago Landmarks." Accessed November 30, 2018. http://webapps1.chicago.gov/landmarksweb/web/listings.htm.

Cohn, Erin P. "Art Fronts: Visual Culture and Race Politics in Mid-Twentieth Century United States." PhD diss., University of Pennsylvania, 2010. https://repository.upenn.edu/edissertations/156.

Coleman, Charles H. *Abraham Lincoln and Coles County, Illinois*. New Brunswick, NJ: Scarecrow, 1955.

Conrad, Glenn R. "Reluctant Imperialist: France in North America." In Galloway, *La Salle*, 93–105.

Cooke, James J. "France, the New World, and Colonial Expansion." In Galloway, *La Salle*, 81–92.

Cornelius, Janet. *A History of Constitution Making in Illinois*. Urbana: University of Illinois Institute of Government and Public Affairs, 1969.

Cromie, Robert. *The Great Chicago Fire*. New York: McGraw-Hill, 1958.

Curry, Andrew. "Ancient Migration: Coming to America." *Nature* 485, May 3, 2012, 31. https://www.nature.com/.

Davis, Allen F. *American Heroine: The Life and Legend of Jane Addams with a New Introduction by the Author*. Chicago: Dee, 2000.

Davis, James E. *Frontier Illinois*. Bloomington: Indiana University Press, 1998.

De Vorsey, Louis, Jr. "The Impact of the La Salle Expedition of 1682 on European Cartography." In Galloway, *La Salle*, 60–78.

Donald, David Herbert. *Lincoln*. New York: Simon and Schuster, 1995.

Downey, Martha Jane. "The Vandalia Statehouse." *Historic Illinois* 2, no. 5 (1980): 1–3.

Drury, John. *Old Illinois Houses*. Edited by Jay Monaghan. Springfield: Illinois State Historical Society, 1948.

Duensing, Darrell. "'A Splendid Ruin': Fort de Chartres as a Historic Site." *Historic Illinois* 3, no. 1 (1980): 6.

Eby, Cecil. "That Disgraceful Affair," the Black Hawk War. New York: Norton, 1973.

Elmen, Paul. *Wheat Flour Messiah: Eric Jansson of Bishop Hill*. Carbondale: Southern Illinois University Press, 1997.

Emerson, Jason. *Giant in the Shadows: The Life of Robert T. Lincoln*. Carbondale: Southern Illinois University Press, 2012.

Emerson, Thomas E. "An Introduction to Cahokia 2002: Diversity, Complexity, and History." *Midcontinental Journal of Archaeology* 27, no. 2 (2002): 127–48. JSTOR.

Emerson, Thomas E., Kristin M. Hedman, and Eve A. Hargrave. "Paradigms Lost: Reconfiguring Cahokia's Mound 72 Beaded Burial." *American Antiquity* 81, no. 3 (2016): 405–25.

Farnsworth, Kenneth B., Thomas E. Emerson, and Rebecca Miller Glenn. "Patterns of Late Woodland/Mississippian Interaction in the Lower Illinois Valley Drainage: A View from Starr Village." In *Cahokia and the Hinterlands: Middle Mississippian Cultures of the Midwest*, edited by Thomas E. Emerson and R. Barry Lewis, 83–118. Urbana: University of Illinois Press, 1991.

Fellows, Paul. "Fort Massac." *Historic Illinois* 4, no. 1 (1981): 1–3, 13.

Ferguson, Gillum. *Illinois in the War of 1812*. Urbana: University of Illinois Press, 2012.

Fitch, Lashonda. "Welcome to Oak Ridge Cemetery, Springfield, Illinois." *City of Springfield, Illinois*, 2020. Accessed April 7, 2020. http://www.oakridgecemetery.org/About.aspx.

Flanders, Robert Bruce. *Nauvoo: Kingdom on the Mississippi*. Urbana: University of Illinois Press, 1965.

Fliege, Stu. *Tales and Trails of Illinois*. Urbana: University of Illinois Press, 2002.

Fogleman, Mary. "The National Lincoln Monument Association." *Historic Illinois* 3, no. 4 (1980): 10–11, 15.

Fortier, John B. "New Light on Fort Massac." In *Frenchmen and French Ways in the Mississippi Valley*, edited by John Francis McDermott, 57–71. Urbana: University of Illinois Press, 1969.

Galloway, Patricia K. *La Salle and His Legacy: Frenchmen and Indians in the Lower Mississippi Valley*. Jackson: University Press of Mississippi, 1982.

Gannett, Lewis. "The Ann Rutledge Story: Case Closed?" *Journal of the Abraham Lincoln Association* 31, no. 2 (2010): 21–60. Accessed June 24, 2017. http://hdl.handle.net/2027/spo.2629860.0031.205.

Garvey, Timothy J. *Public Sculptor: Lorado Taft and the Beautification of Chicago*. Urbana: University of Illinois Press, 1988.

Gericke, Bradley T. "To the Distant Country: The Stirling Expedition to Fort de Chartres, 1765." *Journal of the Illinois Historical Society* 2, no. 2 (1999): 78–100.

Goodell, J. H. "Some Evidences of the Route from the Lakes to the Gulf." *Journal of the Illinois State Historical Society* 5, no. 2 (1912): 212–27.

Gopnik, Adam. "Angels and Ages: Lincoln's Language and Its Legacy." *New Yorker*, May 28, 2007. Accessed June 6, 2018. https://www.newyorker.com/.

Hall, James. "Shawneetown and the Salines." In *Prairie State: Impressions of Illinois, 1673–1967, by Travelers and Other Observers*, edited by Paul M. Angle, 88–93. Chicago: University of Chicago Press, 1968.

Hall, Robert L. "The Archaeology of La Salle's Fort St. Louis on Starved Rock and the Problem of the Newell Fort." In *French Colonial Archaeology: The Illinois Country and the Western Great Lakes*, edited by John A. Walthall, 14–28. Urbana: University of Illinois Press, 1991.

———. "Cahokia Identity and Interaction Models of Cahokia Mississippian." In *Cahokia and the Hinterlands: Middle Mississippian Cultures of the Midwest*, edited by Thomas E. Emerson and R. Barry Lewis, 3–34. Urbana: University of Illinois Press, 1991.

Hallwas, John E., and Roger D. Launius. *Cultures in Conflict: A Documentary History of the Mormon War in Illinois*. Logan: Utah State University Press, 1995.

Hardy, D. A. "And Thus We Shall Survive: The Perseverance of the South Side Community Art Center as a Counter-Narrative, 1938–1959." In *The Palgrave Handbook of Race and the Arts in Education*, edited by Amelia M. Krache, Ruben Gaztambide-Fernandez, and B. Stephen Carpenter II, 119–35. New York: Palgrave, 2018.

Herndon, William H., and Jesse W. Weik. *Herndon's Life of Lincoln: The History and Personal Recollections of Abraham Lincoln as Originally Written by William H. Herndon and Jesse Weik, with Introduction and Notes by Paul M. Angle*. New introduction by Henry Steele Commager. New York: Da Capo, 1983.

Hild, Theodore W. "A Work of Art in Concrete: The Rock River Colossus." *Historic Illinois* 32, no. 5 (2010): 3–6.

Hill, Nancy. "The Transformation of the Lincoln Tomb." *Journal of the Abraham Lincoln Association* 27, no. 1 (2006): 39–56. Accessed June 6, 2018. http://hdl.handle.net/2027/spo.2629860.0027.105.

"History of the Vachel Lindsay Home." *Vachel Lindsay Association*. Accessed October 3, 2018. www.vachellindsay.org/history.html.

Howard, Robert P. *Illinois: A History of the Prairie State*. Grand Rapids, MI: Eerdmans, 1972.

Illinois Department of Conservation. *Lincoln Log Cabin Historic Site*. Land and Historic Sites. Springfield: Illinois Department of Conservation, 1976.

Illinois Department of Natural Resources (IDNR). "About Fort Massac State Park."
     Accessed June 5, 2018. https://www2.illinois.gov/dnr/Parks/About/Pages/
     FortMassac.aspx.
———. "Bishop Hill." *Illinois.gov.* Accessed June 5, 2018. https://www2.illinois.gov/dnr
     historic/.
———. *Fort Massac State Park.* Springfield: IDNR, 2015.
———. *Lowden State Park.* Springfield: IDNR, 1996.
———. *Starved Rock State Park.* Springfield: IDNR, 2006.
Illinois Department of Public Works and Buildings. *New Salem: A Memorial to Abraham
     Lincoln.* 2nd ed. Springfield: Illinois Department of Public Works and Buildings, 1934.
Illinois Historic Preservation Agency (IHPA). *Fort de Chartres State Historic Site.*
     Springfield: IHPA, 1996.
———. *Lincoln Log Cabin State Historic Site.* Springfield: IHPA, 1990.
———. *Lincoln's New Salem State Historic Site.* Springfield: IHPA, n.d.
———. *Vandalia State House State Historic Site.* Springfield: IHPA, 2006.
Illinois Historic Preservation Agency (IHPA) and Bishop Hill Heritage Association. *Bishop
     Hill: Colony of Faith and Freedom.* Bishop Hill: IHPA and Bishop Hill Heritage Assoc.,
     2003.
Illinois Historic Preservation Division. "Fort de Chartres State Historic Site." Accessed
     June 5, 2018. www.fortdechartres.us/.
———. "Lincoln Tomb." *Illinois.gov.* Accessed June 6, 2018. https://www2.illinois.gov/
     dnrhistoric/.
———. "The Vachel Lindsay Home." *Illinois.gov.* Accessed October 18, 2018. https://www2
     .illinois.gov/dnrhistoric/Experience/Sites/Central/pages/vachel-lindsay.aspx.
Illinois Secretary of State. *Illinois Blue Book, 2017–2018.* Springfield: State of Illinois, 2017.
Isaksson, Olov, and Soren Hallgren. *Bishop Hill: A Utopia on the Prairie.* Stockholm: LT,
     1969.
Iseminger, William. *Cahokia Mounds: America's First City.* Charleston, SC: History Press,
     2010.
Jacks, L. V. *La Salle.* New York: Scribner's, 1931.
Johnson, Mark. "Bishop Hill: An 1854 Description by Charles Wilson." Translated by John
     E. Norton. *Journal of Illinois History* 4, no. 1 (2001): 41–54.
Jung, Patrick J. *The Black Hawk War of 1832.* Norman: University of Oklahoma Press, 2007.
———. "Fire along the Mos-co-ho-co-y-nak: The Battle of Apple River Fort during the
     Black Hawk War, 1832." Unpublished manuscript, Apple River Fort Historic Site,
     Elizabeth, Illinois.
Keating, Ann Durkin. *Chicagoland: City and Suburbs in the Railroad Age.* Chicago:
     University of Chicago Press, 2005.

Keene, David. "Fort de Chartres: Archaeology in the Illinois Country." In *French Colonial Archaeology: The Illinois Country and the Western Great Lakes*, edited by John A. Walthall, 29–41. Urbana: University of Illinois Press, 1991.

Kennedy, Roger G., and David Larkin. *When Art Worked*. New York: Rizzoli, 2009.

Kiner, Henry L. *History of Henry County, Illinois*. Vol. 1. Chicago: Pioneer, 1910.

King, Bess, comp. and ed. *The Tomb of Abraham Lincoln*. Springfield, IL: Lincoln Souvenir and Gift Shop, 1941. Internet Archive, 2012. Accessed June 6, 2018. https://archive.org/.

Knight, Louise W. *Citizen: Jane Addams and the Struggle for Democracy*. Chicago: University of Chicago Press, 2005.

———. *Jane Addams: Spirit in Action*. New York: Norton, 2010.

Knupfer, Anne Meis. *The Chicago Black Renaissance and Women's Activism*. Urbana: University of Illinois Press, 2006.

Kramer, Dale. *Chicago Renaissance: The Literary Life in the Midwest, 1900–1930*. New York: Appleton-Century, 1966.

Kronick, Joseph G. "Vachel Lindsay's Life." *Modern American Poetry*. Accessed April 12, 2020. http://maps-legacy.org/poets/g_l/lindsay/lindsay_life.htm.

Kyvig, David A., and Myron A. Marty. *Nearby History: Exploring the Past around You*. 2nd ed. Walnut Creek, CA: AltaMira, 2000.

Larwill, Joseph. "Journal of a Trip to Illinois—1823." *Journal of the Illinois State Historical Society* 34, no. 1 (1941): 136.

Lawler, Lucille. *A Walking Tour of Historic Old Shawneetown*. Southern Illinois Tourism Council and Illinois Humanities Council, 1991.

Leonard, Glen M. *Nauvoo: A Place of Peace, a People of Promise*. Salt Lake City, UT: Deseret, 2002.

Leonard, Stephen, and Melinda F. Kwedar. *The Great Migration: Transportation and Settlement in Illinois, 1800–1850*. Springfield: Illinois State Historical Society, 1989.

Lincoln, Abraham. *Great Speeches*. With historical notes by John Grafton. New York: Dover, 1991.

Lincoln Log Cabin State Historic Site. Lerna, IL: Mattoon and Charleston Tourism Boards and the Lincoln Log Cabin Foundation, n.d.

"Lincoln Tomb: Design & History, The." *Lincoln Monument Association*. Accessed June 7, 2018. http://lincolntomb.org/.

Linder, Douglas O. "Haymarket Trial (1886)." *Famous Trials, UMKC School of Law*, 1995. Accessed June 6, 2018. www.famous-trials.com/haymarket.

Lindsay, Vachel. *The Congo and Other Poems*. New York: Macmillan, 1933.

Lopinot, Neal H., Timothy Schilling, Gayle J. Fritz, and John E. Kelly. "Implications of Plant Remains from the East Face of Monks Mound." *Midcontinental Journal of Archeology* 40, no. 3 (2015): 209–30.

Lowden, Frank O., ed. *Lorado Taft's Indian Statue "Black Hawk": An Account of the Unveiling Ceremonies at Eagle's Nest Bluff, Oregon, Illinois, July the First, Nineteen Hundred and Eleven, Frank O. Lowden Presiding.* Chicago: University of Chicago Press, 1912. https://archive.org/details/loradotaftsindia00heck/page/n14/mode/2up.

Lyles, Stella Pendleton. "Shawneetown." *Journal of the Illinois State Historical Society* 22, no. 1 (1929): 164–91.

Manchester, William. *Portrait of a President.* New York: Macfadden, 1964.

Martin, Robert. "Sacred by Association: The Lincolns and Shiloh Church." Midwest Open Air Museums Magazine 29, no. 1 (2008), 10–18.

Masters, Edgar Lee. *Vachel Lindsay: A Poet in America.* New York: Scribner's, 1934.

Mayer, Harold M., and Richard C. Wade. *Chicago: Growth of a Metropolis.* Chicago: University of Chicago Press, 1969.

McCree, Mary Lynn. "The First Year of Hull House, 1889–1890, in Letters by Jane Addams and Ellen Gates Starr." *Chicago History Magazine,* n.s., 1, no. 2 (1970): 101–4, 106–10, 112–14.

McDonald, William F. *Federal Relief Administration and the Arts.* Columbus: Ohio State University Press, 1969.

Meyer, Douglas K. *Making the Heartland Quilt: A Geographical History of Settlement and Migration in Early Nineteenth-Century Illinois.* Carbondale: Southern Illinois University Press, 2000.

Mikkelsen, Michael A. *The Bishop Hill Colony: A Religious Communistic Settlement in Henry County, Illinois.* Baltimore: Johns Hopkins Press, 1892.

Miller, Donald L. *City of the Century: The Epic of Chicago and the Making of America.* New York: Simon and Schuster, 1996.

Milner, George. *The Cahokia Chiefdom: The Archaeology of a Mississippian Society.* Washington, DC: Smithsonian, 1998.

Mink, Claudia Gellman. *Cahokia: City of the Sun.* Edited by William Iseminger. Rev. ed. Collinsville, IL: Cahokia Mounds Museum Society, 1999.

"Monument of the Chicago Martyrs at Waldheim Cemetery, The." The Dramas of Haymarket: Act V: Raising the Dead: Mourning and Memory. *Chicago History Resources.* Accessed May 22, 2019. chicagohistoryresources.org/.

Muhlstein, Anka. *La Salle: Explorer of the North American Frontier.* Translated by Willard Wood. New York: Arcade, 1994.

Mullen, Bill V. *Popular Fronts: Chicago and African American Cultural Politics, 1935–46.* Urbana: University of Illinois Press, 1999.

Murphy, Edmund Robert. *Henry de Tonty: Fur Trader of the Mississippi.* Baltimore: Johns Hopkins Press, 1941.

National Park Service. "Chicago Avenue Water Tower and Pumping Station." Chicago: A National Register of Historic Places Travel Itinerary. *National Park Service.* Accessed June 6, 2018. https://www.nps.gov/nr/travel/chicago/c4.htm.

———. "Preparing an Expedition." *National Park Service.* Accessed March 26, 2020. https://www.nps.gov/articles/preparing-an-expedition.htm.

———. Registration form, Apple River Fort Site, continuation sheet, sec. 7, 2–3. National Register of Historic Places, National Park Service, US Department of the Interior, October 2, 1997. *State of Illinois.* Accessed June 8, 2018. http://gis.hpa.state.il.us/PDFs/201095.pdf.

National Society Daughters of the American Colonists. "Gateway at Fort de Chartres." NSDAC. Accessed June 6, 2018. http://nsdac.org/work-of-the-society/historical/markers/fort-de-chartres/.

Nelson, Bruce C. *Beyond the Martyrs: A Social History of Chicago's Anarchists, 1870–1900.* New Brunswick: Rutgers University Press, 1988.

Nelson, Larry. "Clark's Kaskaskia Expedition, June 24–July 4, 1778." In *The Life of George Rogers Clark, 1752–1818: Triumphs and Tragedies,* edited by Kenneth C. Carstens and Nancy Son Carstens, 18–31. Contributions in American History 203, edited by Jon L. Wakelyn. Westport, CT: Praeger, 2004.

O'Dea, Thomas F. *The Mormons.* Chicago: University of Chicago Press, 1957.

O'Neill, Linda. *History, Memory, and Ethnic Identification: Rediscovering Community in Bishop Hill, Illinois.* DeKalb: LEPS, 1996.

Pacyga, Dominic A. *Chicago: A Biography.* Chicago: University of Chicago Press, 2009.

Pauketat, Timothy R. *An Archeology of the Cosmos: Rethinking Agency and Religion in Ancient America.* New York: Routledge, 2013.

———. *Cahokia: Ancient America's Great City on the Mississippi.* New York: Viking, 2009.

Pauketat, Timothy R., and Thomas E. Emerson, eds. *Cahokia: Domination and Ideology in the Mississippian World.* Lincoln: University of Nebraska Press, 1997.

Pfister, Tom. "African American Art Center in Chicago Achieves National Register Status." *Forbes,* September 27, 2018. Accessed November 30, 2018. https://www.forbes.com/.

Pierce, Bessie Louise. *A History of Chicago.* 3 vols. Chicago: University of Chicago Press, 1937–57.

Price, Anna. "French Outpost on the Mississippi." *Historic Illinois* 3, no. 1 (1980): 1–4.

Ruggles, Eleanor. *The West-Going Heart: A Life of Vachel Lindsay.* New York: Norton, 1959.

Russell, Herbert K. *The State of Southern Illinois: An Illustrated History.* Carbondale: Southern Illinois University Press, 2012.

Sangamon County Historical Society. "Lincoln Tomb: 'Battle of the Gravesite.'" *Sangamon Link,* October 25, 2014. Accessed June 7, 2018. http://sangamoncountyhistory.org/wp/.

Sauer, Carl O., Gilbert H. Cady, and Henry C. Cowles. *Starved Rock and Its Environs*. Geographic Society of Chicago, 6. Chicago: University of Chicago Press, 1918.

Sawyers, June Skinner. *Chicago Portraits: Biographies of 250 Famous Chicagoans*. Chicago: Loyola University Press, 1991.

Schwartz, Barry. *Abraham Lincoln in the Post-Heroic Era: History and Memory in Late Twentieth-Century America*. Chicago: University of Chicago Press, 2008.

Seigfried, Charlene Haddock. "Cultural Contradictions: Jane Addams's Struggles with the Life of Art and the Art of Life." In *Feminist Interpretations of Jane Addams*, edited by Maurice Hamington, 55–79. University Park: Pennsylvania State University Press, 2010.

Severin, Timothy. *Explorers of the Mississippi*. New York: Knopf, 1968.

Shea, John Gilmary. *Discovery and Exploration of the Mississippi Valley: With the Original Narratives of Marquette, Allouez, Membre, Hennepin, and Anastase Douay*. Clinton Hall, NJ: Redfield, 1852.

Sherfy, Michael. "A Persistent Removal: Black Hawk, Commemoration, and Historic Sites in Illinois." *Journal of the Illinois State Historical Society* 100, no. 3 (2007): 240–67.

Simon, John Y. "Abraham Lincoln and Ann Rutledge." *Journal of the Abraham Lincoln Association* 11, no. 1 (1990): 13–33. *University of Michigan Library*. Accessed June 7, 2018. http://hdl.handle.net/2027/spo.2629860.0011.104.

Simon, Paul. *Lincoln's Preparation for Greatness: The Illinois Legislative Years*. Norman: University of Oklahoma Press, 1965.

Skele, Mikels. *The Great Knob: Interpretations of Monks Mound*. Studies in Illinois Archaeology, 4. Springfield: Illinois Historic Preservation Agency, 1988.

Smith, Carl. *Urban Disorder and the Shape of Belief: The Great Chicago Fire, the Haymarket Bomb, and the Model Town of Pullman*. Chicago: University of Chicago Press, 1995.

Snyder, John Francis. "The Armament of Fort Chartres." *Transactions of the Illinois State Historical Society for the Year 1906*, 11 (January 1906): 219–31.

———. *Captain John Baptiste Saucier at Fort Chartres in the Illinois, 1751–1763*. Rev. ed. Springfield: Illinois State Historical Society, 1919. HathiTrust e-book. Accessed June 7, 2018. http://babel.hathitrust.org/.

Society of Colonial Wars in the State of Illinois. *Welcome to Fort de Chartres State Historic Site*. Kenilworth: Society of Colonial Wars in the State of Illinois, n.d.

"South Side Community Art Center." National Treasures. *National Trust for Historic Preservation*. Accessed December 1, 2018. https://savingplaces.org/places/.

South Side Community Art Center website. Accessed December 1, 2018. www.sscart center.org/.

Steck, Francis Borgia. *The Jolliet-Marquette Expedition, 1673*. Glendale, CA: Clark, 1928.

Steinbacher-Kemp, William. "The Establishment of Starved Rock State Park." *Journal of Illinois History* 2, no. 2 (1999): 123–44.

Stevens, Frank E. *The Black Hawk War: Including a Review of Black Hawk's Life.* Chicago: Stevens, 1903.

Stewart, Jeffrey C. *The New Negro: The Life of Alain Locke.* New York: Oxford University Press, 2018.

Stroble, Paul E., Jr. *High on the Okaw's Western Bank.* Urbana: University of Illinois Press, 1993.

Sutton, Robert P. "An American Elysium: The Icarian Communities." In *America's Communal Utopias,* edited by Donald E. Pitzer, 279–96. Chapel Hill: University of North Carolina Press, 1997.

Tarlach, Gemma. "Earliest American Genome Proves Siberian Origins of Native Peoples." *Discover D-brief,* February 12, 2014. Accessed June 7, 2018. http://blogs.discover magazine.com/d-brief/2014/02/12/earliest-american-genome-proves-siberian -origins-for-native-peoples/.

Taylor, Richard S. "How Illinois Got Its First State Park." *Historic Illinois* 4, no. 1 (1981): 4–5, 13.

Taylor, Richard S., and Mark L. Johnson. "Inventing Lincoln's New Salem: The Reconstruction of a Pioneer Village." Unpublished manuscript, Lincoln's New Salem State Historic Site, New Salem.

Temple, Wayne C., and Sunderine Wilson Temple. *Abraham Lincoln and Illinois' Fifth Capitol.* 2nd ed. Rev. Mahomet, IL: Mayhaven, 2006.

Thomas, Benjamin P. "Lincoln and New Salem." In *An Illinois Reader,* edited by Clyde C. Walton, 113–25. DeKalb: Northern Illinois University Press, 1970.

———. *Lincoln's New Salem.* Springfield, IL: Abraham Lincoln Association, 1934.

Thwaites, Reuben Gold. *On the Storied Ohio: An Historical Pilgrimage of a Thousand Miles in a Skiff from Redstone to Cairo.* Chicago: McClurg, 1903.

Trask, Kerry A. *Black Hawk: The Battle for the Heart of America.* New York: Holt, 2006.

United States. *Miscellaneous Documents of the House of Representatives for the Fifty-Second Congress, 1891–92.* Washington, DC: Government Printing Office, 1895.

"Vachel Lindsay." *Poetry Foundation.* Accessed October 5, 2018. https://www.poetry foundation.org/poets/vachel-lindsay.

Van Wienen, Mark W. "Vachel Lindsay [1879–1931]: Lindsay and Racism," *Modern American Poetry.* Accessed April 12, 2020. http://maps-legacy.org/poets/g_l/lindsay/racism .htm.

Wagner, Jon. "Eric Jansson and the Bishop Hill Colony." In *America's Communal Utopias,* edited by Donald E. Pitzer, 297–318. Chapel Hill: University of North Carolina Press, 1997.

Walczynski, Mark. "The Starved Rock Massacre of 1769: Fact or Fiction." *Journal of the Illinois State Historical Society* 100, no. 3 (2007): 215–36.

Wallace, Anthony F. C. *Prelude to Disaster: The Course of Indian-White Relations Which Led to the Black Hawk War of 1832*. Springfield: Illinois State Historical Library, 1970.

Wallace, Joseph. "Fort de Chartres: Its Origin, Growth and Decline." In *Transactions of the Illinois State Historical Society for the Year 1903*, 105–17. Springfield: Illinois State Historical Library, 1903.

Walthall, John A. "French Colonial Fort Massac: Architecture and Ceramic Patterning." In *French Colonial Archeology: The Illinois Country and the Western Great Lakes*, edited by John A. Walthall, 42–64. Urbana: University of Illinois Press, 1991.

Weller, Allen Stuart. *Lorado Taft: The Chicago Years*. Edited by Robert G. La France and Henry Adams with Stephen P. Thomas. Urbana: University of Illinois Press, 2014.

Werstein, Irving. *Strangled Voices: The Story of the Haymarket Affair*. New York: Macmillan, 1970.

Whitney, Blair. "The Garden of Illinois." In *The Vision of This Land: Studies of Vachel Lindsay, Edgar Lee Masters, and Carl Sandburg*, edited by John E. Hallwas and Dennis J. Reader, 17–28. Macomb: Western Illinois University, 1976.

Wilson, Douglas L. *Lincoln before Washington: New Perspectives on the Illinois Years*. Urbana: University of Illinois Press, 1997.

Woods, John. "The English Settlement, the Illinois Pioneer." In *Prairie State: Impressions of Illinois, 1673–1967, by Travelers and Other Observers*, edited by Paul M. Angle, 76–83. Chicago: University of Chicago Press, 1968.

Zeisler, Sigmund. *Reminiscences of the Anarchist Case*. Chicago: Chicago Literary Club, 1927.

Index

Charles Titus is an emeritus member of the history department at Eastern Illinois University. He is a coeditor of *When the Nation Called a Third Time: Army Officer Candidate School at Fort Knox, Kentucky: The Vietnam Era.*

The University of Illinois Press
is a founding member of the
Association of University Presses.

———————————————

Composed in 10.5/15.5 Lora
with Lora medium display
by Dustin J. Hubbart
at the University of Illinois Press
Manufactured by Versa Press, Inc.

University of Illinois Press
1325 South Oak Street
Champaign, IL 61820-6903
www.press.uillinois.edu